THE COMPASSIONATE INSTINCT

Copyright © 2010 by The Greater Good Science Center

All rights reserved
Printed in the United States of America
First Edition

For information about special discounts for bulk purchases, please contact
W. W. Norton Special Sales at specialsales@wwnorton.com or 800-233-4830

Manufacturing by Courier Westford
Book design by Iris Weinstein
Production manager: Devon Zahn

Library of Congress Cataloging-in-Publication Data

The compassionate instinct : the science of human goodness / edited
by Dacher Keltner, Jason Marsh, and Jeremy Adam Smith. — 1st ed.
p. cm.
Includes index.
ISBN 978-0-393-33728-0 (pbk.)
1. Helping behavior. 2. Compassion. 3. Interpersonal relations. 4. Altruism.
I. Keltner, Dacher. II. Marsh, Jason. III. Smith, Jeremy
Adam, 1970–
BF637.H4C65 2010
155.2'32—dc22

2009022521

W. W. Norton & Company, Inc.
500 Fifth Avenue, New York, N.Y. 10110
www.wwnorton.com

W. W. Norton & Company Ltd.
Castle House, 75/76 Wells Street, London W1T 3QT

1 2 3 4 5 6 7 8 9 0

THE
COMPASSIONATE
INSTINCT

The Science of Human Goodness

Edited by Dacher Keltner,
Jason Marsh, and Jeremy Adam Smith

W. W. NORTON & COMPANY *New York* • *London*

TO ALL THOSE WHO HAVE SUPPORTED
GREATER GOOD MAGAZINE—
READERS, CONTRIBUTORS, AND DONORS

ACKNOWLEDGMENTS

THIS BOOK CONTAINS some of the best essays from *Greater Good* magazine (www.greatergoodmag.org), which for five years has flourished due to the hard work of hundreds of people, from staff and volunteers to writers and editorial board members.

Special thanks to Jill Suttie, our volunteer book review editor, and Alfonso Jaramillo, our design editor. We extend our most profound gratitude to everyone who has contributed to *Greater Good*—and to our dedicated readers and donors—even if space limitations prevent us from thanking each by name.

We would like to express special gratitude to Thomas and Ruth Ann Hornaday and the Herb Alpert Foundation, whose combined support made *Greater Good* possible. Thanks also to Maria Guarnaschelli, the editor at W. W. Norton who championed and helped shape *The Compassionate Instinct*.

The three editors would also like to thank our wives—Mollie McNeil, Meredith Milet, and Olli Doo—for their patience and support.

CONTENTS

PART TWO: HOW TO CULTIVATE GOODNESS IN
RELATIONSHIPS WITH FRIENDS, FAMILY,
COWORKERS, AND NEIGHBORS

The Banality of Heroism
Zeno Franco and Philip Zimbardo
287

CONTRIBUTORS

JESS ALBERTS, PH.D., is President's Professor in the Hugh Downs School of Human Communication at Arizona State University. Her research interests include conflict, relationship communication, and the division of labor.

LISA BENNETT is the communications director for the Center for Ecoliteracy, a nonprofit dedicated to education for sustainable living, and a former fellow at Harvard University's Joan Shorenstein Center on the Press, Politics, and Public Policy. She is writing a book about parenting in the age of global warming.

CHRISTOPHER BOEHM, PH.D., is a professor of anthropology and biological sciences at the University of Southern California and the author of *Hierarchy in the Forest: The Evolution of Egalitarian Behavior* (Harvard University Press).

CAROLYN PAPE COWAN, PH.D., is a professor of psychology emerita at the University of California, Berkeley, and the codirector, with her husband, Philip A. Cowan, of several long-term projects working with families: the Becoming a Family, Schoolchildren and Their Families, and Supporting Father Involvement projects. She has published many articles and books on family relationships and transitions.

PHILIP A. COWAN, PH.D., is a professor of psychology emeritus at the University of California, Berkeley, and the codirector, with his wife, Carolyn Pape Cowan, of several long-term projects working with families. He and his wife also conducted a famed two-decade study of two hundred nuclear families that informed their book *When Partners Become Parents: The Big Life Change for Couples* (Lawrence Erlbaum). He has served as the director of both the clinical psychology program and the Institute of Human Development at UC Berkeley.

PAUL EKMAN, PH.D., is the world's foremost expert on facial expressions and a professor emeritus of psychology at the University of California Medical School in San Francisco. He is the author of fifteen books, including, most recently, *Emotional Awareness* (Times Books), a conversation between himself and the Dalai Lama. He is also a member of *Greater Good*'s editorial board.

ROBERT A. EMMONS, PH.D., has taught in the department of psychology at the University of California, Davis, since 1988. He is the founding editor and editor-in-chief of the *Journal of Positive Psychology* and is the author of *THANKS! How the New Science of Gratitude Can Make You Happier* (Houghton-Mifflin).

ZENO FRANCO is a Ph.D. candidate in clinical psychology at Pacific Graduate School of Psychology in Palo Alto, California. He recently completed a three-year U.S. Department of Homeland Security fellowship.

DANIEL GOLEMAN, PH.D., is an internationally renowned author, psychologist, and science journalist, who for twelve years wrote for the *New York Times*, specializing in psychology and brain sciences. He is the author of numerous books, including the best sellers *Emotional Intelligence* and *Social Intelligence* (Bantam), and writes the "Social Intelligence" column for *Greater Good* magazine. Goleman has received many awards for his writing, including a Career Achievement award for journalism from the American Psychological Association.

LT. COL. DAVE GROSSMAN, a former Army Ranger and para-trooper, taught psychology at West Point and was formerly a professor and chair of the department of military science at Arkansas State University. He is the author of *On Killing: The Psychological Cost of Learning to Kill in War and Society* (Back Bay Books), which was nominated for the Pulitzer Prize for nonfiction.

JONATHAN D. HAIDT, PH.D., is a professor of psychology at the University of Virginia and the author of *The Happiness Hypothesis: Finding Modern Truth in Ancient Wisdom* (Basic Books). His essay draws from his chapter in *Flourishing: Positive Psychology and the Life Well-Lived* (American Psychological Association), a book he coedited with Corey L. M. Keyes.

DACHER KELTNER, PH.D., executive editor of *Greater Good* magazine, is a professor of psychology at the University of California, Berkeley, and the research director of the university's Greater Good Science Center. He is the author of more than eighty scholarly articles and three books, most recently *Born to Be Good* (W. W. Norton).

ALFIE KOHN writes and speaks widely on human behavior, education, and parenting. His essay was originally adapted from *Unconditional Parenting: Moving from Rewards and Punishment to Love and Reason* (Atria Books) for the Spring/Summer 2005 issue of *Greater Good*. For more information, see www.alfiekohn.org.

MICHAEL KOSFELD, PH.D., is a professor of business administration at the University of Frankfurt, Germany.

AARON LAZARE, M.D., is chancellor, dean, and professor of psychiatry at the University of Massachusetts Medical School. He is a leading authority on the medical interview, the psychology of shame and humiliation, and apology. He is the author of many books, including *On Apology* (Oxford University Press).

FRED LUSKIN, PH.D., is the director of the Stanford Forgiveness Projects and an associate professor at the Institute for Transpersonal Psychology. He is the author of *Forgive for Good: A Proven Prescription for Health and Happiness* (HarperSanFrancisco) and *Forgive for Love: The Missing Ingredient for a Healthy and Lasting Relationship* (HarperCollins).

MEREDITH MARAN is the author or coauthor of eight books, including *50 Ways to Support Lesbian and Gay Equality* (New World Library), *Dirty: A Search for Answers inside America's Teenage Drug Epidemic* (HarperOne), and *Class Dismissed: A Year in the Life of an American High School, a Glimpse into the Heart of a Nation* (St. Martin's Press). She writes features, essays, and book reviews for *Playboy, Self, Real Simple, Mother Jones, Health*, the *San Francisco Chronicle*, and *Family Circle*, among others. A different version of her essay originally appeared in *More* magazine.

JASON MARSH is the editor-in-chief of *Greater Good* magazine. Previously he was the managing editor of the quarterly journal *The Responsive Community*, and he is the coeditor (with Amitai Etzioni) of the anthology *Rights vs. Public Safety after 9/11: America in the Age of Terrorism* (Rowman and Littlefield). He has also worked as a documentary producer, kindergarten teacher, and public radio reporter and producer.

MICHAEL E. McCULLOUGH, PH.D., is a professor of psychology at the University of Miami, where he directs the Laboratory for Social and Clinical Psychology. His essay was originally excerpted with permission of the publisher John Wiley & Sons, Inc., from *Beyond Revenge: The Evolution of the Forgiveness Instinct* for the Spring 2008 issue of *Greater Good*.

NEERA MEHTA is an assistant professor of clinical psychiatry and behavioral sciences at Northwestern University's Feinberg School of Medicine. She is also a former fellow of the Greater Good Science Center at UC Berkeley.

KEITH OATLEY, PH.D., is a professor emeritus at the University of Toronto. He is the author of six books on psychology, including *Emotions: A Brief History* (Wiley Blackwell), and two novels, the first of which, *The Case of Emily V.* (Aquitus Books), won the Commonwealth Writers Prize for Best First Novel.

PAMELA PAXTON, PH.D., is an associate professor of sociology at Ohio State University and the coauthor (with Melanie Hughes) of *Women, Politics, and Power* (Sage Publications).

STEVEN PINKER, PH.D., is Harvard College Professor and Johnstone Family Professor in Harvard University's psychology department. He is the author of seven books, two of which were finalists for the Pulitzer Prize. His most recent book is *The Stuff of Thought: Language as a Window into Human Nature* (Penguin). His essay is adapted from a lecture he delivered at the 2007 TED Conference in Monterey, California.

CATHERINE PRICE is a freelance writer for publications including the *New York Times*, *Salon*, and *Men's Journal*, and is founder and editor-in-chief of *Salt* magazine (www.saltmag.net).

ROBERT M. SAPOLSKY, PH.D., is the John A. and Cynthia Fry Gunn Professor of Biological Sciences and a professor of neurology and neurological sciences at Stanford University. He is the author of numerous books, including *Monkeyluv: And Other Essays on Our Lives as Animals* (Scribner). A longer version of this essay appeared in *Foreign Affairs*.

JEREMY ADAM SMITH is the editor of Shareable.net, a contributing editor of *Greater Good* magazine, and author of *The Daddy Shift: How Stay-at-Home Dads, Breadwinning Moms, and Shared Parenting Are Transforming the American Family* (Beacon). His work has appeared in the *San Francisco Chronicle*, *Mothering*, *The Nation*, *Utne Reader*, *Wired*, and many other periodicals and books.

JILL SUTTIE, PSY.D., is a freelance writer and the book review editor for *Greater Good* magazine.

ROBERT I. SUTTON, PH.D., is a professor of management science and engineering at Stanford University's School of Engineering. He is the author of *The No Asshole Rule: Building a Civilized Workplace and Surviving One That Isn't* (Warner Business Books), from which this essay was adapted for the Winter 2007–08 issue of *Greater Good*. His blog is www.bobsutton.net.

ANGELA TRETHEWEY, PH.D., is an associate professor in the Hugh Downs School of Human Communication. She explores the intersections of gender, work, and identity.

DESMOND TUTU, the recipient of the Nobel Peace Prize in 1984, retired as Archbishop of Cape Town, South Africa, in 1996. He then served as chairman of South Africa's Truth and Reconciliation Commission. This essay was adapted from his 2004 book, *God Has a Dream* (Doubleday), for the Fall 2004 issue of *Greater Good*.

FRANS B. M. DE WAAL, PH.D., a Dutch-born primatologist, is the C. H. Candler Professor at Emory University and director of the Living Links Center at the Yerkes National Primate Research Center in Atlanta. This essay was adapted from his book *Our Inner Ape: A Leading Primatologist Explains Why We Are Who We Are* (Riverhead), for the Fall/Winter 2005–06 issue of *Greater Good*.

EVERETT L. WORTHINGTON JR., PH.D., is a professor and chair in the department of psychology at Virginia Commonwealth University. A Campaign for Forgiveness Research, of which he serves as executive director, funded preparation of this essay.

PHILIP ZIMBARDO, PH.D., is a professor emeritus of psychology at Stanford University, a two-time past president of the Western Psychological Association, and a past president of the American Psychological Association. He elaborates on many of the ideas found in this essay in *The Lucifer Effect: Understanding How Good People Turn Evil* (Random House).

THE COMPASSIONATE INSTINCT

PART ONE:

THE SCIENTIFIC ROOTS

OF HUMAN GOODNESS

INTRODUCTION

Dacher Keltner, Jason Marsh,
and Jeremy Adam Smith

W E ARE WITNESSING a revolution in the scientific understanding of human nature. Where once science painted humans as self-seeking and warlike—simplified notions of killer apes and selfish genes that still permeate popular culture—today scientists of many disciplines are uncovering the deep roots of human goodness.

Greater Good magazine, which was launched in 2004, highlights this exciting new scientific research and fuses it with inspiring stories of compassion in action. In the process, it provides a bridge between social scientists and parents, educators, community leaders, and policy makers.

Greater Good magazine is published by the University of California, Berkeley's Greater Good Science Center, an interdisciplinary research center devoted to the scientific understanding of happy and compassionate individuals, strong social bonds, and altruistic behavior. While serving the traditional tasks of a university research center—fostering groundbreaking scientific discoveries—the GGSC is unique in its commitment to helping people apply scientific research to their lives.

In the pages that follow, we present some of the best and most pathbreaking essays to have appeared in *Greater Good* magazine. These essays are the fruits of radical new developments in science: new evolutionary studies of peacemaking among our primate relatives; neuroscientific experiments that have identified the neural bases of emotions like love and compassion; discoveries of how hormones like oxytocin promote trust and generosity; and psychological studies of how and why people can be moved to practice kindness, even when it seems to cut against their own self-interest.

Taken together, this research challenges some long-held notions about human nature, revealing that the good in us is just as intrinsic to our species as the bad. Empathy, gratitude, compassion, altruism, fairness, trust, and cooperation, once thought to be aberrations from the tooth-and-claw natural order of things, are now being revealed as core features of primate evolution.

What's more, as the essays in this volume reveal, this research offers new pathways to healthier bodies, marriages, workplaces, families, and cultures. For example, neuroscience suggests that when we give to others, our brain shows heightened activity in the nucleus accumbens, a region known to have many dopamine receptors and process rewards; in other words, kindness really is its own reward. Moreover, kindness is contagious: research finds that when we offer modest expressions of gratitude—the simple "thank you," smile, or warm gaze—we prompt other people to reciprocate the kindness toward us and toward others.

This research suggests that compassionate behavior not only exemplifies a good, moral way to live, but carries great emotional and physical health benefits for compassionate people, their families, and their communities. More and more, it seems that rather than being irrational and superfluous, behaviors like compassion and kindness are actually conducive to human survival—and essential to human flourishing.

Our expectations for ourselves play a strong role in shaping our behavior. For too long a view of humans has prevailed that presupposes that we are wired to compete, to act aggressively, to pursue unbridled self-interest. These are no doubt facets of human nature, but they represent only half of the story. The essays in this volume reveal another story, one that places goodness at the center of human nature. Our contributors don't deny the existence of the violence and selfishness we see in the world around us. But they do offer scientific evidence that another world is possible.

THE COMPASSIONATE INSTINCT

Dacher Keltner

HUMANS ARE SELFISH. It's so easy to say. The same goes for so many assertions that follow. Greed is good. Altruism is an illusion. Cooperation is for suckers. Competition is natural, war inevitable. The bad in human nature is stronger than the good.

These kinds of claims reflect age-old assumptions about emotion. For millennia, we have regarded the emotions as the fount of irrationality, baseness, and sin. The idea of the seven deadly sins takes our destructive passions for granted. Plato compared the human soul to a chariot: the intellect is the driver and the emotions are the horses. Life is a continual struggle to keep the emotions under control.

Even compassion, the concern we feel for another being's welfare, has been treated with downright derision. Kant saw it as a weak and misguided sentiment: "Such benevolence is called softheartedness and should not occur at all among human beings," he said of compassion. Many question whether true compassion exists at all—or whether it is inherently motivated by self-interest.

Recent studies of compassion argue persuasively for a different take on human nature, one that rejects the preeminence of self-interest. These studies support a view of the emotions as rational, functional, and adaptive—a view that has its origins in Darwin's

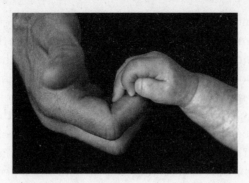

Expression of Emotion in Man and Animals. Compassion and benevolence, this research suggests, are an evolved part of human nature, rooted in our brain and biology, and ready to be cultivated for the greater good.

THE BIOLOGICAL BASIS OF COMPASSION

First consider the recent study of the biological basis of compassion. If such a basis exists, we should be wired up, so to speak, to respond to others in need. Recent evidence supports this point convincingly. University of Wisconsin psychologist Jack Nitschke found in an experiment that when mothers looked at pictures of their babies, they not only reported feeling more compassionate love than when they saw other babies; they also demonstrated unique activity in a region of their brains associated with the positive emotions. Nitschke's finding suggests that this region of the brain is attuned to the first objects of our compassion—our offspring.

But this compassionate instinct isn't limited to parents' brains. In a different set of studies, Joshua Greene and Jonathan Cohen, then both of Princeton University, found that when subjects contemplated harm being done to others, a similar network of regions in their brains lit up. Our children and victims of violence—two very different subjects, yet united by the similar neurological reactions they provoke. This consistency strongly suggests that compassion isn't simply a fickle or irrational emotion, but rather an innate human response embedded into the folds of our brains.

In other research by Emory University neuroscientists James Rilling and Gregory Berns, participants were given the chance to help someone else while their brain activity was recorded. Helping others triggered activity in the caudate nucleus and anterior cingulate, portions of the brain that turn on when people receive rewards or experience pleasure. This is a rather remarkable finding: helping others brings the same pleasure we get from the gratification of personal desire.

The brain, then, seems wired up to respond to others' suffering—indeed, it makes us feel good when we can alleviate that suffering. But do other parts of the body also suggest a biological basis for compassion?

It seems so. Take the loose association of glands, organs, and cardiovascular and respiratory systems known as the autonomic nervous system (ANS). The ANS plays a primary role in regulating our blood flow and breathing patterns for different kinds of actions. For example, when we feel threatened, our heart and breathing rates usually increase, preparing us to either confront or flee from the threat—the so-called fight-or-flight response. What is the ANS profile of compassion? As it turns out, when young children and adults feel compassion for others, this emotion is reflected in very real physiological changes: their heart rate goes down from baseline levels, which prepares them not to fight or flee, but to approach and soothe.

Then there's oxytocin, a hormone that floats through the bloodstream. Research performed on the small, stocky rodents known as prairie voles indicates that oxytocin promotes long-term bonds and commitments, as well as the kind of nurturing behavior—like caring for offspring—that lies at the heart of compassion. It may account for that overwhelming feeling of warmth and connection we feel toward our offspring or loved ones. Indeed, breast-feeding and massages elevate oxytocin levels in the blood (as does eating chocolate). In some recent studies I've conducted, we have found that when people perform behaviors associated with compassionate love—warm smiles, friendly hand gestures, affirmative forward leans—their bodies produce more oxytocin. This suggests that compassion may be self-perpetuating: being compassionate causes a chemical reaction in the body that motivates us to be even more compassionate.

SIGNS OF COMPASSION

According to evolutionary theory, if compassion is truly vital to human survival, it would manifest itself through nonverbal signals. Such signals would serve many adaptive functions. Most importantly, a distinct signal of compassion would soothe others in distress, allow people to identify the good-natured individuals with whom they'd want long-term relationships, and help forge bonds between strangers and friends.

Research by Nancy Eisenberg, perhaps the world's expert on the development of compassion in children, has found that there is a particular facial expression of compassion, characterized by oblique eyebrows and a concerned gaze. When someone shows this expression, they are more likely to help others. My work has examined another nonverbal cue: touch.

Previous research has already documented the important functions of touch. Primates such as great apes spend hours a day grooming each other, even when there are no lice in their physical environment. They use grooming to resolve conflicts, to reward each other's generosity, and to form alliances. Human skin has special receptors that transform patterns of tactile stimulation—a mother's caress or a friend's pat on the back—into indelible sensations as lasting as childhood smells. Certain touches can trigger the release of oxytocin, bringing feelings of warmth and pleasure. The handling of neglected rat pups can reverse the effects of their previous social isolation, going as far as enhancing their immune systems.

My work set out to document, for the first time, whether compassion can be communicated via touch. Such a finding would have several important implications. It would show that we can communicate this positive emotion with nonverbal displays, whereas previous research has mostly documented the nonverbal expression of negative emotions such as anger and fear. This finding would also shed light on the social functions of compassion—how people might rely on touch to soothe, reward, and bond in daily life.

In my experiment, I put two strangers in a room where they were separated by a barrier. They could not see one another, but they could reach each other through a hole. One person touched the other on the forearm several times, each time trying to convey one of 12 emotions, including love, gratitude, and compassion. After each touch, the person touched had to describe the emotion they thought the toucher was communicating.

Imagine yourself in this experiment. How do you suppose you might do? Remarkably, people in these experiments reliably identified compassion, as well as love and the other 10 emotions, from the touches to their forearm. This strongly suggests that compassion is an evolved part of human nature—something we're universally capable of expressing and understanding.

MOTIVATING ALTRUISM

Feeling compassion is one thing; acting on it is another. We still must confront a vital question: Does compassion promote altruistic behavior? In an important line of research, Daniel Batson has made the persuasive case that it does. According to Batson, when we encounter people in need or distress, we often imagine what

their experience is like. This is a great developmental milestone—
to take the perspective of another. It is not only one of the most
human of capacities; it is one of the most important aspects of our
ability to make moral judgments and fulfill the social contract.
When we take the other's perspective, we experience an empathic
state of concern and are motivated to address that person's needs
and enhance that person's welfare, sometimes even at our own
expense.

In a compelling series of studies, Batson exposed participants
to another's suffering. He then had some participants imagine that
person's pain, but he allowed those participants to act in a self-
serving fashion—for example, by leaving the experiment.

Within this series, one study had participants watch another
person receive shocks when he failed a memory task. Then
they were asked to take shocks on behalf of the participant, who,
they were told, had experienced a shock trauma as a child. Those
participants who had reported that they felt compassion for the
other individual volunteered to take several shocks for that person,
even when they were free to leave the experiment.

In another experiment, Batson and colleagues examined whether
people feeling compassion would help someone in distress, even
when their acts were completely anonymous. In this study, female
participants exchanged written notes with another person, who
quickly expressed feeling lonely and an interest in spending time
with the participant. Those participants feeling compassion volunteered to spend significant time with the other person, even when
no one else would know about their act of kindness.

Taken together, our strands of evidence suggest that compassion
is deeply rooted in human nature and has a biological basis in the
brain and body. Humans can communicate compassion through
facial gesture and touch, and these displays of compassion can
serve vital social functions, strongly suggesting an evolutionary
basis of compassion. And when experienced, compassion over-
whelms selfish concerns and motivates altruistic behavior.

CULTIVATING COMPASSION

So we can clearly see the great human propensity for compassion and the effects compassion can have on behavior. But can we actually cultivate compassion, or is it all determined by our genes?

Recent neuroscience studies suggest that positive emotions are less heritable—that is, less determined by our DNA—than the negative emotions. Other studies indicate that the brain structures involved in positive emotions like compassion are more "plastic"—subject to changes brought about by environmental input. So we might think about compassion as a biologically based skill or virtue, but not one that we either have or don't have. Instead, it's a trait that we can develop in an appropriate context. What might that context look like? From children, we are learning some answers.

Some researchers have observed a group of children as they were growing up, looking for family dynamics that might make the children more empathic, compassionate, or likely to help others. This research points to several key factors.

First, children securely attached to their parents, compared to insecurely attached children, tend to be sympathetic to their peers as early as age 3, according to the research of Everett Waters, Judith Wippman, and Alan Sroufe. In contrast, researchers Mary Main and Carol George found that abusive parents who resort to physical violence have less empathic children.

Developmental psychologists have also been interested in comparing two specific parenting styles. Parents who rely on induction engage their children in reasoning when they have done harm, prompting the children to think about the consequences of their actions and how these actions have harmed others. Parents who rely on power assertion simply declare what is right and wrong and resort more often to physical punishment or strong emotional responses of anger. Nancy Eisenberg, Richard Fabes, and Martin Hoffman have found that parents who use induction and reasoning raise children who are better adjusted and more likely to help their peers. This style of parenting seems to nurture the basic tools of compassion: an appreciation of others' suffering and a desire to remedy that suffering.

Parents can also teach compassion by example. A landmark study of altruism by Pearl and Samuel Oliner found that children who have compassionate parents tend to be more altruistic. In the Oliners' study of Germans who helped rescue Jews during the Nazi Holocaust, one of the strongest predictors of this inspiring behavior was the individual's memory of growing up in a family that prioritized compassion and altruism.

A MORE COMPASSIONATE WORLD

Human communities are only as healthy as our conceptions of human nature. It has long been assumed that selfishness, greed, and competitiveness lie at the core of human behavior, the products of our evolution. It takes little imagination to see how these assumptions have guided most realms of human affairs, from policy making to media portrayals of social life.

But recent scientific findings forcefully challenge this view of human nature. We see that compassion is deeply rooted in our brains, our bodies, and in the most basic ways we communicate. What's more, a sense of compassion fosters compassionate behavior and helps shape the lessons we teach our children.

Of course, simply realizing this is not enough; we must also make room for our compassionate impulses to flourish. The rest of this book contains essays that can help us do just that. They provide ample evidence to show what we can gain from more compassionate marriages, schools, hospitals, workplaces, and other institutions, including the United States government and international bodies like the United Nations. They do more than make us reconsider our assumptions about human nature. They offer a blueprint for a more compassionate world.

THE EVOLUTION OF EMPATHY

Frans B. M. de Waal

ONCE UPON A TIME, the United States had a president known for a peculiar facial display. In an act of controlled emotion, he would bite his lower lip and tell his audience, "I feel your pain." Whether the display was sincere is not the issue here; how we are affected by another's predicament is. Empathy is second nature to us, so much so that anyone devoid of it strikes us as dangerous or mentally ill.

At the movies, we can't help but get inside the skin of the characters on the screen. We despair when their gigantic ship sinks; we exult when they finally stare into the eyes of a long-lost lover.

We are so used to empathy that we take it for granted; yet it is essential to human society as we know it. Our morality depends on it. How could anyone be expected to follow the golden rule without the capacity to mentally trade places with a fellow human being? It is logical to assume that this capacity came first, giving rise to the golden rule itself. The act of perspective taking is summed up by one of the most enduring definitions of empathy that we have, formulated by Adam Smith as "changing places in fancy with the sufferer."

Even Smith, the father of economics, best known for emphasizing self-interest as the lifeblood of human economy, understood that the concepts of self-interest and empathy don't conflict. Empa-

An example of consolation among chimpanzees: A juvenile puts an arm around a
screaming adult male, who has just been
defeated in a fight with his rival. Consolation probably relects empathy, as the object
of the consoler seems to be to alleviate the
distress of the other.

thy makes us reach out to others, first just emotionally, but later in
life also by understanding their situation.

This capacity likely evolved because it served our ancestors'
survival in two ways. First, like every mammal, we need to be sensitive to the needs of our offspring. Second, our species depends on
cooperation, which means that we do better if we are surrounded
by healthy, capable group mates. Taking care of them is just a matter of enlightened self-interest.

ANIMAL EMPATHY

It is hard to imagine that empathy—a characteristic so basic to the
human species that it emerges early in life and is accompanied by
strong physiological reactions—came into existence only when our
lineage split off from that of the apes. It must be far older than

that. Examples of empathy in other animals would suggest a long evolutionary history of this capacity in humans.

Evolution rarely throws anything out. Instead, structures are transformed, modified, co-opted for other functions, or tweaked in another direction. The frontal fins of fish became the front limbs of land animals, which over time turned into hoofs, paws, wings, and hands. Occasionally, a structure loses all function and becomes superfluous, but this is a gradual process, and traits rarely disappear altogether. Thus, we find tiny vestiges of leg bones under the skin of whales and remnants of a pelvis in snakes.

Over the last several decades, we've seen increasing evidence of empathy in other species. One piece of evidence came unintentionally out of a study on human development. Carolyn Zahn-Waxler, a research psychologist at the National Institute of Mental Health, visited people's homes to find out how young children respond to family members' emotions. She instructed people to pretend to sob, cry, or choke, and found that some household pets seemed as worried as the children were by the feigned distress of the family members. The pets hovered nearby and put their heads in their owners' laps.

But perhaps the most compelling evidence for the strength of animal empathy came from a group of psychiatrists led by Jules Masserman at Northwestern University. The researchers reported in 1964 in the *American Journal of Psychiatry* that rhesus monkeys refused to pull a chain that delivered food to themselves if doing so gave a shock to a companion. One monkey stopped pulling the chain for 12 days after witnessing another monkey receive a shock. Those primates were literally starving themselves to avoid shocking another animal.

The anthropoid apes, our closest relatives, are even more remarkable. In 1925, Robert Yerkes reported how his bonobo, Prince Chim, was so extraordinarily concerned and protective toward his sickly chimpanzee companion, Panzee, that the scientific establishment might not accept his claims: "If I were to tell of his altruistic and obviously sympathetic behavior towards Panzee, I should be suspected of idealizing an ape."

Nadia Ladygina-Kohts, a primatological pioneer, noticed similar empathic tendencies in her young chimpanzee Joni, whom she raised at the beginning of the last century in Moscow. Ladygina-Kohts, who analyzed Joni's behavior in the minutest detail, discovered that the only way to get him off the roof of her house after an escape—much more effective than any reward or threat of punishment—was by arousing sympathy:

> If I pretend to be crying, close my eyes and weep, Joni immediately stops his plays or any other activities, quickly runs over to me, all excited and shagged, from the most remote places in the house, such as the roof or the ceiling of his cage, from where I could not drive him down despite my persistent calls and entreaties. He hastily runs around me, as if looking for the offender; looking at my face, he tenderly takes my chin in his palm, lightly touches my face with his finger, as though trying to understand what is happening, and turns around, clenching his toes into firm fists.

These observations suggest that apart from emotional connectedness, apes have an appreciation of the other's situation and show a degree of perspective taking. One striking report in this regard concerns a bonobo female named Kuni, who found a wounded bird in her enclosure at Twycross Zoo, in England. Kuni picked up the bird, and when her keeper urged her to let it go, she climbed to the highest point of the highest tree, carefully unfolded the bird's wings and spread them wide open, one wing in each hand, before throwing it as hard as she could toward the barrier of the enclosure. When the bird fell short, Kuni climbed down and guarded it until the end of the day, when it flew to safety. Obviously, what Kuni did would have been inappropriate toward a member of her own species. Having seen birds in flight many times, she seemed to have a notion of what would be good for a bird, thus giving us an anthropoid illustration of Smith's "changing places in fancy."

This is not to say that all we have are anecdotes. Systematic studies have been conducted on so-called "consolation" behavior. Consolation is defined as friendly or reassuring behavior by a bystander toward a victim of aggression. For example, chimpanzee A attacks chimpanzee B, after which bystander C comes over and embraces or grooms B. Based on hundreds of such observations, we know that consolation occurs regularly and exceeds baseline levels of contact. In other words, it is a demonstrable tendency that probably reflects empathy, since the objective of the consoler seems to be to alleviate the distress of the other. In fact, the usual effect of this kind of behavior is that the distressed animal stops screaming, yelping, and exhibiting other signs of distress.

A BOTTOM-UP VIEW OF EMPATHY

The above examples help explain why to the biologist, a Russian doll is such a satisfying plaything, especially if it has a historical dimension. I own a doll of Russian president Vladimir Putin, within whom we discover Yeltsin, Gorbachev, Brezhnev, Kruschev, Stalin, and Lenin, in that order. Finding a little Lenin and Stalin within Putin will hardly surprise most political analysts. The same is true for biological traits: the old always remains present in the new.

This is relevant to the debate about the origins of empathy, especially because of the tendency in some disciplines, such as psychology, to put human capacities on a pedestal. They essentially adopt a top-down approach that emphasizes the uniqueness of human language, consciousness, and cognition. But instead of trying to place empathy in the upper regions of human cognition, it is probably best to start out examining the simplest possible processes, some perhaps even at the cellular level. In fact, recent neuroscience research suggests that very basic processes do underlie empathy. Researchers at the University of Parma, in Italy, were the first to report that monkeys have special brain cells that become active not only if the monkey grasps an object with its hand but also if it merely watches another do the same. Since these cells are activated as much by doing as by seeing someone else do, they are known as mirror neurons, or "monkey see, monkey do" neurons.

It seems that developmentally and evolutionarily, advanced forms of empathy are preceded by and grow out of more elementary ones. Biologists prefer such bottom-up accounts. They always assume continuity between past and present, child and adult, human and animal, even between humans and the most primitive mammals.

So, how and why would this trait have evolved in humans and other species? Empathy probably evolved in the context of the parental care that characterizes all mammals. Signaling their state through smiling and crying, human infants urge their caregiver to take action. This also applies to other primates. The survival value of these interactions is evident from the case of a deaf female chimpanzee I have known named Krom, who gave birth to a succession of infants and had intense positive interest in them. But because she was deaf, she wouldn't even notice her babies' calls of distress if she sat down on them. Krom's case illustrates that without the proper mechanism for understanding and responding to a child's needs, a species will not survive.

During the 180 million years of mammalian evolution, females who responded to their offspring's needs out-reproduced those who were cold and distant. Having descended from a long line of mothers who nursed, fed, cleaned, carried, comforted, and defended their young, we should not be surprised by gender differences in human empathy, such as those proposed to explain the disproportionate rate of boys affected by autism, which is marked by a lack of social communication skills.

Empathy also plays a role in cooperation. One needs to pay close attention to the activities and goals of others to cooperate effectively. A lioness needs to notice quickly when other lionesses go into hunting mode, so that she can join them and contribute to the pride's success. A male chimpanzee needs to pay attention to his buddy's rivalries and skirmishes with others so that he can help out whenever needed, thus ensuring the political success of their partnership. Effective cooperation requires being exquisitely in tune with the emotional states and goals of others.

Within a bottom-up framework, the focus is not so much on the highest levels of empathy, but rather on its simplest forms and how these combine with increased cognition to produce more complex forms of empathy. How did this transformation take place? The evolution of empathy runs from shared emotions and intentions between individuals to a greater self/other distinction—that is, an "unblurring" of the lines between individuals. As a result, one's own experience is distinguished from that of another person, even though at the same time we are vicariously affected by the other's. This process culminates in a cognitive appraisal of the other's behavior and situation: we adopt the other's perspective.

As in a Russian doll, however, the outer layers always contain an inner core. Instead of evolution having replaced simpler forms of empathy with more advanced ones, the latter are merely elaborations on the former and remain dependent on them. This also means that empathy comes naturally to us. It is not something we only learn later in life or that is culturally constructed. At heart, it is a hardwired response that we fine-tune and elaborate on in the course of our lives, until it reaches a level at which it becomes such a complex response that it is hard to recognize its origin in simpler responses, such as body mimicry and emotional contagion.

ON A LEASH

Biology holds us "on a leash," in the felicitous words of biologist Edward Wilson, and will let us stray only so far from who we are. We can design our life any way we want, but whether we will thrive depends on how well that life fits human predispositions.

I hesitate to predict what we humans can and can't do, but we must consider our biological leash when deciding what kind of society we want to build, especially when it comes to goals like achieving universal human rights.

If we could manage to see people on other continents as part of us, drawing them into our circle of reciprocity and empathy, we would be building on, rather than going against, our nature.

For instance, in 2004, the Israeli minister of justice caused political uproar for sympathizing with the enemy. Yosef Lapid questioned the Israeli army's plans to demolish thousands of Palestinian homes in a zone along the Egyptian border. He had been touched by images on the evening news. "When I saw a picture on the TV of an old woman on all fours in the ruins of her home looking under some floor tiles for her medicines, I did think, 'What would I say if it were my grandmother?'" he said. Lapid's grandmother was a Holocaust victim.

This incident shows how a simple emotion can widen the definition of one's group. Lapid had suddenly realized that Palestinians were part of his circle of concern, too. Empathy is the one weapon in the human repertoire that can rid us of the curse of xenophobia.

Empathy is fragile, though. Among our close animal relatives, it is switched on by events within their community, such as a youngster in distress, but it is just as easily switched off with regard to outsiders or members of other species, such as prey. The way a chimpanzee bashes in the skull of a live monkey by hitting it against a tree trunk is no advertisement for ape empathy. Bonobos are less brutal, but in their case, too, empathy needs to pass through several filters before it will be expressed. Often, the filters prevent expressions of empathy because no ape can afford feeling pity for all living things all the time. This applies equally to humans. Our evolutionary background makes it hard to identify with outsiders. We've evolved to hate our enemies, to ignore people we barely know, and to distrust anybody who doesn't look like us. Even if we are largely cooperative within our communities, we become almost a different animal in our treatment of strangers.

This is the challenge of our time: globalization by a tribal species. In trying to structure the world such that it suits human nature, the point to keep in mind is that political ideologues by definition hold narrow views. They are blind to what they don't wish to see. The possibility that empathy is part of our primate heritage ought to make us happy, but we are not in the habit of embracing our nature. When people kill each other, we call them "animals." But when they give to the poor, we praise them for being "humane." We like to claim the latter tendency for ourselves. Yet, it will be hard to come up with anything we like about ourselves that is not part of our evolutionary background. What we need, therefore, is a vision of human nature that encompasses all of our tendencies: the good, the bad, and the ugly.

Our best hope for transcending tribal differences is based on the moral emotions, because emotions defy ideology. In principle, empathy can override every rule about how to treat others. When Oskar Schindler kept Jews out of concentration camps during World War II, for example, he was under clear orders by his society on how to treat people, yet his feelings interfered.

Caring emotions may lead to subversive acts, such as the case of a prison guard who during wartime was directed to feed his charges only water and bread, but who occasionally sneaked in a hard-boiled egg. However small his gesture, it etched itself into the prisoners' memories as a sign that not all of their enemies were monsters. And then there are the many acts of omission, such as when soldiers could have killed captives without negative repercussions but decided not to. In war, restraint can be a form of compassion.

Emotions trump rules. This is why, when speaking of moral role models, we talk of their hearts, not their brains (even if, as any neuroscientist will point out, the heart as the seat of emotions is an outdated notion). We rely more on what we feel than what we think when solving moral dilemmas.

It's not that religion and culture don't have a role to play, but the building blocks of morality clearly predate humanity. We recognize them in our primate relatives, with empathy being most conspicuous in the bonobo ape and reciprocity in the chimpanzee. Moral rules tell us when and how to apply our empathic tendencies, but the tendencies themselves have been in existence since time immemorial.

PEACE AMONG PRIMATES

Robert M. Sapolsky

IT USED TO BE THOUGHT that humans were the only savagely violent primate. "We are the only species that kills its own," narrators intoned portentously in nature films several decades ago. That view fell by the wayside in the 1960s as it became clear that some other primates kill their fellows aplenty. Males kill; females kill. Some use their toolmaking skills to fashion bigger and better cudgels. Other primates even engage in what can only be called warfare—organized, proactive group violence directed at other populations.

Yet as field studies of primates expanded, what became most striking was the variation in social practices across species. Yes, some primate species have lives filled with violence, frequent and varied. But life among others is filled with communitarianism, egalitarianism, and cooperative child rearing.

Patterns emerged. In less aggressive species, such as gibbons or marmosets, groups tend to live in lush rain forests, where food is plentiful and life is easy. Females and males tend to be the same size, and the males lack secondary sexual markers, such as long, sharp canines or garish coloring. Couples mate for life, and males help substantially with child care. In violent species, such as baboons and rhesus monkeys, the opposite conditions prevail.

The most disquieting fact about the violent species was the apparent inevitability of their behavior. Certain species seemed simply to be the way they were, fixed products of the interplay of evolution and ecology, and that was that. And although human males might not be inflexibly polygamous or outfitted with bright red butts and 6-inch canines designed for tooth-to-tooth combat, it was clear that our species had at least as much in common with the violent primates as with the gentle ones. "In their nature" thus became "in our nature." This was the humans-as-killer-apes theory popularized by the writer Robert Ardrey, according to which humans have as much chance of becoming intrinsically peaceful as they have of growing prehensile tails.

That view always had little more scientific rigor than a *Planet of the Apes* movie, but it took a great deal of field research to figure out just what should supplant it. After decades' more work, the picture has become quite interesting. Some primate species, it turns out, are indeed simply violent or peaceful, with their behavior driven by their social structures and ecological settings. More importantly, however, some primate species can make peace despite violent traits that seem built into their natures. The challenge now is to figure out under what conditions that can happen and whether we humans can manage the trick ourselves.

OLD PRIMATES AND NEW TRICKS

To an overwhelming extent, the age-old "nature versus nurture" debate is silly. The action of genes is completely intertwined with the environment in which they function; in a sense, it is pointless to even discuss what gene X does, and we should consider instead only what gene X does in environment Y. Nonetheless, if one had to predict the behavior of some organism on the basis of only one fact, one might still want to know whether the most useful fact would be about genetics or about the environment.

Two classic studies have shown that primates are somewhat independent from their "natures." In the early 1970s, a highly respected primatologist named Hans Kummer was working in a region of Ethiopia containing two species of baboons with markedly different social systems. Savanna baboons live in large troops, with plenty of adult females and males. Hamadryas baboons, in contrast, have a more complex and quite different multilevel society. When confronted with a threatening male, the females of the two species react differently: a hamadryas baboon placates the male by approaching him, whereas a savanna baboon can only run away if she wants to avoid injury.

Kummer conducted a simple experiment, trapping an adult female savanna baboon and releasing her into a hamadryas troop and trapping an adult female hamadryas and releasing her into a savanna troop. The females who were dropped in among a different species initially carried out their species-typical behavior, a major faux pas in the new neighborhood. But gradually, they absorbed the new rules. How long did this learning take? About an hour. In other words, millennia of genetic differences separating the two species, a lifetime of experience with a crucial social rule for each female— and a minuscule amount of time to reverse course completely.

The second experiment was set up by Frans de Waal, of Emory University, and his student Denise Johanowicz in the early 1990s, working with two macaque monkey species. By any human standards, male rhesus macaques are unappealing animals. Their hierarchies are rigid, those at the top seize a disproportionate share of the spoils, they enforce this inequity with ferocious aggression, and they rarely reconcile after fights. In contrast, male stump tail macaques, which share almost all of their genes with their rhesus macaque cousins, display much less aggression, looser hierarchies, more egalitarianism, and more behaviors that promote group cohesion.

Working with captive primates, de Waal and Johanowicz created a mixed-sex social group of juvenile macaques, combining rhesus and stump tails together. Remarkably, instead of the rhesus macaques bullying the stump tails, over the course of a few months, the rhesus males adopted the stump tails' social style, eventually even matching the stump tails' high rates of reconciliatory behavior. It so happens, moreover, that stump tails and rhesus macaques use different gestures when reconciling. The rhesus macaques in the study did not start using the stump tails' reconciliatory gestures, but rather increased the incidence of their own species-typical gestures. In other words, they were not merely imitating the stump tails' behavior; they were incorporating the concept of frequent reconciliation into their own social practices. Finally, when the newly warm-and-fuzzy rhesus macaques were returned to a larger, all-rhesus group, their new behavioral style persisted.

This is nothing short of extraordinary. But it brings up one further question: When those rhesus macaques were transferred back into the all-rhesus world, did they spread their insights and behaviors to the others? Alas, they did not—at least not within the relatively short time they were studied. For that we need to move on to a final case.

LEFT BEHIND

In the early 1980s, "Forest Troop," a group of savanna baboons I had been studying—virtually living with—for years, was going about its business in a national park in Kenya when a neighboring baboon group had a stroke of luck: its territory encompassed a tourist lodge that expanded its operations and, consequently, so did the amount of food tossed into its garbage dump. Baboons are omnivorous, and this "Garbage Dump Troop" was delighted to feast on leftover drumsticks, half-eaten hamburgers, remnants of chocolate cake, and anything else that wound up there. Soon they had shifted to sleeping in the trees immediately above the pit, descending each morning just in time for the day's dumping of garbage. (They soon got quite obese from the rich diet and lack of exercise, but that is another story.)

The development produced nearly as dramatic a shift in the social behavior of Forest Troop. Each morning, approximately half of its adult males would infiltrate Garbage Dump Troop's territory, descending on the pit in time for the day's dumping and battling the resident males for access to the garbage. The particular Forest Troop males who did this shared two traits: they were especially combative (which was necessary to get the food away from the other baboons), and they were not very interested in socializing (the raids took place early in the morning, during the hours when the bulk of a savanna baboon's daily communal grooming occurs).

Soon afterward, tuberculosis, a disease that moves with devastating speed and severity in nonhuman primates, broke out in Garbage Dump Troop. Over the next year, most of its members died, as did all of the males from Forest Troop who had foraged at the dump. (Considerable sleuthing ultimately revealed that the disease had come from tainted meat in the garbage dump. There was little animal-to-animal transmission of the tuberculosis, and so the disease did not spread in Forest Troop beyond the garbage eaters.) The results were that Forest Troop was left with males who were less aggressive and more social than average, and the troop now had double its previous female-to-male ratio.

The social consequences of these changes were dramatic. There remained a hierarchy among the Forest Troop males, but it was far looser than before. Compared with other, more typical savanna baboon groups, high-ranking males rarely harassed subordinates and occasionally even relinquished contested resources to them. Aggression was less frequent, particularly against third parties. And rates of affiliative behaviors, such as males and females grooming each other or sitting together, soared. There were even instances, now and then, of adult males grooming each other—a behavior nearly as unprecedented as baboons sprouting wings.

This unique social milieu did not arise merely as a function of the skewed sex ratio (with half the males having died); other primatologists have occasionally reported on troops with similar ratios but without a comparable social atmosphere. What was key was not just the predominance of females but the type of male who remained. The demographic disaster—what evolutionary biologists term a "selective bottleneck"—had produced a savanna baboon troop quite different from what most experts would have anticipated.

But the largest surprise did not come until some years later. Female savanna baboons spend their lives in the troop into which they are born, whereas males leave their birth troop around puberty; a troop's adult males have thus all grown up elsewhere and immigrated as adolescents. By the early 1990s, none of the original low-aggression/high-affiliation males of Forest Troop's tuberculosis period were still alive; all of the group's adult males had joined after the epidemic. Despite this, the troop's unique social milieu persisted—as it does to this day, some 20 years after the selective bottleneck. In other words, adolescent males that enter Forest Troop after having grown up elsewhere wind up adopting the unique behavioral style of the resident males. As defined by both anthropologists and animal behaviorists, "culture" consists of local behavioral variations, occurring for nongenetic and nonecological reasons, that last beyond the time of their originators. Forest Troop's low-aggression/high-affiliation society constitutes nothing less than a multigenerational benign culture.

Continuous study of the troop has yielded some insights into how its culture is transmitted to newcomers. Genetics obviously plays no role, nor apparently does self-selection: adolescent males that transfer into the troop are no different from those that transfer into other troops, displaying on arrival similarly high rates of aggression and low rates of affiliation. Nor is there evidence that new males are taught to act in benign ways by the residents. One cannot rule out the possibility that some observational learning is occurring, but it is difficult to detect, given that the distinctive feature of this culture is not the performance of a unique behavior but the performance of typical behaviors at atypically extreme rates.

To date, the most interesting hint about the mechanism of transmission is the way recently transferred males are treated by Forest Troop's resident females. In a typical savanna baboon troop, newly transferred adolescent males spend years slowly working their way into the social fabric; they are extremely low ranking—ignored by females and noted by adult males only as convenient targets for aggression. In Forest Troop, by contrast, new male transfers are inundated with female attention soon after their arrival. Resident females first present themselves sexually to new males an average of 18 days after the males arrive, and they first groom the new males an average of 20 days after they arrive, whereas normal savanna baboons introduce such behaviors after 63 and 78 days, respectively. Furthermore, these welcoming gestures occur more frequently in Forest Troop during the early post-transfer period, and there is four times as much grooming of males by females in Forest Troop as elsewhere. From almost the moment they arrive, in other words, new males find out that in Forest Troop, things are done differently.

At present, I think the most plausible explanation is that this troop's special culture is not passed on actively but simply emerges, facilitated by the actions of the resident members. Living in a group with half the typical number of males, and with the males being nice guys to boot, Forest Troop's females become more relaxed and less wary. (This is so, in part, because in a typical baboon troop, a male who loses a dominance interaction with another male will often attack a female in frustration.) As a result, they are more willing to take a chance and reach out socially to new arrivals, even if the new guys are typical jerky adolescents at first. The new males, in turn, finding themselves treated so well, eventually relax and adopt the behaviors of the troop's distinctive social milieu.

NATURAL-BORN KILLERS?

Are there any lessons to be learned here that can be applied to human-on-human violence—apart, that is, from the possible desirability of giving fatal cases of tuberculosis to aggressive people? Can human behavior be as malleable—and as peaceful—as Forest Troop's?

Any biological anthropologist opining about human behavior is required by long-established tradition to note that for 99 percent of human history, humans lived in small, stable bands of related hunter-gatherers. Game theorists have shown that a small, cohesive group is the perfect setting for the emergence of cooperation: The identities of the other participants are known, there are opportunities to play games together repeatedly (and thus the ability to punish cheaters), and there is open-book play (players can acquire reputations). And so, those hunter-gatherer bands were highly egalitarian. Empirical and experimental data have also shown the cooperative advantages of small groups at the opposite human extreme—namely, in the corporate world.

But the lack of violence within small groups can come at a heavy price. Small homogenous groups with shared values can be a nightmare of conformity. They can also be dangerous for outsiders. Unconsciously emulating the murderous border patrols of closely related male chimps, militaries throughout history have sought to form small, stable units; inculcate them with rituals of pseudokinship; and thereby produce efficient, cooperative killing machines.

Is it possible to achieve the cooperative advantages of a small group without having the group reflexively view outsiders as the Other? One often encounters pessimism in response to this question, based on the notion that humans, as primates, are hardwired for xenophobia. Some brain-imaging studies have appeared to support this view in a particularly discouraging way. There is a structure deep inside the brain called the amygdala that plays a key role in fear and aggression, and experiments have shown that when subjects are presented with a face of someone from a different race, the amygdala gets metabolically active—aroused, alert, ready for action. This happens even when the face is presented subliminally, which is to say, so rapidly that the subject does not consciously see it.

More recent studies, however, should mitigate this pessimism. Test a person who has a lot of experience with people of different races, and the amygdala does not activate. Or, as in a wonderful experiment by Susan Fiske, of Princeton University, subtly bias the subject beforehand to think of people as individuals rather than as members of a group, and the amygdala does not budge. Humans may be hardwired to get edgy around the Other, but our views on who falls into that category are decidedly malleable.

In the early 1960s, a rising star of primatology, Irven DeVore, of Harvard University, published the first general overview of the subject. Discussing his own specialty, savanna baboons, he wrote that they "have acquired an aggressive temperament as a defense against predators, and aggressiveness cannot be turned on and off like a faucet. It is an integral part of the monkeys' personalities, so deeply rooted that it makes them potential aggressors in every situation." Thus, the savanna baboon became, literally, a textbook example of life in an aggressive, highly stratified, male-dominated society. Yet in my observation of Forest Troop, I saw members of that same species demonstrate enough behavioral plasticity to transform their society into a baboon utopia.

The first half of the twentieth century was drenched in the blood spilled by German and Japanese aggression, yet only a few decades later it is hard to think of two countries more pacific. Sweden spent the seventeenth century rampaging through Europe, yet it is now an icon of nurturing tranquility. Humans have invented the small nomadic band and the continental megastate and have demonstrated a flexibility whereby uprooted descendants of the former can function effectively in the latter. We lack the type of physiology or anatomy that in other mammals determines their mating system and have come up with societies based on monogamy, polygyny, and polyandry. And we have fashioned some religions in which violent acts are the gateway to paradise and other religions in which the same acts consign one to hell. Is a world of peacefully coexisting human Forest Troops possible? Anyone who says "No, it is beyond our nature" knows too little about primates, including ourselves.

HOPE ON THE BATTLEFIELD

Dave Grossman

D URING WORLD WAR II, U.S. Army Brigadier General
S. L. A. Marshall asked average soldiers how they conducted
themselves in battle. Before that, it had always been assumed
that the average soldier would kill in combat simply because his
country and his leaders had told him to do so and because it might
be essential to defend his own life and the lives of his friends.
Marshall's singularly unexpected discovery was that of every 100
men along the line of fire during the combat period, an average
of only 15 to 20 "would take any part with their weapons." This
was consistently true, "whether the action was spread over a day,
or two days, or three."

Marshall was a U.S. Army historian in the Pacific theater during World War II and later became the official U.S. historian of
the European theater of operations. He had a team of historians
working for him, and they based their findings on individual and
mass interviews with thousands of soldiers in more than 400 infan-
try companies immediately after they had been in close combat
with German or Japanese troops. The results were consistently the
same: only 15 to 20 percent of the American riflemen in combat
during World War II would fire at the enemy. Those who would
not fire did not run or hide—in many cases, they were willing to

risk greater danger to rescue comrades, get ammunition, or run messages. They simply would not fire their weapons at the enemy, even when faced with repeated waves of banzai charges.

Why did these men fail to fire? As a historian, psychologist, and soldier, I examined this question and studied the process of killing in combat. I have realized that there was one major factor missing from the common understanding of this process, a factor that answers this question and more: the simple and demonstrable fact that there is, within most men and women, an intense resistance to killing other people—a resistance so strong that in many circumstances, soldiers on the battlefield will die before they can overcome it.

Indeed, the study of killing gives us good reason to feel optimistic about human nature, for it reveals that almost all of us are overwhelmingly reluctant to kill a member of our own species under just about any circumstance. Yet this understanding has also propelled armies to develop sophisticated methods for overcoming our innate aversion to killing, and as a result, we have seen a sharp increase in the magnitude and frequency of posttraumatic response among combat veterans. Because human beings are astonishingly resilient, most soldiers who return from war will be fine. But some will need help coping with memories of violence.

When those soldiers return from war—especially an unpopular one like Iraq—society faces formidable moral and mental health challenges in caring for and reintegrating its veterans.

RESISTANCE TO KILLING

S. L. A. Marshall's methodology has been criticized, but his findings have been corroborated by many other studies. Indeed, data indicate that soldiers throughout military history have demonstrated a strong resistance to killing other people.

When nineteenth-century French officer and military theorist Ardant du Picq distributed a questionnaire to French officers in the 1860s, he became one of the first people to document the common tendency of soldiers to fire harmlessly into the air simply for the sake of firing. One officer's response stated quite frankly that "a good many soldiers fired into the air at long distances," while another observed that "a certain number of our soldiers fired almost in the air, without aiming, seeming to want to stun themselves."

Missing the target does not necessarily involve firing high, and two decades on army rifle ranges have taught me that a soldier must fire unusually high for it to be obvious to an observer. In other words, the intentional miss can be a very subtle form of disobedience. When faced with living, breathing opponents instead of a target, a significant majority of the soldiers revert to a posturing mode in which they fire over the enemy's heads.

A 1986 study by the British Defense Operational Analysis Establishment's field studies division examined the killing effectiveness of military units in more than 100 nineteenth- and twentieth-century battles. They compared the data from these units with hit rates from simulated battles using pulsed laser weapons.

The analysis was designed (among other things) to determine if Marshall's nonfirer figures were consistent with other, earlier wars. When researchers compared historical combat performances against the performance of these test subjects (who were using simulated weapons and could neither inflict nor receive actual harm from the "enemy"), they discovered that the killing potential in these circumstances was much greater than the actual historical casualty rates.

Battlefield fear alone cannot explain such a consistent discrepancy. The researchers' conclusions openly supported Marshall's findings, pointing to "unwillingness to take part [in combat] as the main factor" that kept the actual historical killing rates significantly below the laser trial levels.

Thus, the evidence shows that the vast majority of combatants throughout history, at the moment of truth when they could and should kill the enemy, have found themselves to be "conscientious objectors"—yet there seems to be a conspiracy of silence on this subject. In his book *War on the Mind*, Peter Watson observes that Marshall's findings have been largely ignored by academia and the fields of psychiatry and psychology.

But they were very much taken to heart by the U.S. Army, and a number of training measures were instituted as a result of Marshall's suggestions. According to studies by the U.S. military, these changes resulted in a firing rate of 55 percent in Korea and 90 to 95 percent in Vietnam. Some modern soldiers use the disparity between the firing rates of World War II and Vietnam to claim that S. L. A. Marshall had to be wrong, for the average military leader has a hard time believing that any significant body of his soldiers will not do its job in combat. But these doubters don't give sufficient credit to the revolutionary corrective measures and training methods introduced over the past half century.

MANUFACTURED CONTEMPT

Since World War II, a new era has quietly dawned in modern warfare: an era of psychological warfare, conducted not upon the enemy, but upon one's own troops. The triad of methods used to enable men and women to overcome their innate resistance to killing includes desensitization, classical and operant conditioning, and denial defense mechanisms.

Authors such as Gwynne Dyer and Richard Holmes have traced the development of boot-camp glorification of killing. They've found it was almost unheard of in World War I, rare in World War II, increasingly present in Korea, and thoroughly institutionalized in Vietnam. "The language used in [marine training camp] Parris Island to describe the joys of killing people," writes Dyer, helps "desensitize [marines] to the suffering of an enemy, and at the same time they are being indoctrinated in the most explicit fashion (as previous generations were not) with the notion that their purpose is not just to be brave or to fight well; it is to kill people."

But desensitization by itself is probably not sufficient to overcome the average individual's deep-seated resistance to killing. Indeed, this desensitization process is almost a smoke screen for conditioning, which is the most important aspect of modern training. Instead of lying prone on a grassy field calmly shooting at a bull's-eye target, for example, the modern soldier spends many hours standing in a foxhole, with full combat equipment draped about his or her body. At periodic intervals, one or two man-shaped targets will pop up in front of the soldier, and he or she must shoot the target.

In addition to traditional marksmanship, soldiers are learning to shoot reflexively and instantly while mimicking the act of killing. In behavioral terms, the man shape popping up in the soldier's field of fire is the "conditioned stimulus." On special occasions, even more realistic and complex targets are used, many of them filled with red paint or ketchup, which provide instant and positive reinforcement when the target is hit. In this and other training exercises, every aspect of killing on the battlefield is rehearsed, visualized, and conditioned.

By the time soldiers do kill in combat, they have rehearsed the process so many times that they are able to, at one level, deny to themselves that they are actually killing other human beings. One British veteran of the Falklands, trained in the modern method, told Holmes that he "thought of the enemy as nothing more or less than Figure II [man-shaped] targets."

There is "a natural disinclination to pull the trigger when your weapon is pointed at a human," says Bill Jordan, a career U.S. Border Patrol officer and veteran of many gunfights. "To aid in overcoming this resistance it is helpful if you can will yourself to think of your opponent as a mere target and not as a human being. In this connection you should go further and pick a spot on your target. This will allow better concentration and further remove the human element from your thinking."

Jordan calls this process "manufactured contempt."

THE HIDDEN COST OF KILLING

The success of this conditioning and desensitization is obvious and undeniable. In many circumstances, highly trained modern soldiers have fought poorly trained guerilla forces, and the tendency of poorly prepared forces to instinctively engage in posturing mechanisms (such as firing high) has given significant advantage to the more highly trained force. We can see the discrepancy in dozens of modern conflicts, including in Somalia, where 18 trapped U.S. troops killed an estimated 364 Somali fighters, and in Iraq, where small numbers of U.S. troops have inflicted terrible losses on insurgents. Though we might be quick to credit technology for American deadliness, keep in mind that the lopsided casualty rates apply even in situations of close, small-arms combat, where the technological gap between opposing forces is not a decisive factor.

The ability to increase the firing rate, though, comes with a hidden cost. Severe psychological trauma becomes a distinct possibility when military training overrides safeguards against killing. In a war when 95 percent of soldiers fired their weapons at the enemy, it should come as no surprise that between 18 and 54 percent of the 2.8 million military personnel who served in Vietnam suffer from posttraumatic stress disorder (PTSD)—far higher than in previous wars.

It's important to note that contrary to stereotype, numerous studies have demonstrated that there is not any distinguishable threat of violence to society from returning veterans. Statistically, there is no greater a population of violent criminals among veterans than there is among nonveterans. What the epidemic of PTSD among Vietnam vets has caused is a significant increase in suicides, drug use, alcoholism, and divorce.

In 1988, a major study by Jeanne and Steven Stellman at Columbia University examined the relationship between PTSD manifestations and a soldier's involvement in the killing process. This study of 6,810 randomly selected veterans is the first in which combat levels were quantified. Stellman and Stellman found that the victims of PTSD are almost solely veterans who participated in high-intensity combat situations. These veterans suffer far higher incidence of divorce, marital problems, tranquilizer use, alcoholism, joblessness, heart disease, and ulcers. As far as PTSD symptoms are concerned, soldiers who were in noncombat situations in Vietnam were found to be statistically indistinguishable from those who spent their entire enlistment in the United States. During the Vietnam era, millions of American adolescents were conditioned to engage in an act against which they had a powerful resistance. This conditioning is a necessary part of allowing a soldier to succeed and survive in the environment where society has placed him. If we accept that we need an army, then we must accept that it has to be as capable of surviving as we can make it. But if society prepares a soldier to overcome his resistance to killing and places him in an environment in which he will kill, then that society has an obligation to deal forthrightly, intelligently, and morally with the psychological repercussions upon the soldier and the society. Largely through an ignorance of the processes and implications involved, this did not happen for Vietnam veterans—a mistake we risk making again as the war in Iraq becomes increasingly deadly and unpopular.

THE RESENSITIZATION OF AMERICA

Today I am on the road, almost 300 days a year, speaking to numerous military organizations going in and out of the combat zone. I explain to them the two dangers that they must guard against. One danger is the "Macho Man" mentality that can cause a soldier to refuse to accept vital mental health services. But the other danger is what I call the "Pity Party." There is a powerful tendency for human beings to respond to stress in the way that they think they should. If soldiers and their spouses, parents, and others are all convinced that the returning veteran will have PTSD, then it can create a powerful self-fulfilling prophecy.

Thus, there is a careful balancing act in which our society is morally obligated to provide state-of-the-art mental health services to returning veterans and the returning soldier is obligated to partake of such care if needed. But we also must remember (and even create an expectation) that most combat veterans will be okay. For those who do have a problem, we must make it clear to them that PTSD is treatable and can be curable, and when finished with it they can potentially be stronger individuals for the experience.

Most importantly, if we do want to build a world in which killing is increasingly rare, more scientists, soldiers, and others must speak up and challenge the popular myth that human beings are "natural-born killers." Popular culture has done much to perpetuate the myth of easy killing. Indeed, today many video games are actually replicating military training and conditioning kids to kill—but without "stimulus discriminators" to ensure that they only fire under authority. Even at elite intellectual levels, the natural-born killer myth is too often embraced uncritically and promoted aggressively, sometimes at the service of an ideological agenda.

We may never understand the nature of the force in humankind that causes us to strongly resist killing fellow human beings, but we can be thankful for it. And although military leaders responsible for winning a war may be distressed by this force, as a species we can view it with pride. It is there, it is strong, and it gives us cause to believe that there may just be hope for humankind after all.

POLITICAL PRIMATES

Christopher Boehm

RECENT AMERICAN POLITICS has been defined by a series of bitter power struggles—as when, for example, the Bush administration was accused of overstepping its authority with wiretaps and torture. In such conflicts we can see traces of countless earlier struggles, from the American Revolution to Watergate. Similar struggles for dominance and power take place in countries all over the world, and we even see them crop up in our local communities and family life.

Because they seem so universal, we have to consider that these problems might be intertwined with our genetic code, that they're part of our evolutionary history. Indeed, if we are to fully understand why and how these conflicts arise, we must examine what comes naturally to us as a highly political species: Are humans predisposed to live freely, side by side as equals? Or are we more likely to form hierarchies where one person or group tries to dominate or subjugate another?

This question has generated long-standing philosophical disputes, but we now have enough data to propose some definite answers. Discoveries in the fields of anthropology and primatology suggest that though we may have a deeply rooted instinct to exert power over others, we also have what may be an equally strong aversion to abuses of power, along with some natural tendencies to punish people who commit those abuses.

Consider this fact: Before 10,000 years ago, only egalitarian societies existed on our planet—tiny societies with no strong leaders at all. Keeping in mind that gene selection requires at least a thousand generations to change our nature significantly, we must assume that most of our genes have evolved from the genetic makeup of people living in these small Paleolithic bands. This includes our "political genes," if I may call them that. Yet, of course, we do not only see egalitarian societies in the world today; we also see nations ruled by fierce despots. So, somehow, prehistoric egalitarians set us up to live not only in egalitarian democracies but in these despotic nations as well.

I am careful to say "set us up," for we are not speaking of hardwired, innately fixed patterns of action like an eyeblink or an uncontrollable scream of fear. Rather, we are talking about softwiring—behavioral propensities that make it very easy to learn certain kinds of behavior rather than others.

Over the years, researchers have tried to hypothesize what our softwired political and social propensities may be. But it was only in 1987 that Harvard primatologist Richard Wrangham made a major breakthrough in his study of how human behavior relates to that of our closest primate relatives. In view of the fact that humans, gorillas, bonobos, and chimpanzees share a recent ancestor and more than 98 percent of their genes, Wrangham determined that any behaviors that all four of these species exhibit today must also have been present in their shared predecessor, which would have lived about 7 million years ago. He called this ancient ape the "common ancestor."

Wrangham identified some social behaviors shared by all four species, including the tendency to live in groups and the willingness to attack members of the same species. But with respect to the common ancestral uses of power, he faced a problem: bonobos, chimpanzees, and gorillas were distinctly hierarchical, with aggressive alpha males; by contrast, human hunter-gatherers were egalitarian, suggesting that our species lacked both innate hierarchical tendencies and tendencies to develop leaders. This inconsistency made it impossible for Wrangham to determine how this ancestor used power, and therefore made it difficult to offer any definitive conclusions about human nature.

Puzzled by this human anomaly, I surveyed almost 50 small, nonliterate cultures, both bands and tribes—to see exactly how egalitarian they were, and why. I discovered that their egalitarian political arrangements were quite deliberate. They believed devoutly in maintaining political parity among adults. This belief was so strong that males who turned into selfish bullies or even tried to boss others around for reasons useful to the group were treated brutally, as moral deviants. The fact that on all continents, hunter-gatherers faced bullies or self-aggrandizing political upstarts—and faced them in spite of these strong egalitarian beliefs—told me that if these people had not so vigilantly worked against inequality, they would have soon turned hierarchical.

This new interpretation meant that by nature, today's hunter-gatherers were prone to try to dominate one another, just like the three species of living apes—and therefore so were the common ancestor and humans all down the evolutionary line. In fact, because this urge to dominate is so intrinsic to humans' political nature, hunter-gatherers who wish to stay egalitarian have to use not only ostracism and shaming but also ejection from the group and sometimes even capital punishment to hold down power-hungry political upstarts. We must ask, then, why a species so inclined to domination has been motivated to insist that power be shared so equally. And here, I believe, is the answer: Just as all four of the aforementioned species have strong propensities to domination and submission, so do they also naturally resent being dominated.

This is obvious enough in a human hunting band, where upstarts who attempt to dominate others are dealt with so harshly. But it's also obvious with chimpanzees that have been studied extensively. Both wild and captive males are extremely ambitious politically, and they invariably form political coalitions to try to unseat the alpha male. More striking is the fact that large coalitions can form in the wild to challenge domineering former alphas and run them out of the community. Emory University primatologist Frans de Waal's studies with captive chimpanzees show that females, too, can band together to partially control their alphas. Captive gorillas, like wild and captive chimpanzees, may attack a dominant silverback they don't like. And bonobos have relatively small female coalitions that routinely raise the power of female subordinates to a degree that puts females virtually on a par with the individually dominant males in competitive situations.

Because such rebellious behavior is found in all four primate species, the roots of this behavior appear to stretch back at least 7 million years. The common ancestor not only disliked being dominated; it ganged up actively in coalitions to cut down the power of its alphas or would-be alphas. And once we recognize that humans throughout prehistory have had to cope with this tension between attraction to power and desire for social parity, it's much easier to see why power has always posed such a problem for our species—and why there can be such variety in human expressions of power today.

Nations are so large that it takes considerable concentration of power at the political center just to make them run, and they come, basically, in two brands. At one extreme is a centralized, autocratic government that has so much military or police power that it can impose degrees of political control beyond a chimpanzee alpha male's wildest dreams. Typically, people ruled in this way—whether in the former Soviet Union or contemporary Iran—are highly ambivalent about the authority above them.

As a practical matter we may, of course, see benefits in having a strong, highly powerful figure govern us, especially when our groups become large and unwieldy. And if those in power are both generous and sensitive to people's natural inclinations to dislike being dominated, even a strong dictatorship may be popularly accepted as "benign." The problem with this unguarded approach is that the next strong leader to come along may be a selfish individual with despotic tendencies.

At the other extreme is our American democracy, in which people realize they need to be governed by a central authority but are determined to keep their leaders from accumulating power beyond what is necessary to keep the nation functioning. The basic assumption about human nature is that leaders will just naturally want to aggrandize their power. That's why all democracies write checks and balances into their constitutions, which curb the power of leaders and guarantee rights to citizens. Democratic nations are never as egalitarian as hunting bands, yet the political dynamics are similar. For instance, just as an arrogant hunter can be deposed as band leader, Richard Nixon's abuse of power led to his being forced to resign from office.

I do not mean to oversimplify the picture. As psychiatrist Erich Fromm has claimed, people may sometimes appreciate a powerful and even ruthlessly despotic leader. And long before Hitler came to power, sociologist Max Weber argued that people may submit their autonomy to an especially charismatic leader. (Think not only of Hitler but of the revered Japanese emperor Hirohito, a figure like Lenin, and perhaps, to a lesser degree, President Hugo Chavez of Venezuela.) But of course, many despots are without charisma and use bald coercive force to dominate resentful populations. In such situations, change may come either through violent revolution or, often enough, by historical evolution when a tyrant like Stalin dies.

For the most part, though, human history has rebuffed the claims of those political thinkers, most notably Thomas Hobbes, who have assumed that strong, authoritarian leadership is required to rule our inherently unruly species. Humans became both anatomically and culturally modern at least 45,000 years ago, and it's a safe bet that the main political behavior we see today in foraging bands—their uniform insistence on keeping their political life reasonably egalitarian—goes even further back than that.

In effect, these egalitarian bands did something very special about the problem of power. They arrived at a largely implicit "social contract," by which each political actor conceded his or her personal pursuit of dominance in order to remain at political parity with his or her peers. In doing so, hunter-gatherers were able to cooperate effectively because their societies were so small. Similarly, a large national democracy can do its best to vigilantly limit power and uphold civil rights. But just like a hunting band, it must watch carefully for would-be dictators in order to preemptively curb their power if need be and stand up to them decisively if they do get the bit in their teeth.

This theory about our political evolution helps us understand why we are so often ambivalent about power. Our genetic nature makes both its abuse and our counterreactions equally likely. And if these counterreactions don't come strongly enough and in a timely fashion, this may bode badly for a nation's citizens, subjecting them to harsh restrictions of their pursuits of liberty and happiness. Indeed, if that nation happens to be a world superpower, this can have disastrous consequences for an entire world of nations.

THE FORGIVENESS INSTINCT

Michael E. McCullough

EARLY ON THE MORNING of October 26, 2001, 25-year-old Chante Mallard was driving home along Interstate 820, just southeast of Fort Worth, Texas, after a long night of partying. Fatigue, combined with the many substances in her bloodstream—alcohol, marijuana, ecstasy—had impaired her judgment and slowed her reaction time. As she rounded the horseshoe-shaped curve to merge onto Route 287, Mallard drove her car straight into a man who had been walking along the dark highway. Gregory Biggs, 37 years old, was catapulted onto the hood of Mallard's car. His head and upper body went crashing through the windshield and landed on the passenger-side floorboard. His legs remained trapped inside the windshield.

With all of the drugs and the noise and the broken glass, Mallard was so disoriented at first that she didn't even know that a human being was stuck in her windshield. When she realized what had happened, she stopped the car, got out, and went around to try and help. But as soon as she touched Biggs's leg, she panicked. In her drug-addled state, she couldn't figure out what to do next. So with Biggs still immobilized in the windshield, she drove the final mile back to her house, pulled into the garage, and closed the garage door behind her. Mallard let Biggs bleed to death right there in the garage. Over and over, Biggs begged Mallard to help him, but Mallard, a nurse's aide, insisted there was nothing she could do for him. So she left him to die. Medical examiners would later testify that Biggs would surely have survived the crash had he received prompt medical attention.

The next night, Mallard and two friends dumped Biggs's body in a nearby park. An informant told police that she had joked about the event later.

It was several months before the police received the tip that would lead them to Mallard. After her arrest, Mallard was tried and convicted of murder. She was sentenced to 50 years in prison. At her sentencing hearing, Biggs's son Brandon had the opportunity to make a victim impact statement. Instead of using this opportunity to request the harshest possible sentence, Brandon said to the court and to Mallard's family, "There's no winners in a case like this. Just as we all lost Greg, you all will be losing your daughter." Later, Brandon would go on to say, "I still want to extend my forgiveness to Chante Mallard and let her know that the Mallard family is in my prayers."

An act of forgiveness like this is astonishing, but Brandon Biggs is hardly unique. In more than a decade of researching forgiveness, I've come across hundreds of stories like Brandon's—acts of forgiveness for transgressions small and large. Over and over, I've been amazed by stories of people who seem to transcend the natural urge for revenge and, instead, find a way to forgive.

But for every one of those stories, you could probably counter with an equally astonishing story of vengeance. I also know these stories well: The grieving father who murders the air traffic controller he blames for his family's death. The disenfranchised loner who, feeling abused by the system, takes a giant bulldozer, converts it into an assault vehicle, then razes the homes and workplaces of people who have caused him pain. The men whose desire for vengeance against what they view as an unjust foreign occupation leads them to capture westerners, behead them, and incinerate their bodies for the world to see.

In light of these outrageous, often tragic stories of revenge, you might be tempted to assume that people like Brandon Biggs possess some special trait that enables them to bypass the desire for vengeance. At the same time, it may seem that people who act on those urges for revenge are somehow defective, sick, or morally misshapen.

Both of those assumptions are wrong. My research on forgiveness has led me to this unsettling conclusion: The desire for revenge isn't a disease that afflicts a few unfortunate people; rather it's a universal trait of human nature, crafted by natural selection, that exists today because it helped our ancestors adapt to their environment.

But there's some good news, too. Evolutionary science leads us squarely to the conclusion that the capacity for forgiveness, like the desire for revenge, is also an intrinsic feature of human nature, crafted by natural selection. Because revenge and forgiveness both solved problems for ancestral humans, these capacities are now typical of modern humans.

If the capacity to forgive and the desire for revenge really are standard-issue human social instincts, then there's a hopeful possibility waiting in the wings: that we can make the world a less vengeful, more forgiving place, even when we're forced to work with a fixed human nature. How do we do that? By making our social environments less abundant in the factors that elicit the desire for revenge and more abundant in the factors that elicit forgiveness. In other words, to increase forgiveness in the world, it doesn't make sense to try to change human nature. It makes a lot more sense to try to change the world around us.

But to do that, we need to make sure that we're seeing human nature for what it really is. Consider these three simple truths about forgiveness and revenge and their place in human nature.

TRUTH #1: THE DESIRE FOR REVENGE IS A BUILT-IN FEATURE OF HUMAN NATURE

A century of research in the social and biological sciences reveals a crucial truth: Though we might wish it were otherwise, the desire for revenge is normal—normal in the sense that every neurologically intact human being on the planet has the biological hardware for it.

When evolutionary biologists Martin Daly and Margo Wilson looked at data on 60 different societies from around the world, they tried to determine how many of those societies showed evidence of blood feuds, capital punishment, or the desire for blood revenge. They found that 57 of the 60 societies they examined—95 percent—had "some reference to blood feud or capital punishment as an institutionalized practice, or specific accounts of particular cases or, at the least, some articulate expression of the desire for blood revenge."

"What our survey suggests," Daly and Wilson write in their book *Homicide*, "is that the inclination to blood revenge is experienced by people in all cultures, and that the act is therefore unlikely to be altogether 'absent' anywhere."

When a behavior is this universal, that suggests it's not just the product of particular cultures or social factors. Instead, it's essential to what it means to be human.

There are three very good reasons why revenge might have evolved in humans. First, revenge may have deterred would-be aggressors from committing acts of aggression against our ancestors. Ancestral humans were group-living creatures who lived, worked, and ate in the presence of others. Thus, the outcomes of their aggressive encounters with other individuals quickly became public knowledge. If our ancestors saw that someone didn't seek revenge after being harmed, they may have concluded that he was an easy mark, then tried to take advantage of him themselves.

Research suggests that these social dynamics still play out today. Social psychologists have shown in the laboratory that a victim will retaliate more strongly against his or her provoker when an audience has witnessed the provocation, especially if the audience lets the victim know that he or she looks weak because of the abuse he or she suffered. In fact, when people find out that bystanders think less of them because of the harm they've endured, they'll actually go out of their way—even at substantial cost to themselves—to retaliate against their provokers. Moreover, when two men have an argument on the street, the mere presence of a third person doubles the likelihood that the encounter will escalate from an exchange of words to an exchange of blows.

Second, when ancestral humans were harmed by others, the propensity for revenge may have helped them deter the aggressors from harming them again. In highly mobile modern societies such as ours, often we can simply end relationships in which we've been betrayed. But in the close societies in which our earliest hominid ancestors lived, moving away usually wasn't a good option. In fact, ostracism from the group was often a severe punishment that carried the risk of death. Therefore, our ancestors often had to find more direct ways to cope with the despots and bullies in their midst. One way to cope with someone who has taken advantage of you is to make it less profitable for that person to do so again.

This punishment function of revenge is quite prevalent in many animal societies. For example, if a rhesus macaque monkey finds a source of a highly valued food but doesn't issue one of the "food calls" used to alert others to the big discovery, the animal is likely to be attacked when others realize what he's done. In a scenario like this, you can almost see the evolutionary logic at work: If you don't want to share your food with us, then we're going to make it less profitable for you to try and be sneaky about it. In this way, revenge may have evolved because of its ability to teach our aggressors that crime doesn't pay.

Finally, revenge may have been useful for punishing (and

reforming) "free riders," people who enjoy the benefits of a group's efforts without contributing to those efforts. To spur humans' prodigious tendencies for cooperation, our ancestors had to ensure that when free riders failed to "pitch in" and make appropriate contributions to the common good, they suffered dire consequences.

With these adaptive functions in mind, it gets easier to accept the idea that revenge is a built-in feature of human nature, despite its dreadful effects in the world today. We might rightly view revenge as a modern-day problem, but from an evolutionary point of view, it's also an age-old solution.

TRUTH #2: THE CAPACITY FOR FORGIVENESS IS A BUILT-IN FEATURE OF HUMAN NATURE

So revenge is an authentic, standard-issue, bred-in-the-bone feature of human nature. But that doesn't imply that forgiveness is a thin veneer of civility, slapped on top of a brutish, vengeful core. Nothing could be further from the truth. In fact, when you use the conceptual tools of evolutionary science, you can't help but conclude that our capacity for forgiveness is every bit as authentic as our capacity for revenge.

For example, there's evidence that forgiveness is just as universal among humans as revenge is. Although Martin Daly and Margo Wilson found that blood revenge has emerged as an important social phenomenon in 95 percent of the societies they examined, my own analysis revealed that the concepts of forgiveness, reconciliation, or both have been documented in 93 percent of those same societies.

Is it possible that forgiveness and reconciliation really didn't exist among that remaining 7 percent? The evolutionary biologist David Sloan Wilson has observed that "it is actually difficult to find descriptions of forgiveness in hunter-gatherer societies, not because forgiveness is absent but because it happens so naturally that it often goes unnoticed." I think Wilson may be correct, and not just about hunter-gatherers but about all societies. Forgiveness and reconciliation may be so common and so taken for granted by anthropologists as to be regarded, quite literally, as nothing to write home about.

And just as with revenge, research has found that forgiveness is also widespread across the animal kingdom, offering further evidence of its evolutionary significance. More than two decades ago, primatologist Frans de Waal and a colleague published results showing that friendly behaviors such as kissing, submissive vocal sounds, touching, and embracing were actually quite common after chimpanzees' aggressive conflicts. In fact, these were the chimpanzees' typical responses to aggressive conflicts. The researchers observed 350 aggressive encounters and found that only 50, or 14 percent, of those encounters were preceded by some sort of friendly contact. However, 179, or 51 percent, of the aggressive encounters were followed by friendly contact. This was a staggering discovery: friendly contact was even more common after conflict than it was during conflict-free periods. Chimps kiss and make up in the same way people do.

Chimpanzees aren't the slightest bit unique in this respect. Other great apes, such as the bonobo and the mountain gorilla, also reconcile. And it gets more interesting still, for reconciliation isn't even limited to primates. Goats, sheep, dolphins, and hyenas all tend to reconcile after conflicts (rubbing horns, flippers, and fur are common elements of these species' conciliatory gestures). Of the half dozen or so nonprimates that have been studied, only domestic cats have failed to demonstrate a conciliatory tendency. (If you own a cat, this probably comes as no surprise.)

So why might animals (humans included) be so willing to forgive and reconcile? Why might evolution have outfitted us with such an ability? Biologists have offered several hypotheses. I'm especially fond of the "valuable relationship" hypothesis, espoused by de Waal and many other primatologists. It goes like this: Animals reconcile because it repairs important relationships that have been damaged by aggression. By forgiving and repairing relationships, our ancestors were in a better position to glean the benefits of cooperation between group members—which, in turn, increased their evolutionary fitness.

Research with seven pairs of female long-tailed macaques offers perhaps the most striking evidence of how the value of a relationship affects whether a conflict will be reconciled. In the first phase of their experiment, researchers Marina Cords and Sylvie Thurnheer simply examined how often these seven pairs of individuals reconciled. Averaging across the seven pairs, about 25 percent of their conflicts got reconciled. In phase two, the seven pairs were trained to cooperate with each other in order to get food. If one partner wanted to eat, she had to wait until the other one wanted to eat. Then they could work together to gain access to the food. No cooperation, no food. In other words, the researchers used experimental methods to turn the macaques' relationships into valuable relationships. After they had been trained to work together in order to obtain food, the average rate of reconciliation doubled to about 50 percent. When group-living animals are given the choice between (a) reconciling with a valuable partner who has harmed them or (b) holding on to their grudges but going hungry, they generally choose the reconciled relationship and the full belly.

Needless to say, even if natural selection has caused forgiveness and reconciliation to become universal features of human nature, that doesn't imply that these behaviors are universally practiced in the same way or with the same frequency. There are cultural differences in what people are willing to forgive and how they go about doing it. However, it seems a safe bet that under the right social conditions, most people will be motivated to take the time and trouble to forgive. So what are those social conditions that can help promote forgiveness?

TRUTH #3: TO MAKE THE WORLD A MORE FORGIVING, LESS VENGEFUL PLACE, DON'T TRY TO CHANGE HUMAN NATURE— CHANGE THE WORLD!

Human nature is what it is: the outcome of billions of years of biological evolution, the details of which are managed by a genetic cookbook. In other words, it's pretty well locked in.

But it's also exquisitely sensitive to context. Human nature ensures that people are capable of a wide range of behaviors; the behaviors we actually express depend on our changing circumstances.

This is especially true for forgiveness and revenge. They both emerged as adaptive solutions to problems that humans persistently encountered during evolution, and people still encounter many of those problems today. When people live in places where crime and disorder are high, policing is poor, governments are weak, and life is dangerous, they will tend to use revenge as a problem-solving strategy. They'll do so because revenge's ability to punish aggressors, its ability to deter would-be aggressors, and its ability to discourage cheaters made it adaptive in our ancestral environment.

Likewise, we'll see higher rates of forgiveness under those conditions that made forgiving adaptive in our ancestral environments. This means we'll see more forgiveness in places where people are highly dependent on complex networks of cooperative relationships, policing is reliable, the system of justice is efficient and trustworthy, and social institutions are up to the task of helping truly contrite offenders make amends with the people they've harmed.

Cultural changes can also produce changes in revenge and forgiveness even when we can't change social and environmental factors directly. This is because culture's function, as far as forgiveness and revenge are concerned, is to help people learn rules about when it's appropriate to forgive and when it's appropriate to seek revenge. Indeed, research with other primates has shown that the propensity to forgive can be shaped heavily by one's cultural experiences. Separate infant monkeys from their mothers, and they'll grow up to be less conciliatory than is typical for their species. Raise them among individuals from a more conciliatory species, and they'll become more conciliatory than is typical.

Because we are cultural learners, we can learn valuable lessons about where and when to seek revenge and about where and when to forgive, simply by observing our parents, siblings, friends, associates, teachers, and mentors. We also learn culturally through religious teachings, myths, traditions, the arts, advertisements, items in the news, and other formal vehicles for transmitting cultural lessons. The informal codes that govern people's social behavior in many U.S. inner cities, for example, convey reams of revenge-promoting cultural information. Likewise, the Amish are fed a steady diet of pro-forgiveness religious teachings and other cultural inputs that make them into the superforgivers they are. Most of us are in between the two extremes, raised on a diet of mixed cultural inputs, some of which promote revenge and others of which encourage forgiveness.

In certain cases, we can see macrolevel cultural changes developing to make the world a more forgiving place. One of those changes has taken shape over the past decade. Few people knew very much about the idea of a "truth and reconciliation commission" before the early- to mid-1990s, when El Salvador and South Africa put commissions in place to investigate human rights abuses during civil war (in the case of El Salvador) and apartheid (in the case of South Africa). Since then, the truth and reconciliation commission idea has been disseminated worldwide, and many people who've learned about it have helped establish similar commissions within their own nations—often to great effect. The United States Institute of Peace documents more than 20 nations that have used truth and reconciliation commissions following civil war. This is cultural learning at its finest, and on a truly global scale.

If the hundreds of scientific articles on human forgiveness—coupled with decades of work from evolutionary biology, primatology, and anthropology—show us anything, it's that forgiveness is easier to achieve when we presume that natural selection has endowed the human mind with a "forgiveness instinct." In that light, forgiveness is not an elusive or mystical force but rather a skill that the mind already possesses. Making the world a more forgiving place, then, does not require that we make miracles happen. It just requires that we learn to use a tool that's already well within humanity's reach.

THE NEW SCIENCE OF FORGIVENESS

Everett L. Worthington Jr.

WHEN CHRIS CARRIER was 10 years old, he was abducted near his Florida home, taken into the swamps, stabbed repeatedly in the chest and abdomen with an ice pick, and then shot through the temple with a handgun. Remarkably, hours after being shot, he awoke with a headache, unable to see out of one eye. He stumbled to the highway and stopped a car, which took him to the hospital.

Years later, a police officer told Chris that the man suspected of his abduction lay close to death. "Confront him," suggested the officer. Chris did more than that. He comforted his attacker during the man's final weeks of life and ultimately forgave him, bringing peace to them both.

Chris Carrier's act of forgiveness might seem unfathomable to some, an act of extreme charity or even foolishness. Indeed, our culture seems to perceive forgiveness as a sign of weakness, submission, or both. Often we find it easier to stigmatize or denigrate our enemies than to empathize with or forgive them. And in a society as competitive as ours, people may hesitate to forgive because they don't want to relinquish the upper hand in a relationship. "It is much more agreeable to offend and later ask forgiveness than to be offended and grant forgiveness," said the philosopher

Friedrich Nietzsche. I think many people today are inclined to agree with him.

Surely now is a time when the world could use some more forgiveness. Americans resent the Muslim world for September 11. Iraqis and much of the Middle East feel humiliated by the United States. Diplomats in the United Nations bicker and insult each other, igniting or reigniting national rivalries. Still, many people hesitate to ask for or grant forgiveness when they feel they have nothing to gain in return.

But a new line of research suggests something different. This research has shown that Chris Carrier's story isn't an anomaly. Forgiveness isn't just practiced by saints or martyrs, nor does it benefit only its recipients. Instead, studies are finding connections between forgiveness and physical, mental, and spiritual health and evidence that it plays a key role in the health of families, communities, and nations. Though this research is still young, it has already produced some exciting findings—and raised some important questions.

FORGIVENESS AND HEALTH

Perhaps the most basic question to address first is, What is forgiveness? Though most people probably feel they know what forgiveness means, researchers differ about what actually constitutes forgiveness. I've come to believe that how we define forgiveness usually depends on context. In cases where we hope to forgive a person with whom we do not want a continuing relationship, we usually define forgiveness as reducing or eliminating resentment and motivations toward revenge. My colleagues Michael McCullough, Kenneth Rachal, and I have defined forgiveness in close relationships to include more than merely getting rid of the negative. The forgiving person becomes less motivated to retaliate against someone who offended him or her and less motivated to remain estranged from that person. Instead, he or she becomes more motivated by feelings of goodwill, despite the offender's hurtful actions. In a close relationship, we hope, forgiveness will not only move us past negative emotions, but move us toward a net positive feeling. It doesn't mean forgetting or pardoning an offense.

Unforgiveness, by contrast, seems to be a negative emotional state where an offended person maintains feelings of resentment, hostility, anger, and hatred toward the person who offended him. I began with Chris Carrier's story because it is such a clear example of forgiveness. Although he never forgot or condoned what his attacker did to him, he did replace his negative emotions and desire for retribution with feelings of care and compassion and a drive toward conciliation.

People can deal with injustices in many ways. They don't have to decide to forgive, and they don't necessarily need to change their emotions. But if they don't change their response in some way, unforgiveness can take its toll on physical, mental, relational, and even spiritual health. By contrast, new research suggests that forgiveness can benefit people's health.

In one study, Charlotte vanOyen Witvliet, a psychologist at Hope College, asked people to think about someone who had hurt, mistreated, or offended them. While they thought about this person and his or her past offense, she monitored their blood pressure, heart rate, facial muscle tension, and sweat gland activity. To ruminate on an old transgression is to practice unforgiveness.

Sure enough, in Witvliet's research, when people recalled a grudge, their physical arousal soared. Their blood pressure and heart rate increased, and they sweated more. Ruminating about their grudges was stressful, and subjects found the rumination unpleasant. It made them feel angry, sad, anxious, and less in control. Witvliet also asked her subjects to try to empathize with their offenders or imagine forgiving them. When they practiced forgiveness, their physical arousal coasted downward. They showed no more of a stress reaction than normal wakefulness produces.

In my own lab, we wanted to determine whether people's stress levels are related to their ability to forgive a romantic partner. We measured levels of cortisol in the saliva of 39 people who rated their relationship as either terrific or terrible. Cortisol is a hormone that metabolizes fat for quick response to stress (and after the stress ends, deposits the fat back where it is easily accessible— around the waist). People with poor (or recently failed) relationships tended to have higher baseline levels of cortisol, and they also scored worse on a test that measures their general willingness to forgive. When they were asked to think about their relationship, they had more cortisol reactivity—that is, their stress hormone jumped. Those jumps in stress were highly correlated with their unforgiving attitudes toward their partner. People with very happy relationships were not without stresses and strains between them. But forgiving their partner's faults seemed to keep their physical stress in the normal range.

The physical benefits of forgiveness seem to increase with age, according to a recent study led by Loren Toussaint, a psychologist at Luther College, in Iowa. Toussaint—along with David Williams, Marc Musick, and Susan Everson—conducted a national survey of nearly 1,500 Americans, asking the degree to which each person practiced and experienced forgiveness (of others, of self, and even if they thought they had experienced forgiveness by God). Participants also reported on their physical and mental health. Toussaint and his colleagues found that older and middle-aged people forgave others more often than did young adults and also felt more forgiven by God. What's more, they found a significant relationship between forgiving others and positive health among middle-aged and older Americans. People over 45 years of age who had forgiven others reported greater satisfaction with their lives and were less likely to report symptoms of psychological distress, such as feelings of nervousness, restlessness, and sadness.

Why might that relationship between unforgiveness and negative health symptoms exist? Consider that hostility is a central part of unforgiveness. Hostility also has been found to be the part of type A behavior that seems to have the most pernicious health effects, such as a heightened risk of cardiovascular disease. Forsaking a grudge may also free a person from hostility and all its unhealthy consequences.

It probably isn't just hostility and stress that link unforgiveness and poor health. According to a recent review of the literature on forgiveness and health that my colleague Michael Scherer and I recently published, unforgiveness might compromise the immune system at many levels. For instance, our review suggests that unforgiveness might throw off the production of important hormones and even disrupt the way our cells fight off infections, bacteria, and other physical insults, such as mild periodontal disease.

FORGIVENESS AND RELATIONSHIPS

Forgiveness has proved beneficial to a range of relationships, whether it's a family, romantic, or professional relationship. Forgiveness within close relationships is not harder or easier than forgiving absent individuals, such as strangers who rob or assault us or people who have moved away or died since hurting us. In ongoing relationships, forgiveness is simply different. A present partner can make things better or worse. An absent person can't be confronted, but also can't reject a confrontation or compound harms with new hurts.

Johan Karremans and Paul Van Lange, in the Netherlands,

and Caryl Rusbult, at the University of North Carolina, have, in collaboration and separately, investigated forgiveness in close relationships. People are usually more willing to forgive if they sense trust and a willingness to sacrifice from their partner. The authors predicted that forgiving would be associated with greater well-being, especially in relationships of strong rather than weak commitment. They figured that people in highly committed relationships have more to lose if the relationship fails and so would be willing to make certain sacrifices. They used several methods, such as having people fill out questionnaires, recall past relationships, and assess their present relationships. What they found was that if people were unwilling to sacrifice at times—if they wanted to exact revenge rather than practice forgiveness—they often suffered conflict, negative emotions, and poor abilities to compromise when inevitable differences arose.

The researchers also found that the relationship between forgiveness and well-being in marriages was stronger than in other relationships. Their findings suggest that the more we invest in a relationship, the more we need a repertoire of good strategies to guide it through troubled times—and the more these strategies will prove satisfying and rewarding. Forgiveness is one of those strategies.

Colleagues and I developed a scale to measure forgiveness between people. We asked people to remember a specific offense in which someone harmed them, and then asked about their motives for revenge and for avoiding the perpetrator. People who showed high motivations for revenge and avoidance had lower relationship satisfaction. People who tended to forgive reported greater relationship quality and also greater commitment to relationships.

Frank Fincham and Julie Hall, at the University of Buffalo, and Steven Beach, at the University of Georgia, recently reviewed 17 empirical studies on forgiveness in relationships. By their analysis, the studies suggest that when partners hurt each other, there is often a shift in their goals for their relationship. They might have previously professed undying love and worked hard to cooperate with their partner, but if this partner betrays them, suddenly they become more competitive. They focus on getting even and keeping score instead of enjoying each other. They concentrate on not losing arguments rather than on compromise. They use past transgressions to remind the partner of his or her failings. Forgiveness, assert Fincham and his colleagues, can help restore more benevolent and cooperative goals to relationships.

LEARNING FORGIVENESS

These findings suggest that forgiveness has benefits such as high self-esteem, better moods, and happier relationships. But skeptical scientists will be quick to ask, "Couldn't it simply be that when people feel good about themselves, feel happy, and feel satisfied with their relationships, they'll forgive almost anything? Could it be that happiness drives forgiveness, not the other way around?" Sometimes that might well be the case. But one way to test this idea is to see whether people—cheerful, sad, and everywhere in between—could learn to become more forgiving and, if they do, how that might affect their mental and physical health. This would imply that forgiveness could be possible for almost anyone, not just the perpetually happy and well-adjusted.

Interventions have been designed for partners seeking to make their marriages better, for parents, victims of incest, men offended because their partner aborted a pregnancy, people in recovery for drug and alcohol problems, divorced partners, and love-deprived adolescents.

Through all these interventions, no one has yet found a silver bullet that helps people forgive instantly. But evidence so far suggests that people of various backgrounds and temperaments can learn to forgive. For instance, Robert Enright has developed a specific 20-step intervention that he has tested rigorously, with encouraging results. In one study, men who reported being hurt by their partner's decision to have an abortion went through 12 90-minute weekly sessions designed to help them forgive. These men showed a significant increase in their levels of forgiveness and significant reductions in their levels of anxiety, anger, and grief when compared with a control group. Enright has reported similar results with other populations, including victims of incest.

Not everyone responds equally to these interventions, and a lot of work still must be done to determine exactly what makes forgiveness interventions most effective. British researchers Peter Woodruff and Tom Farrow are doing some of this important work. Their research suggests that the areas in the brain associated with forgiveness are often deep in the emotional centers, in the region known as the limbic system, rather than in the areas of the cortex usually associated with reasoned judgments. In one study, they asked people to judge the fairness of a transgression and then consider whether to forgive it or empathize with the transgressor. Ten individuals evaluated several social scenarios while the researchers recorded images of their brain activity. Whether people empathized or forgave, similar areas in the emotion centers of the brain lit up. When those same people thought about the fairness of the same transgression, though, the emotion centers stopped being as active. This could be a clue for interventionists. To help people forgive, help them steer clear of dwelling on how fair a transgression was or how just a solution might be. Instead, get people to see things from the other person's perspective.

There are other clues for encouraging forgiveness. Charlotte Witvliet, Nathaniel Wade, Jack Berry, and I have conducted a set of three studies that show that when people feel positive emotions toward transgressors—such as when they receive apologies or restitution for offenses—they experience changes in physiology, including lowered blood pressure, heart rate, and sweat activity as well as lowered tension in the frown muscles of the face. When they experience positive emotions toward transgressors, they are also more likely to forgive them. Sincere apologies helped people forgive and calm down. Getting fair restitution on top of an apology magnified the effect. Insincere or incomplete apologies actually riled people up more.

It's important to stress again that forgiveness usually takes time. In fact, in a meta-analysis of all research that measured the impact of forgiveness interventions, Nathaniel Wade and I found that a factor as simple as the amount of time someone spent trying to forgive was highly related to the actual degree of forgiveness experienced.

So, the question I posed at the beginning of this section—does forgiveness drive happiness or vice versa?—seems at least in part answerable by saying that forgiveness is not necessarily something that just comes naturally to people with high self-esteem and stable relationships. Instead, it is something all different kinds of people can learn. With the right kind of practice, its benefits can be available to most of us.

Teaching people to forgive raises some important questions. Are some offenses so heinous that they ought never to be forgiven? Are there times when justice should trump forgiveness? Justice and forgiveness do clash at times. I do not advocate forgiving under all circumstances (unless a person's religion dictates it). But I know that a sincere apology, restitution, or a punishment imposed by the proper authorities can often make it easier for victims to grant forgiveness. The big transgressions are not necessarily "unforgivable" because they are big. Instead, big transgressions are often the ones that, if they are ever to be surmounted, must be forgiven.

WHAT WE DON'T KNOW

While we have learned a lot over the past few years, we also realize that our knowledge fills only a teacup when there is a giant swimming pool of unknowns awaiting discovery.

We know little about how children forgive or how they can learn to forgive. We know that not everyone responds equally to the interventions to promote forgiveness. Who does and doesn't benefit by different forgiveness interventions? How long should interventions last?

We still need to discover how forgiveness can be better promoted in society at large. How can schools, parents, and sports coaches work together in communities to foster cooperation and forgiveness instead of violence? Given the role of forgiveness in religious traditions, should youth programs be created to promote forgiveness at churches, mosques, or synagogues? Can the media serve as a tool for effective education, or can forgiveness education work as an adjunct to therapy by mental health professionals?

Conflicts and transgressions seem inevitable as humans rub against each other. The sharp corners of our personalities irritate and scuff against those with whom we interact on a daily basis. But if the new science of forgiveness has proved anything, it's that these offenses don't need to condemn us to a life of hurt and aggravation. For years, political and religious figures, such as Nelson Mandela and Archbishop Desmond Tutu in South Africa, have demonstrated the beauty and effectiveness of forgiveness in action. Through a harmony of research and practice, I trust that we can continue to foster forgiveness—and continue to study the effects scientifically—to bring health to individuals, relationships, and societies as a whole.

BRAIN TRUST

Michael Kosfeld

IMAGINE A BARE ROOM and two players sitting face to face, about to play a game. The first player is the "investor"; the second player is the "trustee."

At the outset of the game, both players are endowed with a set number of points—say, 12 each—with each point equivalent to real money.

The investor can transfer any amount to the trustee. On the way to the trustee, the investor's transfer is tripled. So if the investor decides to transfer 8 points, the trustee receives 24 points on top of her original 12, for a total of 36.

The trustee can then return any amount of her points back to the investor. After she has made her transfer back, that's it. The game is over. Each player tallies her points and the money she'll receive.

The investor's decision in this game is a decision of trust, which is why social scientists refer to this as the "trust game" and use it to test trusting behavior in different situations. The more the investor transfers to the trustee, the more she stands to profit in the end. But she must trust that the trustee will return a sufficiently large amount—at least as large as the original transfer—for the game to be profitable for her. And what if the trustee returns nothing?

The game nicely captures the fundamental dilemma of trust in human society. The decision to trust always entails the risk of being exploited or betrayed. Yet if people trust and the trust is rewarded, everyone is typically better off. To gain the benefits that come with trust, the trusting person must always overcome her natural aversion to the risk of betrayal.

Conventional economic theory maintains that people will always behave in a purely self-interested manner. According to this worldview, it makes no sense to trust, whether in a trust game or in real life, as any trust will be exploited. The trustee will always keep her entire windfall for herself, so the investor would be better off not transferring any money in the first place.

And yet when researchers like Joyce Berg and others have had people play the trust game with real monetary stakes, they have repeatedly found that the average investor will transfer half of her initial endowment and receive similar amounts in return. Through the trust game, researchers have also discovered a number of factors that seem to drive levels of trust. Familiarity breeds trust—players tend to trust each other more with each new game. So does introducing punishments for untrustworthy behavior or even just reminding players of their obligations to each other.

These studies have demonstrated the strength of human trust and that humans are truly worthy of this trust from one another. They have also improved our understanding of the social factors that determine trust. But two important questions remain: Is trust truly a biologically based part of human nature, and if so, what is it in the brain that makes humans trust each other?

BIOLOGY OF TRUST

This question might sound complex, but there is a simple hypothesis about what steers the human brain to trust another human: a hormone called oxytocin.

Oxytocin is produced in the brain's hypothalamus and stored

in the posterior pituitary gland. We know that it helps smooth muscle contractions in childbirth and in breast-feeding mothers. But recently we've discovered that its applications go beyond the maternal. It turns out that oxytocin also reduces social anxiety and helps people meet and bond with each other. A man and woman involved in the mating dance are releasing oxytocin; so are friends having a good time at dinner.

Forming relationships like these involves trust, but is there a direct connection between trust and oxytocin?

To find out, my colleagues and I conducted an experiment in which participants took either oxytocin or a placebo. Fifty minutes later, participants played the trust game against four different anonymous partners. They played with real money, with each point worth almost half a Swiss franc.

The results revealed that oxytocin does indeed seem to grease the wheels of trust. Of the 29 investors who had taken oxytocin, 45 percent transferred the maximum amount of 12 points in each interaction. By contrast, only 21 percent of the placebo-group investors did so. The average transfer made by the oxytocin-group investors was 9.6 points, compared with 8.1 points by the placebo-group investors.

Interestingly, the investors' expectations about the back-transfer from the trustee did not differ between the oxytocin and placebo recipients. Oxytocin increased the participants' willingness to trust others, but it did not make them more optimistic about another person's trustworthiness.

The results indicate that oxytocin does indeed somehow help humans overcome distrust. But does oxytocin really increase trust, or does it merely make us feel so good that we lose our aversion to risk and betrayal?

To figure that one out, we conducted a second experiment, in which investors faced the same choices as in the trust game. The investors in this experiment were again in a risky situation, but this time there was no human being on the other side of the table; instead, investors faced a computer that generated random numbers of points. Everything else in the "risk experiment" was identical to the trust experiment.

The result? Investors who'd received oxytocin behaved no differently than those in the placebo groups. We therefore concluded that the effect of oxytocin is, indeed, specific to trusting other people and the willingness to take risks in social situations. Oxytocin does not affect human attitudes toward risk and uncertainty in situations where there are no other human beings involved.

In short, trust is very much a biologically based part of the human condition. It is, in fact, one of the distinguishing features of the human species. An element of trust characterizes almost all human social interactions. When trust is absent, we are, in a sense, dehumanized.

APPLIED TRUST

The discovery that oxytocin increases trust in humans is likely to have important clinical applications for patients suffering from mental disorders like social phobia or autism. Social phobia ranks as the third most common mental health disorder after depression and alcoholism; sufferers are severely impaired during social interactions and are often unable to show even basic forms of trust toward others.

Given the results of our trust studies, the administration of oxytocin, in combination with behavioral therapy, might yield positive effects for the treatment of these patients, particularly in light, too, of its relaxing effects in social situations.

At the same time, however, the results from these experiments raise fears of abuse. Some might suppose that unscrupulous employers or insurance companies could use oxytocin to induce trusting behavior in their employees or clients. Dishonest car salesmen might spray customers with the hormone before steering them toward a lemon.

Fortunately, most of these fears are baseless: the surreptitious administration of a substantial dose of oxytocin—for example, through air conditioning, food, or drinks—is technically impossible. Of course, one could always force the spray up another's nose. But it's safe to say that this would alarm recipients enough to override any glow they might get from the oxytocin.

It is more likely that advertisers might find ways to cleverly design stimuli to trigger the release of oxytocin in consumers through, for example, strategically placed smiling faces or warm handshakes or perhaps even by measuring people's oxytocin levels in focus groups. All this might make these consumers more inclined to trust the claims made by the advertisers. Of course, advertisers (and most socially intelligent humans) have always intuitively understood ways to manipulate perception and build trust; this just gives them one more tool for their kit. However, knowledge can cut both ways: by better understanding the underlying biological mechanisms of these stimuli, research into oxytocin could be even more useful for protecting consumers from the manipulative strategies of marketing departments.

To some people, these findings about oxytocin might raise another concern: that trust is not subject to rational control—that it's "all hormones." This seems to stand in stark contrast to the traditional idea of trust being the outcome of a cognitive, rational process.

In my view, trust is both, just like other human social behaviors. We cannot deny that many of our decisions are governed by cognitive processes, which in the case of trust take into account the available information about the trustee's motivation, the likelihood of a repeated interaction, and so on.

Nevertheless, research like this shows that our behavior is also influenced by a large number of very complex, yet identifiable, biological processes. Future research should help us understand how cognitive and biological processes interact in shaping our decisions about whom to trust.

But there's no denying the important role trust plays in cooperative behaviors or that humans have a deeply rooted ability to trust. It's up to us to earn that trust from one another.

PAY IT FORWARD

Robert A. Emmons

ELIZABETH BARTLETT is a professor of political science at a midwestern university. At the age of 42, her irregular heartbeat had become life-threatening. A heart transplant was her last hope, and she was fortunate to receive one. In a book chronicling her journey, she writes that she felt thankful for her new lease on life—but simply feeling thankful wasn't enough.

> I have a desire to do something in return. To do thanks. To give thanks. Give things. Give thoughts. Give love. So gratitude becomes the gift, creating a cycle of giving and receiving, the endless waterfall. Filling up and spilling over and perhaps not even to the giver but to someone else, to whoever crosses one's path. It is the simple passing on of the gift.

What Bartlett describes is true gratitude. As this brief passage illustrates, gratitude is more than a pleasant feeling; it is also motivating. Gratitude serves as a key link between receiving and giving: it moves recipients to share and increase the very good they have received. Because so much of human life is about giving, receiving, and repaying, gratitude is a pivotal concept for our social interactions. The famed sociologist Georg Simmel declared

that gratitude is "the moral memory of mankind." If every grateful action, he went on to say, were suddenly eliminated, society would crumble.

Yet gratitude's benefits are rarely discussed these days; indeed, in contemporary American society, we've come to overlook, dismiss, or even disparage the significance of gratitude.

Part of the problem, I think, is that we lack a sophisticated discourse for gratitude because we are out of practice. The late philosopher Robert Solomon noted how relatively infrequently Americans talk about gratitude. Despite the fact that it forms the foundation of social life in many other cultures, in America, we usually don't give it much thought—with a notable exception of one day, Thanksgiving. On the other hand, we tend to scrutinize anger, resentment, happiness, and romantic love.

It has been argued that males in particular may resist experiencing and expressing gratefulness insomuch as it implies dependency and indebtedness. One fascinating study in the 1980s found that American men were less likely to regard gratitude positively than were German men, and were likely to view it as less constructive and useful than their German counterparts. Gratitude presupposes so many judgments about debt and dependency that it is easy to see why supposedly self-reliant Americans would feel queasy about even discussing it.

We like to think that we are our own creators and that our lives are ours to do with as we please. We take things for granted. We assume that we are totally responsible for all the good that comes our way. After all, we have earned it. We deserve it. A scene from *The Simpsons* captures this mentality: When asked to say grace at the family dinner table, Bart Simpson offers the following words: "Dear God, we paid for all this stuff ourselves, so thanks for nothing."

In one sense, of course, Bart is right. The Simpson family did earn their own money. But on another level, he is missing the bigger picture. The grateful person senses that much goodness happens independently of his actions or even in spite of himself. Gratitude implies humility—a recognition that we could not be who we are or where we are in life without the contributions of others. How many family members, friends, strangers, and all those who have come before us have made our daily lives easier and our existence freer, more comfortable, and even possible? It is mind-boggling to consider.

Indeed, contemporary social science research reminds us that if we overlook gratitude, it will be at our own emotional and psychological peril. After years of ignoring gratitude—perhaps because it appears, on the surface, to be a very obvious emotion, lacking in interesting complications—researchers have found that gratitude contributes powerfully to human health, happiness, and social connection.

I first started studying gratitude ten years ago. While the emotion initially seemed simplistic to me, I soon discovered that gratitude is a deep, complex phenomenon that plays a critical role in human happiness. My research partnership with Michael McCullough at the University of Miami has led to several important findings about gratitude. We've discovered scientific proof that when people regularly work on cultivating gratitude, they experience a variety of measurable benefits: psychological, physical, and social. In some cases, people have reported that gratitude led to transformative life changes. And even more importantly, the family, friends, partners, and others who surround them consistently report that people who practice gratitude seem measurably happier and are more pleasant to be around. I've concluded that gratitude is one of the few attitudes that can measurably change people's lives.

THE SCIENCE OF GRATITUDE

At the outset of our research, Mike McCullough and I assumed that regularly practicing gratitude should enhance people's psychological and social functioning; we then based a series of experiments on that assumption.

In our first study, Mike and I randomly assigned participants one of three tasks. We decided to encourage some participants to feel gratitude and others to be negative and irritable. We also created a third, neutral group by which to measure the others. Once a week for ten weeks, the study's participants kept a short journal listing five things that had occurred over the past week. Either they briefly described, in a single sentence, five things for which they were grateful ("the gratitude condition") or they did the opposite, describing five hassles that displeased them ("the hassles condition"). The neutral control group was simply asked to list five events or circumstances that had affected them each week, and they were not told to accentuate the positive or negative aspects of those circumstances.

To give a flavor for what participants wrote about, examples of gratitude-inducing experiences included "waking up this morning," "the generosity of friends," "God for giving me determination," and "the Rolling Stones." Examples of hassles were "hard to find parking," "messy kitchen no one will clean," "finances depleting quickly," and "doing a favor for a friend who didn't appreciate it."

Although I believed we'd see the benefits of gratitude, I wasn't sure this result would be inevitable or unequivocal. To be grateful means to allow oneself to be placed in the position of a recipient—to feel indebted, aware of one's dependence on others, and obligated to reciprocate. An exercise like ours might remind people that they need to repay the kindness of others, and they may resent these obligations and even report strong negative feelings toward their benefactors.

So I was surprised at how dramatically positive our results were. At the end of the ten weeks, participants who'd kept a gratitude journal felt better about their lives as a whole and were more optimistic about the future than participants in either of the other two conditions. To put it into numbers, according to the scale we used to calculate well-being, they were a full 25 percent happier than the other participants. Those in the gratitude condition reported fewer health complaints and even spent more time exercising than control participants did, and significantly more time exercising than those in the hassles condition (nearly 1.5 hours more per week). This is a massive difference. The gratitude-group participants also experienced fewer symptoms of physical illness than those in either of the other two groups.

In a second study, we asked participants to keep journals every day for two weeks. People assigned to express gratitude again showed an impressive array of benefits: On surveys we gave all study participants, people who kept a gratitude journal reported feeling more joyful, enthusiastic, interested, attentive, energetic, excited, determined, and strong than those in the hassles condition. They also reported offering others more emotional support or help with a personal problem—supporting the notion that gratitude motivates people to do good. And this was not limited to what they said about themselves. We sent surveys to people who knew them well, and these significant others rated participants in the gratitude group as more helpful than those in the other groups (these friends were not aware of which experimental condition the participants were in).

We got similar results in a study of adults with neuromuscular disorders, many of whom suffered from fatigue, slowly progressive muscle weakness, muscle and joint pain, and muscular atrophy. Little is known about factors affecting the quality of life among people with neuromuscular disorders. This study gave us a unique opportunity to determine if the gratitude intervention could help improve the well-being of these people coping with a chronic physical disease.

Participants in the gratitude condition showed significantly more positive emotions and satisfaction with life than a control group, while also showing fewer negative emotions. They also felt more optimism about the upcoming week and felt closer and more connected to others, even though many lived alone and did not increase their actual contact time with others. Remarkably, these positive emotional and psychological changes weren't only apparent to the participants themselves: based on reports we received from the spouses of study participants, people in the gratitude condition seemed outwardly happier than people in the control group.

Participants in the gratitude condition also reported getting more hours of sleep each night, spending less time awake before falling asleep, and feeling more refreshed upon awakening. This finding is enormous, in that sleep disturbance and poor sleep quality have been identified as central indicators of poor overall well-being, as well as increased risk for physical disease and premature death. It may sound simplistic, but the evidence cannot be ignored: If you want to sleep more soundly, count blessings, not sheep.

One of the important features of all of these studies is that we randomly assigned participants to conditions. Many people who tend toward pessimism may have been placed in the gratitude group, just as optimists may have been placed in the other conditions. Plus, few studies have been able to successfully create interventions to increase happiness or well-being; we were able to do so with an exercise that required minimal effort. Other studies have corroborated our findings and further testified to gratitude's benefits, especially for social connections. For example, additional research Mike and I conducted has shown that individuals who report habitually experiencing gratitude engage more frequently in kind or helpful behaviors than do people who experience gratitude less often.

We've also identified people with strong dispositions toward gratitude and asked their friends to tell us about them. We then compared their friends' responses to feedback we received from the friends of less grateful people. According to their friends, grateful people engaged in more supportive, kind, and helpful behaviors (for example, loaning money or providing compassion, sympathy, and emotional support) than did less grateful people. Some particularly informative research has been conducted by David DeSteno and Monica Bartlett at Northeastern University. In their creative studies, participants worked on a computer-generated task; when they were about to receive their score, the screen suddenly went blank. Another person in the room—a "confederate," someone secretly working with the researchers—"discovered" that the monitor's plug had been pulled partially out of the power strip and then helped display the participant's scores. Upon leaving the laboratory, the participants were asked if they would volunteer to assist in another, ostensibly unrelated experiment, which involved completing a tedious and taxing survey.

Compared to people who didn't receive the favor, including some who were put in a good mood by watching a funny video clip, the people who received the favor and felt grateful toward the confederate were more likely to go through the trouble of filling out the survey. This suggests the unique effects of gratitude in motivating helping behavior, more so than the general effects of simply being in a positive mood.

WHY IS GRATITUDE GOOD?

So why is gratitude good? For two main reasons, I think. First, gratitude strengthens social ties. It cultivates an individual's sense of interconnectedness. This was beautifully illustrated in a story by Roger, a man we interviewed in our research on patients with chronic neuromuscular disease.

Faced with escalating medical bills and an extended period of unemployment, Roger was on the verge of losing his home—until friends organized a benefit party to raise money for him. He wrote in his gratitude journal:

> Well the big day came after much anticipation. About 200 people showed up, bought raffle tickets, drank, danced, partied and ate till 1 a.m. closing! We went up on stage to thank everyone amid joy, tears, and hugs. My manager cut me a check for over $35,000 the next week! Without that check my house/car would have been on the market. . . . We saw so many friends and coworkers it was truly a great night. The $1,000 first prize was donated back to us by the winner (a stranger!). My doctor and nurse also attended and our priest stopped by for a few beers—I keep thinking of more highlights as I write. I truly felt like George Bailey in *It's a Wonderful Life*! I feel myself almost tearing up as I write. My heart warms as I see the people that attended. I also feel a need to help or reach out to others whenever I can help by speaking or just listening.

In Roger's response to that evening and his desire to help others as a result, we can see how gratitude truly serves as "the moral memory of mankind."

A second reason supporting the power of gratitude is that gratitude increases one's sense of personal worth. When we experience gratitude, we understand that another person wishes us well, and in turn, we feel loved and cared for. If someone has incurred a personal cost by helping me out, then how can I not conclude that I have value in that person's eye?

It might be this link that explains why gratitude can be a powerful antidote to a depressed view of life. One of the reasons gratitude makes us happier is that it forces us to abandon a belief that may accompany severe depression—that the world is devoid of goodness, love, and kindness and is nothing but randomness and cruelty. By recognizing patterns of benevolence, the depressed person may change his or her self-perception ("I guess I'm not such a loser after all"). By feeling grateful, we are acknowledging that someone, somewhere, is being kind to us. And therefore, we can see not just that we are worthy of kindness, but that kindness indeed exists in the world and, therefore, that life may be worth living.

We are receptive beings, dependent on the help of others, on their gifts and their kindness. As such, we are called to gratitude. Life becomes complete when we are able to give to others what we ourselves received in the past. In one of our studies, a 33-year-old woman with spinal muscular atrophy captured this dynamic:

> All of my life, people have been involved to assist me in getting dressed, showered, to work/school, etc. It was my hope that one day, I would be able to do something really significant for someone else, like others have always done for me. I met a man who was married and very unhappy. He and his wife had a little boy born to them and then die at 7 months of age. For ten years they remained married, trying to have another baby. They were never able to have a child again. They divorced and he became my friend and lover. He told me of his life's dream of having another child. I got pregnant from him and had a miscarriage. I got pregnant again and had an ectopic pregnancy. (No loss of my tube, thank God!) A shot took care of the problem. I got pregnant a third time; our beautiful son was born on 12/20/98. I have never felt as grateful for anything in my life. I was actually able to give something back to someone. Me, who was supposed to die before I was 2 years old.

It is gratitude that enables us to receive and it is gratitude that motivates us to return the goodness that we have been given. In short, it is gratitude that enables us to be fully human.

WIRED TO BE INSPIRED

Jonathan Haidt

HERE'S A PUZZLE: Why do we care when a stranger does a good deed for another stranger? Most theories in the social sciences say that people's actions and feelings are motivated by self-interest. So why are we sometimes moved to tears by the good deeds or heroic actions of others?

I believe we cannot have a full understanding of human morality until we can explain why and how human beings are so powerfully affected by the sight of a stranger helping another stranger. For the past several years, I have studied this feeling, which I call "elevation." I have defined elevation as a warm, uplifting feeling that people experience when they see unexpected acts of human goodness, kindness, courage, or compassion. It makes a person want to help others and to become a better person himself or herself.

Elevation is widely known across cultures and historical eras. You probably recognize it yourself. But for some reason, no psychologist has studied it empirically. Instead, psychologists have focused most of their energies on the negative moral emotions, especially guilt and anger. Psychologists have thought about morality primarily as a system of rules that prevents people from hurting each other and taking their possessions.

But I believe that morality is much richer and more balanced.

Most people don't want to rape, steal, and kill. What they really want is to live in a moral community where people treat each other well and in which they can satisfy their needs for love, productive work, and a sense of belonging to groups of which they are proud. We get a visceral sense that we do not live in such a moral world when we see people behave in petty, cruel, or selfish ways. But when we see a stranger perform a simple act of kindness for another stranger, it gives us a thrilling sense that maybe we do live in such a world. The fact that we can be so responsive to the good deeds of others—even when we do not benefit directly—is a very important facet of human nature. Yes, people can be terribly cruel, and we must continue our study of racism, violence, and other social ills. But there is a brighter side to human nature, too, and psychology ought to look more closely at it.

BEYOND DISGUST

I started examining elevation only after years of studying its opposite: disgust. It makes good evolutionary sense that human beings should have an emotion that makes us feel repulsion toward rotten food, excrement, dead bodies, and other physical objects that are full of dangerous bacteria and parasites. It also makes sense that disgust should make us hypersensitive to contagion—that is, we feel disgust toward anything that touched something that we find disgusting.

But when my colleagues and I actually asked people in several countries to list the things they thought were disgusting, we repeatedly found that most people mentioned social offenses, such as hypocrisy, racism, cruelty, and betrayal. How on earth did a food-based and very corporeal emotion become a social and moral emotion? The short version of our attempt at an answer is that while disgust may motivate people to distance themselves from physical threats, it is well suited for dealing with social threats as well. When we find social actions disgusting, they indicate to us that the person who committed them is in some way morally defective.

In this light, we seem to place human actions on a vertical dimension that runs from our conception of absolute good (God) above, to absolute evil (the Devil) below. This vertical dimension is found in many cultures—for example, in Hindu and Buddhist ideas that people are reincarnated at higher or lower levels, depending on their moral behavior in this life.

Social disgust can then be understood as the emotional reaction people have to witnessing others moving "down," or exhibiting their lower, baser, less God-like nature. Human beings feel revolted by moral depravity, and this revulsion is akin to the revulsion they feel toward rotten food and cockroaches. In this way, disgust helps us form groups, reject deviants, and build a moral community.

I thought about the social nature of disgust in this way for years and about what exactly it means when someone moves "down" on the vertical dimension from good to evil. But then, one day in 1997, I looked up. I had never thought about what emotion we feel when we see someone move higher on the vertical dimension, acting in an honorable or saintly way. But once I began to investigate, I saw a whole new emotional response triggered by virtuous, pure, or superhuman behavior. I called this emotion "elevation" because seeing other people rise on the vertical dimension toward goodness seems to make people feel higher on it themselves. Once I began looking for elevation, I found it easily. I saw that most people recognize descriptions of it, and the popular press and Oprah Winfrey talk about it (as being touched, moved, or inspired). Yet research psychologists had almost nothing to say about it. I have now done several experiments on elevation, and here is what I have learned.

STUDYING ELEVATION

First, my students and I asked people to write in detail about five kinds of situations that we thought seemed likely to produce different kinds of positive emotions, including happiness and elevation. We then asked specific questions about their bodily changes, thoughts, actions, and motivations in these different situations. In the question that was supposed to prompt people to share their experiences of elevation, we asked participants to write about "a specific time when you saw a manifestation of humanity's 'higher' or 'better' nature." The stories told in response were often moving and beautiful.

The most commonly cited circumstances that caused elevation involved seeing someone else give help or aid to a person who was poor or sick or stranded in a difficult situation. A particularly powerful and detailed case captures the flavor of these situations:

> Myself and three guys from my church were going home from volunteering our services at the Salvation Army that morning. It had been snowing since the night before, and the snow was a thick blanket on the ground. As we were driving through a neighborhood near where I lived, I saw an elderly woman with a shovel in her driveway. I did not think much of it when one of the guys in the back asked the driver to let him off here. The driver had not been paying much attention so he ended up circling back around towards the lady's home. I had assumed that this guy just wanted to save the driver some effort and walk the short distance to his home (although I was clueless as to where he lived). But when I saw him jump out of the back seat and approach the lady, my mouth dropped in shock as I realized that he was offering to shovel her walk for her.

When participants saw unexpected acts of goodness like this one, they commonly described themselves as being surprised, stunned, and emotionally moved. Their descriptions imply that under the surface, they were changing their views about humanity in a more optimistic way and triggering higher goals for themselves. When asked, "Did the feeling give you any inclination toward doing something?" the most common response was to describe general desires to help others and to become a better person.

Several participants described the kind of openness and urge to be playful that psychologist Barbara Fredrickson has ascribed to joy. The woman who wrote about the snow-shoveling episode also wrote:

> I felt like jumping out of the car and hugging this guy. I felt like singing and running, or skipping and laughing. Just being active. I felt like saying nice things about people. Writing a beautiful poem or love song. Playing in the snow like a child. Telling everybody about his deed.

A common theme in most of the narratives is a social focus—a desire to be with, love, and help other people. The effects of these feelings appear to have potentially life-altering effects. One participant described how moved he was when so many people came to visit and support his family while his grandfather was dying. He said he still had those feelings seven years later and that those feelings helped inspire his decision to become a doctor. Feelings of elevation seem particularly capable of fostering love, admiration, and a desire for closer affiliation with the doer of the good deed. The woman in the snow-shoveling incident wrote:

> My spirit was lifted even higher than it already was. I was joyous, happy, smiling, energized. I went home and gushed about it to my suite-mates, who clutched at their hearts. And, although I have never seen this guy as more than just a friend, I felt a hint of romantic feeling for him at this moment.

Love and a desire for affiliation appear to be a common human response to witnessing saints and saintly deeds or even to hearing about them secondhand. If disgust is a negative emotion that strengthens ego boundaries and defenses against a morally reprehensible other, then elevation is its opposite—a desire to associate with those who are morally admirable.

A second study confirmed this general portrait of elevation. This study induced elevation in a laboratory by showing one group of participants video clips from a documentary about Mother Teresa. Control groups saw other videos, including an emotionally neutral but interesting documentary and a comedy sequence from the television show *America's Funniest Home Videos*. Compared to participants who watched the control videos, participants who watched the elevating video clip reported feeling more loving and inspired; they more strongly wanted to help and affiliate with others, and they were more likely to actually volunteer to work at a humanitarian charity organization afterward.

In both studies, we found that participants in the elevation conditions reported different patterns of physical feelings and motivations when compared to participants in the control conditions. Elevated participants were more likely to report physical feelings in their chests—especially warm, pleasant, or "tingling" feelings—and they were more likely to report wanting to help others, become better people themselves, and affiliate with others. In both studies, reported feelings of happiness energized people to engage in private or self-interested pursuits, while feelings of elevation seemed to open people up and turn their attention outward, toward other people.

Based on this research, I believe that elevation carries many benefits, including individual benefits like the energy and playfulness of the woman in the earlier example. However, elevation is particularly interesting because of its social benefits—its power to spread, which could improve entire communities.

If frequent bad deeds trigger social disgust, cynicism, and hostility toward one's peers, then frequent good deeds may have a type of social undoing effect, raising the level of compassion, love, and harmony in an entire society. Efforts to promote and publicize altruism may therefore have widespread and cost-effective results. I am now looking into the possibility that elevation can be used in moral education programs, inspiring young people in ways that more traditional teaching techniques cannot.

GETTING ELEVATED

It is a surprising and very beautiful fact about our species that each of us can be moved to tears by the sight of a stranger helping another stranger. It is an even more beautiful fact that these feelings sometimes inspire us to change our own behavior, values, and goals. Narratives of the lives of Jesus, Buddha, Mother Teresa, and other inspiring figures are full of stories of people who, upon meeting the saintly figure, dropped their former materialistic pursuits and devoted themselves to advancing the mission of the one who elevated them.

Indeed, a hallmark of elevation is that, like disgust, it is contagious. When an elevation story is told well, it elevates those who hear it. Powerful moments of elevation, whether experienced first- or secondhand, sometimes seem to push a mental "reset" button, wiping out feelings of cynicism and replacing them with feelings of hope, love, optimism, and a sense of moral inspiration. This thought is for the moment an unsubstantiated speculation, but a clear description of such a case was recently sent to me by a man named David Whitford.

Several years ago, David's Unitarian church asked each of its members to write his or her own "spiritual autobiography," an account of how he or she became a more spiritual person. While reflecting on his spiritual experiences, David grew puzzled over why he is so often moved to tears during the course of church services. He concluded that there are two kinds of tears. The first he called "tears of compassion," such as those he shed during a sermon on Mother's Day about children who were growing up abandoned or neglected. He wrote that these cases felt to him like "being pricked in the soul," after which "love pours out" for those who are suffering.

But the second kind of tears was very different. He called them "tears of celebration," but he could just as well have called them "tears of elevation." I will end this article with his words, which give a more eloquent description of elevation than anything I could write:

> A few weeks after Mother's Day, we met here in the sanctuary after the service and considered whether to become a Welcoming Congregation [a congregation that welcomes gay people]. When John stood in support of the resolution, and spoke of how, as far as he knew, he was the first gay man to come out at First Parish, in the early 1970s, I cried for his courage. Later, when all hands went up and the resolution passed unanimously, I cried for the love expressed by our congregation in that act. That was a tear of celebration, a tear of receptiveness to what is good in the world, a tear that says it's okay, relax, let down your guard, there are good people in the world, there is good in people, love is real, it's in our nature. That kind of tear is also like being pricked, only now the love pours in.

PART TWO:

HOW TO CULTIVATE GOODNESS

IN RELATIONSHIPS WITH

FRIENDS, FAMILY, COWORKERS,

AND NEIGHBORS

INTRODUCTION

Dacher Keltner, Jason Marsh,
and Jeremy Adam Smith

IT'S ONE THING to recognize the potential for human goodness, as contributors did in the previous section; it's something
else to realize that potential.

The essays that follow are intended to help us do just that. Each
one offers concrete, research-tested steps for building stronger,
more compassionate relationships with spouses, coworkers, friends,
family, and other people in our daily lives.

It goes without saying that it can be difficult to take these steps,
for human relationships are complicated and shaped by social
context. Take, for example, empathy, a skill that is a fundamental building block to our individual happiness and well-being, as
well as to a peaceful society. Like many pieces of advice, the age-
old adages to "put yourself in someone else's shoes" and "see the
world from someone else's perspective" can sound painfully naive.
Indeed, they seem to go against human nature, serving as moralis-
tic attempts to rein in our tendencies toward self-interest. Can we
truly understand what other people are thinking or feeling—and
if so, how?

Those are the questions at the heart of many of the following essays, several of which explore the human capacity for empathy and how it is related to behaviors like gratitude, forgiveness, and altruism. But it's not always clear what the term *empathy* means and how it differs from other concepts, like sympathy. In this section, many contributors highlight what is sometimes called "perspective taking": understanding what another person is seeing and feeling to the point that you actually begin to feel those same emotions yourself. (By contrast, sympathy involves recognizing the suffering of another person and feeling sorry for that person, but not sharing his or her sad or distressed emotions.)

With that definition of empathy in mind, it's not hard to see why we should try to cultivate it. Perspective taking enables us to see things from our spouse's point of view or helps us to build workplaces that demonstrate care and compassion for employees. Our sense of justice and fairness stems from our ability to really understand other people's emotions and therefore respond to their suffering.

Gratitude is another seemingly simple skill that just doesn't seem to fit into contemporary American society. Indeed, argues psychologist Robert Emmons in Part I of this book, "We've come to overlook, dismiss, or even disparage the significance of gratitude." It's easy to understand why. After all, "thank you" is one of the first phrases we teach children to say—how complicated could the concept be? We see gratitude as a basic form of politeness, like chewing with your mouth closed, and we don't usually consider what deeper significance it may hold.

Yet the fact that we try to make "thank you" such an essential part of a child's vocabulary and that children (and adults) often have a hard time bringing themselves to utter those two words suggests that gratitude is more complex than we typically assume. Indeed, as many contributors to this book make clear, true gratitude is more a state of mind than a single act, and it takes real effort to cultivate. The same can be said of forgiveness and apology and indeed any act that acknowledges our interdependence with other people and deepens our social ties.

Fortunately, we have good reason to believe that most of us can develop empathy and gratitude, as well as forgiveness and apology and other related skills—and there's overwhelming evidence to suggest that we should. As several essays in this book reveal, skills like these can serve as powerful tools to build health, trust, cooperation, and respect between people in a number of daily situations, from home to work to politics.

The essays in this section do not deny that humans are capable of great selfishness and insensitivity and that there's sometimes no greater challenge than simply getting out of our own skin and identifying with another human being. But while the advice to see from another person's perspective may at times sound unrealistic, the following essays make clear that it's advice we can all learn to follow.

FEELING LIKE PARTNERS

Philip A. Cowan, Carolyn Pape Cowan,
and Neera Mehta

RICK AND ANNA met on a blind date and immediately became enchanted with each other. They moved in together four months later, and after two more years they decided to get married. They planned to have kids after four years, and that worked like a charm. Jason came along right on schedule and his sister Debby arrived two years later. Unfortunately, somewhere over the years, not everything went according to plan. As we look in on Rick and Anna after they've been together for almost ten years, their early enchantment seems to exist only in wistful memory.

Rick returned home from work about half an hour ago. He's slumped on the couch when Anna sees him in the living room.

ANNA: How come you didn't put your stuff away after you came home?

RICK: I'll do it in a minute.

ANNA: It's been a whole bunch of minutes already. Now I've got your sweater and papers dumped in the dining room, the kids' toys in the kitchen, and me tripping over everything while I'm trying to make dinner.

RICK: Give me a break, Anna. I had a horrible afternoon at work and I'm just fried.

ANNA: You haven't asked about my afternoon. Your mother kept me on the phone for an hour, yelling about some cousin of yours who insulted her.

RICK: And I suppose you were your usual sweet and patient self, trying to help her calm down?

ANNA: (No answer)

RICK (voice raised): I've had it, Anna. You're out of control.

ANNA: Maybe you need a more patient wife.

RICK (leaving the room): Maybe I do.

It didn't take Rick and Anna long to go from a small complaint about putting away "stuff" to a discussion about the survival of their relationship. Readers familiar with self-help books or the professional literature on couples therapy will probably say that Rick and Anna need to learn more effective communication skills. After they recover from their heated exchange, Rick and Anna will probably say the same thing.

We think their problem goes deeper than that. In our careers as family researchers and couples therapists, we have conducted long-term studies of more than 300 families, following many from their first child's birth through the preschool, elementary school, and high school years. We've seen couples confronted and even overwhelmed by the challenges in their relationship, but we've also seen many partners find ways to overcome these problems. We've found that it's simply not enough to teach couples like Rick and Anna the "right" thing to say in the middle of a fight or ask them to follow communication "rules," such as "Summarize what your partner just said before responding to him" or "Make 'I' rather than 'you' statements." Couples' relationships suffer less from a failure of words than from a failure of imagination—an ability to imagine what a partner is thinking and feeling. We believe that the key ingredient missing from Rick and Anna's conversation—and from the relationships of countless other couples—is empathy.

BEYOND WORDS

What do we mean by empathy? There's a thinking component of empathy that involves the ability to take another person's point of view ("I can see why you find it so hard to talk to my mother when she complains all the time") and an emotional capacity to feel what the other is feeling ("Oh honey, it hurts when I see you so upset"). Both of these aspects describe what might be going on inside one partner when the other is feeling intense emotions—often negative (sad, angry, frightened) but sometimes positive (elated, delighted, joyful). Another important aspect of empathy involves behavior consistent with that empathic position. The simple statement "I feel your pain" isn't really evidence of empathy unless the speaker actually does something to show a true understanding of the listener's experience. If Anna had explained to Rick how overwhelmed she was feeling about caring for the children and taking care of their home, Rick could have shown her that he "gets it" by helping to pick up the toys or working with Anna to prepare dinner.

A number of researchers have investigated whether accuracy in "reading" one's partner is an important ingredient of couple satisfaction. Are partners happier in their relationships if they can conjure up an accurate picture of what the other person is feeling and experiencing? Indeed, studies have found that people who gauge their partner's thoughts and feelings more accurately during disagreements are generally more satisfied with their overall relationship. But for empathy to be truly beneficial, both partners need to experience it. If Rick had responded empathically to Anna's frustration about her conversation with his mother but Anna ignored or dismissed his response, Rick would likely have been left feeling even less empathic and more distant from his wife.

Clearly, both Rick and Anna failed to demonstrate empathy in their exchange. Rick discarded his papers and sweater on the floor and didn't move to pick them up when Anna complained. Anna didn't respond to Rick's statement about his terrible day, and in turn, Rick was sarcastic, almost contemptuous, of Anna's description of her conversation with his mother. As their hostile exchange quickly escalated, the specter of not being the right partners for each other overshadowed everything else. In a more empathic mode, Anna might have greeted Rick before complaining, asked about his day, and softened her complaint once she heard how difficult it was. If she had done that, Rick might have been more inclined to place his belongings out of the line of traffic and ask about Anna's day the next time he came home.

That's often easier said than done. As we all know, it's especially difficult to take other people's points of view, feel what they're feeling, and act on those feelings when we are stressed ourselves. Some people seem to be not very good at this at all, but even the most empathic people occasionally find it psychologically difficult and emotionally taxing to empathize with their partner—and the tone of family relationships often reflects those difficulties.

The good news is that there are ways partners can learn to empathize with one another. Our own research and clinical experience, and that of a number of colleagues, suggest several methods for fostering empathy between spouses. While there isn't one recipe that guarantees partners' empathy in every situation, we believe there are enough tools to help couples like Rick and Anna not only survive adversity, but use it in a way to strengthen their relationship.

FOSTERING EMPATHY

Empathy seems to come more easily to some partners than others. Yet although we tend to describe some people as empathic and others as lacking empathy, empathy is not a fixed trait—a stable characteristic that a person expresses similarly in all situations. We believe that under ideal conditions, everyone can be at least somewhat empathic in the moment.

We see five main conditions necessary for fostering empathy in couples' lives. These are when both partners (1) are reasonably mentally healthy; (2) have grown up in empathic families; (3) work collaboratively in parenting their children; (4) have relatively low levels of stress external to the family or sources of support to cope with the stresses they face; and (5) have what they consider to be a fair division of labor and an effective way of solving the problems that confront them.

Even if they don't meet one or more of these conditions, partners can still work on ways to overcome that problem and empathize with each other.

The first major impediment to understanding "where a partner is coming from" is either partner's serious cognitive or emotional problems. These problems can prevent them from reading others accurately or may trigger disabling levels of anxiety or symptoms of depression. For example, one aspect of depression is the tendency to see and expect the worst in other people. It is extremely difficult for a depressed person to understand that a loving partner can do something hurtful unintentionally. It is also hard for the nondepressed spouse to understand why the depressed partner is reacting in such an unrelentingly negative way. One option for couples that find themselves in the middle of escalating negative exchanges is for one partner to talk to the other about seeking outside help as a couple to deal with the emotional problems. Empathy may come easier once the couple has started to address these issues.

Many researchers and therapists also look at how childhood

attachment to parents affects partners' abilities to empathize with each other as adults. Studies of attachment across generations suggest that parents who make their children feel secure and reassured during times of stress prime them to feel empathic in their adult relationships. Adults whose childhood experiences led them to expect caring, understanding responses from loved ones when they were upset find it easier to be optimistic and empathic when relationship problems stir their emotions, even if their partner doesn't act empathically in the moment. By contrast, partners whose caretakers dismissed their childhood fears feel anxious and not worthy of care. They are then more likely to feel threatened and react negatively to a spouse who doesn't seem to understand their feelings.

Also, for many partners, the relationship between their parents has provided a salient model of what they can expect from couple relationships. If both partners' parents typically disparaged and insulted one another, it will be more difficult for the couple to establish a civil way of solving problems. Some couples whose parents were always in high conflict tend to mirror that pattern, while others try to avoid upsetting conversations altogether. In a couple where one partner experienced constant shouting and arguing in his family and members of the other partner's family never raised their voices, neither partner has a useful model for tackling the differences that partners inevitably need to resolve. Although it isn't possible to change what happened to us when we were children, it is not too late for adults to understand more about their own and their partner's early relationships. This often leads to insight about how partners' styles of responding to conflict may be a reaction to the way they were treated by the closest figures in their lives years ago.

Working from this perspective, psychologist Susan Johnson talks about how strengthening a feeling of security in romantic relationships can compensate for old wounds and allow partners to be more empathic and flexible in the meanings they attribute to their partner's behavior (for example, "Rick must have had a difficult day and that's why he just dumped his stuff when he got home. It's not that he's doesn't care about what I need"). As a therapist, Johnson uses empathy herself to help couples feel more secure. In exploring the roots of each partner's reactions, she acts as a model for how to be an empathic partner. She might say to Rick, "It sounds as if you can't imagine that anyone will take your needs and desires seriously. So you feel as if you have no choice but to agree when Anna says you may need to find someone else rather than work it out with her." In this way, Johnson explores Rick's fears and reformulates his negative reaction as an understandable position, with the goal of strengthening both Rick's and Anna's feelings of empathy for one another.

NEW CHALLENGES FOR COUPLES

Becoming parents increases opportunities for disagreements between partners, especially when new parents discover that they have some different ideas about parenting. Some disagreements can be resolved by having discussions when things are calm, rather than when emotions are running high. On some issues, it may be possible to let each parent handle the children in a different fashion, so that each parent has a unique relationship with them. On other core issues, they may need to work out a way of responding to their children that satisfies both of their instincts.

Either way, when partners are parents, as Rick and Anna are, the conditions for empathy can be difficult to create because time and attention get shifted from the couple to the children. Modern parents who are typically juggling at least two jobs and care of the home and children have few occasions when they are alone together and reasonably well rested. Because they are already working away from home for so many hours, parents feel guilty about stealing time as a couple. Yet family research with parents of young children reveals that children suffer academically, socially, and often emotionally when their parents are unhappy. The results of our years of working with partners who are parents have provided a clear message: If you feel you can't take time to work on your relationship for yourselves, do it for your children. We know that children will reap the benefits of their parents' more satisfying exchanges—both because they'll have models of empathic behavior to emulate and because they'll be more free to concentrate on their own learning and development, instead of becoming preoccupied with their parents' distress.

Inevitably, all couples also experience stress outside the family that spills over into their lives at home—strain at work, with friends, in the neighborhood, and so on. Partners who are distracted by these stressors find it difficult to listen fully, to place themselves in each other's position, or to imagine how the other person is feeling. There are no simple solutions to this problem. What we suggest is that partners develop an experimental attitude and try small changes that might bring some relief. When Rick comes home from work, Anna could support his having 10 minutes to "chill out" while she ignores the belongings he dumped in the living room, as long as he has agreed to pick them up and join her in the kitchen to help afterward.

Although these examples illustrate that many of the conditions that support or interfere with empathy don't start with the couple, the final condition—partners' division of family work and care of the children and their effectiveness at solving problems—focuses more specifically on aspects of the couple relationship.

In our longitudinal studies, we have found that these issues play a critical role in both partners' satisfaction with their overall relationship. Some researchers and couples argue that the secret of a satisfying relationship is a traditional arrangement of roles, with separate, well-defined tasks for men and women, whereas others argue that modern marriage calls for an egalitarian arrangement of a 50–50 division of family tasks and care of children, based on the partners' available time, skills, and preferences. Our research suggests that more important than the specific arrangement of "who does what" is whether each partner feels that their arrangement fits their ideals and is fair.

Another key to couple satisfaction is the partners' confidence that they have effective ways of tackling problems when they do arise. When partners are unable to work collaboratively to meet the challenges of family life, they are likely to be less empathic with one another and less satisfied with their overall relationship.

Collaboration relies on, and helps facilitate, clear and honest communication. While we said earlier that Rick and Anna don't just need communication skills training, we hope that increased empathy will lead to more satisfying communication. Along these lines, couples therapist Dan Wile writes about how empathy isn't just an attitude that partners can choose to adopt, but develops out of the couple's interaction. As a therapist, Wile tries to help couples "get on a platform" from which they can look at their problems jointly and empathically and begin resolving their difficulties together. He discusses how empathy can be self-perpetuating, since an empathic exchange can help partners shift from behaving like enemies or strangers to feeling like allies. For instance, Rick might have said, "Anna, I can see that I created another mess, but I'm so wiped out by how my boss stole my ideas at work that I can't move right this minute. What kind of time extension could you give me here?" This would have been more likely to put Anna at ease and take her out of an adversarial mindset. She might have found herself responding, "I'm sorry I snapped at you. I was tense because my day has been so frustrating, and I feel as if we haven't connected for days."

How can couples get on a "platform" in order to have nonadversarial discussions? Although it may sound like the last thing to do in the middle of a fight, they could try this: when one partner becomes upset, the other can start by asking questions about where the feelings are coming from, rather than attacking the partner or defending against the perceived attack. This can lead the troubled spouse to feel the partner's empathy and be more willing to give a fuller explanation of what is upsetting about the situation.

Andrew Christensen and the late Neil Jacobson wrote about how empathic exchanges can turn problems "into vehicles for greater intimacy." According to these researchers, one way to get partners to unite empathically with each other is to get at the soft feelings, such as sadness and fear, that underlie the more frequently and easily expressed hard feelings, like anger and resentment. Trying to understand where the other person is coming from can lead to both partners feeling as if their experience has been heard, which in turn allows them to feel safe expressing pain without blame. In this way, empathy can lead to acceptance and forgiveness. Psychologist and marital therapist John Gottman suggests that a way for one partner to understand the other's upsets is to take time to have regular discussions about each of their goals, dreams, and worries. Gottman suggests that these "love maps" of partners' inner lives encourage them to be aware of each other's changing needs so that they can be understanding and supportive when things go wrong.

Of course, managing to meet all five of these conditions that promote empathy all of the time is impossible, even for couples with many advantages in their lives. We know that it's not enough to simply say, "Be more empathic" and "Don't resort to blaming, unforgiving, contemptuous, or icy-silent behaviors." Most couples would do these things if they could. What we are saying is this: empathy is so important to a relationship that if it appears to be low, partners must talk about ways that they can help each other to take a more empathic position. A first step in that direction might be to review an "empathy conditions checklist" to see whether anything can be done about any of the barriers to empathy that are affecting their lives.

WHAT IF COUPLES NEED HELP?

Our longitudinal studies of hundreds of families make it clear that life is stressful for most modern partners. Couples should pursue outside help if the partners have tried to create conditions to encourage more empathy and have failed to change the atmosphere between them. A consultation with a mental health professional might help get them started. An empathic helper who understands couples can often help improve the climate in which partners tackle their problems. Partners can learn gradually to take on this role themselves so that they can deal with future problems in more empathic and constructive ways.

Let's return to Rick and Anna. After stewing in silence in different rooms, wondering whether their relationship will survive and wishing they could avoid these hurtful exchanges, Rick and Anna considered two choices. The first was to try to use some time together, possibly with the aid of some self-help books, to try to resolve some of the issues behind their conflicts. The second was to seek the help of a professional marriage counselor or couples therapist to teach them how to communicate more effectively. We are not able to predict which alternative would be more effective for them or for couples in similar situations. We do know that their impasse at this moment doesn't necessarily mean that they've lost the chance to feel that early enchantment again. At the moment, they are struggling with demands that make it difficult for them to empathize with one another and to feel the delight that they experienced when they first met. But we are confident that there are practical and realistic steps that Rick and Anna can take to begin to work through this challenge to their relationship. If they can renew their ability to feel empathy for each other, we believe that they will be capable of recapturing the friendship, romance, and happiness they experienced years ago.

LOVE, HONOR, AND THANK

Jess Alberts and Angela Trethewey

Q: Are you grateful for your partner's household labor?
HIM: Uh, yeah, I guess so.
Q: How do you express it?
HIM: She just knows.
—*From a focus group conducted by the authors*

THE DIVISION OF HOUSEHOLD LABOR is one of the most frequent sources of conflict in romantic relationships. As research by Philip and Carolyn Cowan has shown, when partners feel that the division of labor (a combination of housework and paid work) in their relationship is unfair, they are more dissatisfied with their marriage and more likely to think they would be better off divorced. However, even an equitable division of labor may not be enough to ensure that partners are satisfied with their relationship.

As sociologist Arlie Hochschild and others have argued, a successful relationship doesn't just depend on how partners divide labor, but on how they each express gratitude for the labor the other one contributes. This can be as true for single-income couples as for dual-income ones. When you perform work around the house—from cooking to laundry to checking your kids' homework—it often feels like a burden to yourself and a gift to your partner. So if you don't feel that your partner is grateful for your efforts, especially if you perform the lion's share of domestic labor, that's likely to exacerbate feelings of inequity and dissatisfaction, making a difficult situation even worse.

In our research, we set out to test this theory—that it's not just the division of labor but the expression of gratitude that's key to a strong and lasting relationship. Through focus groups, interviews, and surveys with people in heterosexual and same-sex relationships, we've found evidence that gratitude isn't just a way to mitigate the negative effects of an unequal division of labor. Rather, a lack of gratitude may be connected to why that division of labor is so unequal to begin with.

Fortunately, through our research we've started to understand how couples can identify different reasons behind their unbalanced workloads and achieve more equity in their division of labor—cultivating a greater sense of fairness, satisfaction, and gratitude in their relationships.

WHY DOESN'T HE SEE IT?

H E R : The house is a wreck! Why didn't you put a load of laundry in the wash, put the dishes in the dishwasher, or just take out the garbage that's overflowing?

H I M : I didn't notice.

We have found that this conversation resonates with virtually all of our research participants—either as the complainer or the complained about. Complainers say, incredulously, "How can he (or she) not see it!?" Their partners claim earnestly that they really didn't notice the mess and don't understand why their partners are so upset. To make matters worse for the complainers, not only do their unaware partners fail to notice the dirty windows, piles of laundry, or overflowing garbage; they don't even notice when someone else takes care of these problems. Although gender is a strong predictor of who will perform household labor (conservative estimates suggest that women perform two-thirds of all household tasks, not including child care), it isn't entirely clear why women take on this burden even in cases where they earn 50 percent or more of a family's income.

Our research suggests that one of the keys to determining who will perform a specific household task is each partner's "response threshold," which describes the degree of disorder that must exist before someone is sufficiently bothered to perform a task that's not being done. Individuals with low response thresholds for a specific task are moved to perform the task earlier than those who have a higher threshold. Interestingly, this theory is originally based on studies of social networks and division of labor among ants and bees. In her research, entomologist Jennifer Fewell found that certain bees were almost always the ones to take action once the level of honey in the hive had dropped to a particular level. In addition, she discovered that their work reduced the chance that other, higher-threshold bees would perform the job in the future.

We've all seen the same dynamics play out among humans. For example, if Joan's partner Ted is disturbed when the trash in the wastebasket approaches the rim, whereas it doesn't bother her until the trash spills onto the floor, Ted will take out the trash before Joan is moved to do so. If the difference in their disturbance levels is great enough, Joan never will empty the trash, because Ted will always take care of it before it bothers her, possibly before she ever even notices the garbage.

What's more, if one partner does something well, that increases the chance he'll perform that task again, just as failing at the task (or a lack of opportunity to complete it) decreases the chance he'll get another turn. Then consider that before long, the partner who performs a task more frequently will likely be seen as a specialist at it. Taken together, these facts explain how one partner can get stuck with a household chore.

Consider Cristina and Stephen: Cristina began doing the laundry because she had a lower threshold for piles of dirty clothes, but through repetition, she became an "expert" at laundry, and ultimately, she and Stephen came to see the task as "hers." Partners may have different thresholds for many (or even most) tasks. If one partner's threshold level consistently is lower than the other's, then that first partner will take on a greater share of the housework. He might be able to tolerate this imbalance if his partner appreciated his extra work, but too often it's taken for granted.

WHY ISN'T SHE GRATEFUL?

HER: So that roommate that I had last year was horrible. She never thanked me for anything, she never cleaned the house—it was horrible. Yeah, I wouldn't live with her again.

Arlie Hochschild's theory of "the economy of gratitude" explains why underperformers often aren't grateful for their partner's efforts and don't pitch in their fair share. Hochschild argues that in relationships, individuals offer each other "gifts," which are something extra, beyond what is expected. Therefore, if the laundry (or trash, or dishes, or all of the above) is defined as "yours," then your partner is unlikely to feel gratitude toward you for doing it. After all, you are just doing what you are "supposed" to do, what you are "so much better" at doing. In fact, he may argue, since the undone task bothers you, that you aren't doing it for him, but for yourself. Thus, he is unlikely to feel gratitude—because he doesn't view your efforts as a gift to him.

In terms of the division of labor, then, household partners often develop this pattern: the person with the lower threshold performs tasks before the partner is moved to do so; the tasks come to be defined as "hers"; the partner does not feel responsible for performing the task—and he does not feel grateful, because the overperformer is just doing "her" job, all of which makes him less likely to lend a hand in the future.

Importantly, gratitude can help alter the dynamics of couples' division of labor. Expressing gratitude reminds the underperforming partner that the division of labor is not fair and that his partner's contributions are a gift. And since people who receive gifts typically feel obligated to reciprocate, this insight can lead the underperforming partner to offer "gifts" of his own by contributing more to household tasks. In addition, the overperforming partner is likely to experience less resentment and frustration once her efforts are recognized and appreciated.

The economy of gratitude, then, helps to explain the fact that husbands and wives are most satisfied in their marriage when they perceive that their spouses do more than their fair share of the work. That is, when one views a partner's household labor as a gift, over and above what is expected, then one is grateful and happy in the marriage. And, in turn, we have found that individuals who feel appreciated by their partners do indeed express less resentment over the division of labor and greater satisfaction with their relationships than do other study participants.

APPRECIATING GIFTS

So how can couples cultivate gratitude, compensate for different tolerances of disorder, and thus create more equitable divisions of household labor—and greater satisfaction with their relationship?

Part of the answer comes from simply being aware of these phenomena. Once one understands that, in a sense, one's partner truly did not "see" the dirty dishes, piles of laundry, and overflowing garbage, one tends to be less angry and can discuss the issue more calmly and in a less accusatory fashion—which in turn can help one's partner be less defensive.

In general, it is best to anticipate problems before they arise.

Overperformers should avoid repetitively performing a task they don't want to "own," especially when first living with their partner. In other words, when you first move in with your romantic partner, be careful not to cook dinner every night—or you can expect to continue cooking it every night for the rest of your relationship. Take turns in the beginning so that you can both own the task down the line.

Overperformers can also communicate to their partner when a task should be performed, rather than waiting for the partner's threshold level to be reached—and resenting them for their lack of awareness. Also, although underperformers may not perform a task to their partner's standards, statements of appreciation—rather than criticism for not doing it right or for doing it too late—are more likely to encourage repetition.

It also helps if underperformers understand that their partners are more disturbed by a messy house, so they need to develop strategies to respond to the differences in threshold levels, such as performing a task even before it bothers them. Each partner can take responsibility for specific tasks that they perform on a schedule, regardless of whether they are disturbed by it—for instance, by taking out the garbage every Monday and Thursday, whether or not they think it needs to be done.

Finally, domestic partners may find it helpful to write down a list of their tasks and then switch lists for a week or month to better understand their partner's contributions. They may be surprised to discover that their partner does far more than they thought. When her husband Jim was on crutches for two weeks, one of us (Jess) discovered that she did, in fact, perform more routine household labor, but she also discovered that Jim performed many of the "dirty" tasks that she really didn't want to do. She then began to see the division of labor as more equitable.

The gratitude issue is thornier. But understanding the role of gratitude in the division of labor can encourage overperformers to take responsibility for fewer tasks so that these tasks are not taken for granted as "his" or "hers." Also, understanding the economy of gratitude can help underperformers recognize that they do benefit from their partner's efforts—that this work is, in fact, a gift to them, wrapped in clean laundry and vacuumed rugs. They might not be disturbed by disorder as early as their partners, but eventually they would be and would have to do the tasks themselves. Thus, their partners are performing tasks that, rightly, belong to both of them. And if partners practice some of the steps outlined above to create a more equitable division of labor, they're likely to gain newfound appreciation for the work the other performs for them.

It's unlikely that these suggestions will eliminate conflict around couples' division of labor. But we do believe that they can help partners reduce the frequency of their conflict, increase their expressions of gratitude, and improve their overall feelings about their relationship. Most of all, they can help partners avoid the trap of taking each other for granted and help them start to appreciate all the gifts—big and small—that they give to one another.

STUMBLING TOWARD GRATITUDE

Catherine Price

I HAVE A CONFESSION: When I go to a bookstore, I like hanging out in the self-help section. I don't know if it's because I think I'll find a book that will solve all my problems or if seeing all the books on problems I don't have makes me feel better about myself. But whatever it is, I keep going back.

On recent visits, I've noticed a trend: The market has been glutted by books promising the secrets to happiness. That might not seem new, but these aren't touchy-feely self-help titles—they're books by scientific researchers, who claim to offer prescriptions based on rigorous empirical research. It's all part of the "positive psychology" movement that has spilled out of academic journals and into best-selling books, popular magazine articles, and even school curricula.

As I glanced through a few of these titles, two things quickly became clear. First, positive psychologists claim that you can create your own happiness. Conventional wisdom has long held that each of us is simply born with a happiness "set point" (meaning that some people are constitutionally more likely to be happy than others). That's partially true—but according to positive psychologists Sonja Lyubomirsky and Ken Sheldon, research now suggests that up to 40 percent of our happiness might stem from intentional activities in which we choose to engage.

Second, in trying to explain which activities might actually help us cultivate happiness, positive psychology keeps returning to the same concept: gratitude. In study after study, researchers have found that if people actively try to become more grateful in their everyday lives, they're likely to become happier—and healthier— as well.

So how do positive psychologists recommend that you increase your level of gratitude—and therefore happiness? They endorse several research-tested exercises. These include keeping a "gratitude journal," where you record a running list of things for which you're grateful; making a conscious effort to "savor" all the beauty and pleasures in your daily life; and writing a "gratitude letter" to some important person in your life who you've never properly thanked.

These gratitude exercises all sounded pleasant enough, but would they work for me? While I'm not currently depressed, I'm very aware that depression runs in my family: I'm the only person—including the dog—who has not yet been on Prozac. So I decided to indulge in all three of these exercises over a six-week period, risking the possibility that I might become an insufferably happy and cheerful person.

I e-mailed University of Miami psychologist Michael McCullough, a leading gratitude researcher, to ask what he thought I could expect as a result of my gratitude overdose.

"If you're not experiencing more happiness and satisfaction in your life after this six-week gratitude infusion," he wrote back, "I'll eat my hat!"

GETTING GRATEFUL

My first step was to get a gratitude journal. Luckily, a year earlier my recently retired father had stumbled across a bookstore that sold "quotable journals"—blank books with inspiring quotes on their covers. My father, always a sucker for inspiration, sent me seven of them. I settled on one with a cover that said, in all caps, "Life isn't about finding yourself. Life is about creating yourself." Given my experiment in manufactured happiness, this seemed appropriate.

Journal at my side, I decided to start by taking a happiness inventory (available, along with a bunch of other quizzes, at authen tichappiness.org, the Web site run by positive psychology guru Martin Seligman). I scored a 3.58 out of 5, putting myself ahead of 77 percent of participants, but still leaving plenty of room for improvement—as evidenced by my first journal entry.

"It's been a somewhat depressing day," starts my gratitude journal. "Or, rather, week."

At first, it felt a little awkward to keep a journal specifically for gratitude—I felt as if I should plaster my car in cheesy bumper stickers ("Happiness is") and call it a day. But even on that first downbeat afternoon, my journal did make me feel a little better about things. Listing things I was grateful for made me feel, well, grateful for them—and since I'd also decided to jot down moments each day that had made me happy (another positive psychology–endorsed exercise), I had a concrete list of cheerful experiences to look back on when I was feeling down. Thanks to my journal, I know that on January 18 I was happy because I'd exercised, had a good Chinese lesson, and spent 15 minutes dancing around my room to Shakira's "Hips Don't Lie." On January 30, I was grateful for my perseverance, the Pacific Ocean, and the fact that I have really, really good cholesterol.

I've always kept a journal, but once my initial excitement about my new project had passed, my writing schedule felt a bit contrived—I often had to force myself to stay awake for a few minutes before bedtime so that I wouldn't miss an entry. But I quickly found that encouraging myself to focus on the good in my life instead of dwelling on the bad was helping me gain a bit of perspective on things. "The actions in my day-to-day life are actually quite pleasant," I wrote on January 21, in a moment of insight. "It's anxieties that get me derailed."

It was also good to get in the habit of countering bad things in my day with reflections on the good. For example, on February 1—which I described as "having a lot going against it"—I wrote that I "spent a bunch of the day cleaning my room and trying to get my new phone to work, went on fruitless errands, ripped out part of a sweater I was knitting, and when I e-mailed the pattern designer—who goes by "Yarn Boy"—to ask if he could help me figure out where I'd gone wrong, he sent me an e-mail back telling me to 'take it to a yarn shop.' Thanks a lot, Yarn Ass." And yet the entry ends as follows: "But I did get my phone set up and cleaned my room a bit. Chinese went well. I got cute new barrettes. I worked out even though I didn't feel like it, then I savored the feel of my calf muscles."

That might not sound like much, but trust me: it's an improvement.

Despite my calf muscle appreciation, I wasn't exactly sure how to practice my "savoring" exercise, so I e-mailed Todd Kashdan, a psychology professor at George Mason University who teaches an immensely popular class called "Science of Well-Being and Character Strengths." Kashdan, who worked on the floor of the stock exchange until a late-night revelation on a golf course made him realize he'd rather spend his life studying creativity and happiness, wrote back quickly.

"You can do something simple, such as stop and notice an instance of natural beauty, e.g., a sunrise, a flower, a bird singing, a couple gazing at each other," he suggested. "Or start keeping a journal of beautiful moments in which you write down each day the most beautiful things you saw and then return to it before you go to sleep."

Not wanting to start another journal, I instead tried to take more time to appreciate my surroundings. On an 8-mile run on a fire trail, I stopped at a bench on top of a steep hill to give myself a chance to "savor." I felt a bit like I was cheating—after all, the real reason I'd stopped was that if I hadn't, I'd have thrown up—but as my heart rate slowed, I allowed myself to appreciate what was around me: the view of San Francisco, the warmth of the sun, the cool breeze, and the sounds of the birds. It made me feel nice, and since it didn't involve jogging, I continued to savor for 20 minutes before forcing myself back on the trail.

Surprisingly, that exercise made me want to try to savor other small things in my day: watching a mechanic on break from work crack open a beautiful ripe pomegranate, noticing rays of light outside my kitchen window—even enjoying the feeling, weird as it might sound, of brushing my own hair. These were all small, private moments, but consciously trying to find things to savor was kind of like looking for manhole covers on the street: once you start paying attention, they're everywhere.

For my gratitude letter, I decided to write one to my grandmother back in New York for her 84th birthday. It took me three weeks to build up the emotional energy to do it (something about putting all that emotion down on paper made me procrastinate), and, as expected, as soon as I started writing, I began to cry. "I remember you singing me to sleep when I was little," I wrote. "And helping me with my math homework and quizzing me on spelling while I tried to do handstands in the living room, and picking me up from the school bus, and coming into school for grandparents' day— I was always so proud to have you there." I told her how lucky I felt to have her in my life, how much I respected her for having raised my mother on her own, and how much it meant to me that we were so close. By the time I finished writing the letter, I was exhausted— and when I called to read it to her (since she lives across the country, I couldn't do it in person), we both ended up in tears.

NEGATIVITY BIAS

Halfway through my experiment, I was running into problems. I had been trying to appreciate happy moments in my life, but that didn't stop me from getting into a verbal fight with a mechanic, who became so angry that he threatened to have me arrested. I had delivered my gratitude letter to my grandmother, which did make us both happy, but also made her think I was writing her eulogy; she told me, pointedly, that she wasn't planning to die yet. And when I tried to savor a beautiful afternoon by taking a hike along the coast with my boyfriend, we got poison oak.

What's more, I noticed that when I was particularly stressed or angry or feeling down, I didn't want to reflect on things I was happy or grateful for. During those moments, thinking about reasons my life was good just made me more anxious.

I decided to call Julie Norem, professor and chair of the psychology department at Wellesley College, for reassurance. She told me my reaction made sense.

"If you're trying to be grateful all the time but are in a really sucky situation," she said, "then you set yourself up for feeling like things are even worse than they were before because you didn't get cured by this gratitude thing that was supposed to make you happy."

Granted, Norem has her biases. She's the author of a book called *The Positive Power of Negative Thinking* and believes that for some people, whom she calls defensive pessimists, trying to be constantly positive and optimistic can lead to more stress. But apparently, I'm biased, too, because as I read through her Web site, I could feel myself identifying with it.

"Defensive pessimists lower their expectations to help prepare themselves for the worst," says her Web site. "Then they mentally play through all the bad things that can happen. Though it sounds like it might be depressing, defensive pessimism actually helps anxious people focus away from their emotions so they can plan and act effectively."

Intrigued, I took the quiz on Norem's Web site titled "Are you a defensive pessimist?" and scored exactly in the middle between optimism and defensive pessimism—which makes sense, given the fact that I do try to be positive about things, but use negativity to cope. It goes along with a saying I learned from my grandmother: "Hope for the best; expect the worst."

Perhaps ironically, thinking about pessimism made me feel better, especially when University of Michigan psychologist Christopher Peterson admitted to me that even positive psychologists like himself are not always brimming with joy. "I'm not a Pollyanna," he said when I called to ask how positive psychology had affected his life. "And obviously, someone who's unrelentingly cheerful can be a pain in the ass."

HAPPY MEAL

But how about unrelenting gratitude? To celebrate finishing my experiment—not to mention filling up my journal—I took my boyfriend out for dinner at a restaurant here in Berkeley called Café Gratitude. It's a place that is anathema to my cynical New York roots: cheery waitresses who call everyone "darling," posters on the walls that ask questions like, "Can you surrender to how beautiful you are?" and, worst of all, a menu of organic, vegan dishes, all named with life-affirming sentences. For example, saying to your server, "I am fabulous" means that you would like some lasagna. "I am fun" indicates that you want some toast. Unfortunately, there is no organic, vegan interpretation of "I am about to vomit."

My boyfriend and I settled on being generous, fulfilled, and accepting (guacamole, a large café salad, and a bowl of rice), and in honor of my experiment, I insisted on ordering the "I am thankful" (Thai coconut soup, served cold). To offset the restaurant's unrelenting cheer, we both ordered alcohol (luckily, even in Café Gratitude, a beer is just a beer).

While nibbling on carrot flaxseed crackers ("I am relishing"), we talked about the past six weeks. McCullough doesn't need to eat his hat—I definitely had experienced moments of feeling happier and more consciously grateful as a result of the exercises, and by the end of my experiment, my happiness index had gone up to 3.92.

But I also found that there are times when I need to allow myself to feel bad without fighting against my negative emotions. And my cynical side continues to dream of opening a rival restaurant next door called the Cantankerous Café, with menu items like "I am depressed" and "I am resentful."

My biggest question was how long these exercises' effects would last.

"Sometimes positive psychologists sound like we're trying to sell miracles to people. There are no miracles. . . . There are no long-term quick fixes for happiness," said Peterson, when I asked him how I could maintain my happiness boost. "So if you become a more grateful person and you add those exercises to your repertoire, you'll be different six months or a year from now. But if you say okay, I'm done with the story and I'm going back to the way I was, it'll just have been a six-week high. There's nothing wrong with that, but it's not going to permanently change you."

Perhaps that's why, when I got home from dinner, I went straight to my bookcase where I keep stuff my dad has sent me—and picked out another journal.

THE CHOICE TO FORGIVE

Fred Luskin

D ELORES WAS GOOD-NATURED and attractive, but I could
see the hurt in her eyes and the sorrow in the way she held
herself. Though her parents were successful businesspeople who
raised her in an upper middle-class neighborhood, her mother
was cold and critical, while her father was quiet and aloof. Delores
grew up feeling unattractive and uncared for, and she struggled to
create strong relationships.

When Delores was 30, her fiancé Skip decided he was more
interested in sleeping with local waitresses than remaining faithful to her. One day she came home and found him in bed with
someone else. She saw this betrayal as an example of how unfair
the world was—as proof that she never got a break. She was angry,
hurt, confused, scared, and lonely. Skip moved out, but Delores
constantly thought of begging him to return.

I met Delores when she came to a class I teach to help people
learn to forgive others. She rarely spoke without mentioning at least
one of the many people who had done her wrong. When she began
the forgiveness training, she doubted it would do her any good. She
was there because her therapist had recommended the class.

I've known many people like Delores. There's no shortage of
people in the world who've been hurt—by someone they love, by

a friend, by someone they didn't know at all. My classes rest on the simple and radical notion that how we react to these hurts is up to us. I teach people to make forgiving choices.

For eight years, I have directed the Stanford Forgiveness Projects, the largest interpersonal forgiveness training research projects ever conducted. In conjunction with this research, I teach classes and workshops that offer a concrete method for forgiving others. I stress that while pain and disappointment are inevitable, they need not control us. It is vital to our health and well-being that we handle what comes our way without getting mired in blame and suffering.

Through my research and teaching, I have found that forgiveness isn't just wishful thinking. It's a trainable skill. My colleagues and I have developed a nine-step method for forgiving almost any conceivable hurt. We have tested this method through a series of studies with people who had been lied to, cheated, abandoned, beaten, abused, or had their children murdered. They ranged from neglected spouses to the parents of terrorist victims in Northern Ireland.

What we have found is that forgiveness can reduce stress, blood pressure, anger, depression, and hurt, and it can increase optimism, hope, compassion, and physical vitality. For instance, in a study we conducted with Protestants and Catholics from Northern Ireland who had lost a family member in the violence there, participants reported a 40 percent decline in symptoms of depression after undergoing the forgiveness training. Another study involved people who had suffered a variety of hurts, from business partners lying to them to best friends abandoning them. Six months after their forgiveness training, these people reported a 70 percent drop in the degree of hurt they felt toward the person who had hurt them, and they said they felt more forgiving in general.

This does not mean that forgiveness is ever easy. It certainly wasn't easy for Delores. But forgiveness was something she could learn to practice, even if it didn't come naturally to her. Difficult as it was, Delores's experience is emblematic of many others I've seen through this forgiveness training. Each story is different, but most follow a similar trajectory across the nine steps of forgiveness.

FIRST STEPS

Delores had mastered the first step before we even met: she determined what she did not like about her fiancé's behavior and knew in gruesome detail how she felt about it. She told anyone willing to listen what a louse Skip was.

Learning the second and third steps of forgiveness was more difficult. Even a year after Skip had cheated on her, Delores was in so much pain that she could not think straight. At first, healing meant only that she would revive her relationship with Skip. It was a struggle for her to want to heal just for her own well-being. In fact, Delores considered taking her fiancé back because she did not think other men would ever find her attractive. In her mind, Skip was the cause of, and the solution to, her problem.

Delores thought forgiving condemned her to being a doormat her entire life. She thought it meant staying with Skip and overlooking his cheating. She suffered under the misconception that forgiving Skip meant condoning his actions, or that it meant forgetting what had happened.

In truth, these things are very different. Forgiving someone does not mean forgetting or approving of hurtful events in the past. Rather, it means letting go of your hurt and anger, and not making someone endlessly responsible for your emotional well-being. Delores struggled to understand how controlling the way she felt in the present was more important than reviewing what happened to her in the past. She had trained herself to talk relentlessly of her past and of how her parents and poor relationships limited her options and happiness. It was hard for her to understand that constantly focusing on the past was the reason for her current distress.

I emphasized to Delores that she could not change the hurtful parts of the past, but only how much space she rented to them in her mind. By putting less blame on the past, she could change the way she felt in the present.

GLIMMERS OF PEACE

Delores got her first glimpse at an alternate way of living when she started to practice stress management every time she thought of Skip. She saw, if only for an instant, that breathing slowly and deeply affected how she felt. It gave her body and mind a break, and a glimmer of peace. When she did not practice, she remained in a state of upset and continually blamed her ex-fiancé for how she felt. After a few weeks of this pattern, she started to understand that she could reclaim her emotional life.

Delores simultaneously experimented with challenging what I call "unenforceable rules." By unenforceable rules, I mean the desires we have that we are simply powerless to turn into realities. For instance, while Delores wanted Skip to love and be faithful to her, it was clear that there was no way to make him do so. His behavior was a constant reminder that he did what he wanted and she had limited power over him. Delores also started to examine her theory that her parents had ruined her life. She noticed that she had an "unenforceable rule" that her parents must love her and treat her with kindness. Her parents had treated Delores the best they could, which included some cruelty and lack of care. Her parents' behavior was a reminder that no matter how much Delores wanted things to go her way, she did not have the power to control either the past or other people's behavior. By continuing to insist that her past should somehow change, Delores was dooming herself to endless blame, offense, and suffering.

As the forgiveness training progressed, Delores began to look at her suffering and ask herself what "unenforceable rule" she was trying to enforce. I reminded her that she would not be so upset unless she was trying to change something that was impossible for her to change. Delores saw that trying to change her ex-fiancé's behavior would always lead to pain and helplessness. She saw that just because she hoped for something, it did not have to come true. She understood that she would not be continuously upset if her rules for life were more in line with reality.

Therefore, Delores took it upon herself to create more enforceable rules. She was finally able to ask herself the revealing question, "What do I really want?" What she wanted was happiness, confidence, and peace of mind—things only she could provide for herself. Through asking this question, she saw that Skip and her parents did not have to remain in control of her life. Because of this insight, she started to work on her "positive intention," or life goals described only in positive terms. She realized that her positive goals were to learn how to value herself and her actions, as opposed to capturing someone to affirm her. She saw that it was more important for her to feel good about herself than it was for other people to feel good about her. Identifying these goals helped Delores to focus more on creating her future and less on lamenting her past.

In response, she concentrated on learning about herself and approving of herself. She talked about blaming other people and holding onto the past as impediments to her goal of healing. She told me how she was entering counseling, looking for male friends and not lovers, and appreciating her good qualities. She did not gloss over the difficulties she faced—there is no miracle cure for life's struggles.

Delores found that this strategy helped her free up mental space so she could uncover other ways to meet her needs. She realized that neither Skip nor her parents were ever going to approve of her in the way she wanted. She was going to have to find that in herself. Her old habit had been to see her glass as empty. She started retraining her mind to see where her cup might already be full.

Delores looked at her life and saw that she had good friends and was capable of doing well at work. She found appreciation for her parents' business acumen and the freedom their financial success granted her to attend college full-time without accruing any loans. She started to enjoy the beautiful area in which she lived, and she gave herself credit for her excellent exercise routine.

Delores also practiced gratitude when doing ordinary, everyday tasks. She found that one can be thankful for anything at any time, whether it's the beauty of the trees one passes while driving, the phenomenon of one's breathing, or the embarrassing riches of twenty-first-century America. When shopping, she made it a point to marvel at the opportunities she had to purchase a stupendous array of items. She learned to stop for a minute at the local shopping mall and say thanks to all of the people working there. She would walk into her local supermarket and take a moment to appreciate the abundance of food choices in front of her.

Delores had experienced the pain of parents who were more interested in their business than in caring for her. She had dwelled for years on what she had lost. Now she saw that her parents' financial success was also a blessing. She was able to appreciate the hard work they put in to provide a life for her. Delores practiced and saw the value of the old adage that a life well lived is the best revenge.

MOVING ON

When I bumped into Delores a year after her forgiveness classes ended, it was rewarding to see the changes in her. She was filled with energy and showed a lovely smile. When I asked her about Skip, she almost responded, "Skip who?" Instead of Skip, she wanted to talk about how much she had learned about herself. When I asked about her parents, she said her relationship with them had improved. Delores accepted what they could offer and realized their enormous emotional limitations. As an adult she understood that she was the one with the best chance to create a good life for herself. She was learning to let her parents off the hook. She forgave them for their mistakes.

The biggest change in Delores was the way she turned her grievances into more positive stories about herself. She talked with pride of forgiving Skip and learning how to take care of herself. Delores was a woman who took her forgiveness training to heart. She completed the full nine steps and now presented herself as a hero and not a victim. Forgiveness brought her a sense of peace that had previously eluded her.

Of course, she did not always have it easy. She still longed for a loving and tight family and a faithful partner. When she found the longing overpowering, she told herself to make the best of what she had. She would take a walk and remind herself of the blessings of a beautiful day or the possibilities the future might bring. And sometimes, like the rest of us, there were times when she was simply unhappy.

To become a forgiving person, we have to practice forgiving smaller grievances. Then, when a bigger insult comes, we are ready, willing, and able to deal with it. Alternatively, like Delores, once we learn to forgive a major grievance, we can understand the value of limiting the power that pain and anger hold over us the next time we are hurt. No one can make the people in life behave kindly, fairly, or honestly at all times. We cannot end the cruelty on this planet. What we can do is forgive the unkindness that comes our way and put energy toward meeting our positive goals. Then we can help others do the same.

Forgiveness, like other positive emotions such as hope, compassion, and appreciation, is a natural expression of our humanity. These emotions exist within a deep part of each of us. Like many things, they require practice to perfect, but with this practice they become stronger and easier to find. Ultimately, they can be as natural to us as anger and bitterness. It takes a willingness to practice forgiveness day after day to see its profound benefits to physical and emotional well-being and to our relationships. Perhaps the most fundamental benefit of forgiveness is that over time it allows us access to the loving emotions that can lie buried beneath grievances and grudges.

COMPASSION ACROSS CUBICLES

Jill Suttie

FIVE-FOOT TALL PANELS divide the physician's billing department into a maze of cubicles at Foote Hospital, in Jackson, Michigan. Each cubicle contains one of the 39 employees who make up the billing office staff. Most of the employees are women, many are single mothers, and they spend each day on the phone trying to collect unpaid debts owed to the hospital. The work is repetitive and may seem uninspiring. Yet the hospital staff widely considers this department one of the best places to work at Foote.

"Our department is special," said Sarah Boik, head of the billing unit. "People care about each other here."

Deb LeJeune agrees. LeJeune had been on Boik's staff for only five months when her husband needed a kidney transplant. She said she was worried and distracted in the days leading up to his operation and couldn't concentrate at work. She needed to take six weeks off without pay to care for her husband, a financial strain she wasn't sure she could handle. When her coworkers learned of her situation, they pitched in to make her a basket full of puzzles, books, and snacks she could take to the hospital, took up a collection to help her make her house payments, gave her gas cards to use for the drives back and forth from the hospital, and visited her at home just to check in on her.

"It was amazing!" said LeJeune. "I couldn't have gotten through without their support. They are like family to me."

These days, it's rare to find people who consider their workplace "special" and feel close to their coworkers, let alone call them "family." Denise Rousseau, a professor of organizational behavior at Carnegie Mellon University, traces that fact to a steady deterioration in employer-employee relationships that began in the 1980s, when changes in technology, globalization, and a volatile stock market pushed major manufacturers to lay off large numbers of employees. Other organizations followed suit, and soon managers were hiring and firing their workers at will. "The downsizing surge in the '80s left employees feeling betrayed," said Rousseau. "Employees no longer felt they could trust their employer to provide for them, so they had less attachment and loyalty toward their places of work." Rousseau's statements are borne out by statistics from a recent Gallup poll, which found that 59 percent of American workers are disengaged from work—putting in their time, but with no energy or passion for it—while another 14 percent are actively disengaged, acting out their unhappiness at work and undermining coworkers.

But a growing number of researchers, mainly at business schools across the country, are working to determine what's behind anomalies like the Foote billing department, where ennui and malaise are displaced by excitement and compassion. This movement, called positive organizational scholarship, or POS, breaks with traditional business research. Instead of analyzing organizational failures, POS looks for examples of "positive deviance"—cases in which organizations successfully cultivate inspiration and productivity among workers—and then tries to figure out what makes these groups tick, so that others might emulate them. "We're a combination of positive psychology, sociology, and anthropology," said Jane Dutton, a professor of psychology and business at the University of Michigan and a leader in the POS movement. "POS seeks to cultivate hope and a sense of possibility that people don't always know is there."

Over the last six years, Dutton and her colleagues have studied an array of organizational settings, including hospitals, universities, and businesses like Newsweek, Reuters, Macy's, and Cisco Systems, using a combination of surveys, structured interviews, and observation to learn how organizations respond to employees experiencing personal difficulty. Their studies yielded some stories of compassion, where distressed workers received cards, flowers, financial help, emotional support, or time off from work; in other cases, workers complained of receiving little sympathy or help. "We found that employees who'd experienced compassion at work saw themselves, their coworkers, and the organization in a more positive light," said Dutton. "Statistically, they demonstrated more positive emotions, such as joy and contentment, and more commitment toward the organization." Interestingly, she added, these results held regardless of whether employees received compassion directly or merely witnessed it.

Dutton sees compassion as a natural response of people witnessing others in pain or distress—something we are hardwired to do. The problem with bringing compassion into the workplace, she explains, is that people don't know what's acceptable to express in that setting. Many workers assume that they are supposed to check their personal problems at the door when they enter the office. "Ever since organizations began moving toward more bureaucracy and measuring success by reliability and efficiency, the relational aspects of work have been de-emphasized," said Dutton. But when stress at home inevitably spills into the workplace, Dutton added, it can contribute to lost productivity and higher health care costs, and compassion becomes a vital response. "If compassion heals, as our research suggests, then people will be able to get back to work more quickly, to bounce back from life's setbacks," she said. "This has to be of interest to employers."

Thomas Wright, a researcher in the University of Nevada's managerial sciences department, agrees that managers would do well to pay more attention to the mental health of their employees. In several studies, Wright has found that psychological well-being accounted for 10 to 25 percent of an employee's job performance and was predictive of positive employee evaluations up to five years in the future. "Organizations that are able and willing to foster a psychologically well workforce and work environment are at a distinct competitive advantage," said Wright. "Managers should take note."

Apparently, some are. At Cisco Systems, a California company that creates technologies for the Internet, whenever an employee suffered a significant loss, such as a death in the family, CEO John Chambers made it a policy to contact that employee within 48 hours to offer his condolences and help. His example gave others within the organization a green light to act compassionately toward their coworkers, and employees consistently rate the company as one of the best places to work in the country. "When an organization's capacity for compassion comes from the top, it can result in a kind of compassion contagion that sweeps the whole organization," said Dutton.

Of course, not all organizations have charismatic leaders to serve as compassionate role models, but that's not necessarily an obstacle to building a compassionate workplace. According to Monica Worline, a professor of organization and management at Emory University and a POS scholar, overt displays of compassion usually come from coworkers, not management. But through in-depth case studies of several organizations, she has found that organizations that implicitly encourage positive contact among employees, through regular meetings or by providing spaces for employees to gather together informally, tend to have higher levels of compassion. Frequent interaction gives workers more opportunities to notice when someone needs help and to offer it; when workers share news and ideas, it helps foster empathy between them. "An organization which has high-quality connections between people will have much more fertile ground for compassion to happen," said Worline.

Still, many organizations have neither a compassionate manager nor an environment that fosters compassion among colleagues. One financial analyst, who works for a large national bank in the San Francisco Bay Area and asked to remain anonymous for fear of reprisal, spoke in an interview about his office environment, where employees work side by side every day but barely acknowledge each other. Having come from a smaller, more familial software company, he was surprised by the lack of camaraderie at the bank. But he soon found himself adjusting to the new environment, keeping his own natural friendliness in check. Then a coworker on his floor died suddenly over the holidays. "I expected a supervisor or someone to at least explain why he wasn't there, but nobody talked about it. It was really weird," he said. "I didn't learn he'd died until I needed an office space for a new hire, and they suggested I use his." Given the culture of his office, the incident wasn't surprising, he said, but it made him question the heart of the organization.

Worline said that such environments take their toll on people working within them. "In extreme cases, employees leave," she said. "But even those that stay will often quit doing the discretionary things they used to do for the organization, when they thought it cared."

It isn't always easy for a boss to accommodate employees, even when one is committed to demonstrating compassion. "All supervisors have to balance the needs of the corporation—which is all about money, earnings per share, and profitability—with the needs of the worker," said Renee Knee, a senior vice president for SAP, a leading software company. She cited an example of a senior employee who had to leave the country suddenly because of a death in his family, just before the deadline of a multimillion-dollar project for which he was responsible. Though Knee gave him the time off, the ill-timed departure created extra stress in an office already under deadline pressure.

Organizations, especially businesses in competitive industries, always walk a fine line when giving employees time off in emergencies. But Worline suggests that the POS message about compassion sometimes gets misconstrued, as managers only focus on the bigger acts of compassion, such as time off and monetary gifts, which may make a big difference to workers but are not always easy to provide. "Just stopping by and listening to an employee in pain can make all the difference," insists Worline. When giving talks to groups of managers, she tries to convey the importance of just paying attention to employees and noticing when they need help.

Worline, Dutton, and their POS colleagues recognize that problems can arise in practicing compassion at work. They note that compassionate acts must be tailored to the particular needs of each person. If a person suffers a traumatic event and wishes to remain private about it, he or she may not welcome attention or help from others, well-meaning as it might be. Programs like vacation pools, where employees donate small amounts of vacation time for coworkers in need, can create complicated ethical dilemmas: If an employee doesn't contribute to the vacation pool, should she be allowed to dip into it herself? "Compassion, if applied differently to different employees, may create a perception of inequity," said Worline. If applied in this spirit, it may even alienate employees, she argues.

Then there are the researchers who take issue with some of the basic objectives of POS. Ben Hunnicutt, a professor of leisure studies at the University of Iowa, argues that efforts to make work life more rewarding and pleasurable distract from what he considers bigger goals for workers, like higher pay and shorter workweeks. Encouraging people to pursue satisfaction through work means that they'll spend more time there and have less left for family, health, art, religion—the things, he argues, that really give meaning to people's lives. "Work can never replace these important aspects of life, and we shouldn't expect it to," he said. "Instead of trying to make work better, we should all be working less."

Dutton agrees that working less may help improve people's lives, but she thinks American society is a long way from moving in that direction. If anything, people are working more than they used to, she said, and economic realities require people to spend more time at work. And she added that her work on compassion is not just relevant to work settings, but to organizational settings in general. The conditions that foster compassion at work apply to other contexts as well. "Whether we're talking about work, schools, churches, or hospitals, we all spend time in organizations," said Dutton. "POS is trying to understand how all organizations can be places of healing, where people feel alive and can flourish."

There are signs that Dutton and her colleagues' ideas are gaining wider recognition, including the publication of POS scholarly work in journals aimed at business managers and the inclusion of a chapter on compassion in two recent management textbooks. When a POS article appeared in the *Harvard Business Review* in January 2005, over 200 individuals from businesses, schools, and hospitals called in to participate in an online conference with the authors, arranged by the magazine. Dutton says none of this would have happened even a few years ago.

"It's exciting to see how interested people are in our work, how it energizes them," she said. "They want to move toward more humane interactions at work, more compassionate responding. This is deeply motivating to me and my colleagues."

ARE YOU A JERK AT WORK?

Robert I. Sutton

WHEN I ARRIVED at Stanford University as a 29-year-old researcher, I was an inexperienced, ineffective, and extremely nervous teacher. I got poor teaching evaluations in my first year on the job, and I deserved them. I worked to become more effective in the classroom and was delighted to win the best-teacher award in my department (by student vote) at the graduation ceremony at the end of my third year.

But my delight evaporated when a more senior colleague ran up to me immediately after the ceremony, gave me a big hug, and whispered in my ear in a condescending tone (while sporting a broad smile for public consumption), "Well, Bob, now that you've satisfied the babies here on campus, perhaps you can settle down and do some real work." She secretly and expertly extracted every ounce of joy I had been experiencing.

When I encounter a mean-spirited person like this, the first thing I think is, "Wow, what an asshole!"

I bet you do, too. You might call such people bullies, creeps, jerks, weasels, tormentors, tyrants, serial slammers, despots, or unconstrained egomaniacs, but for me at least, "asshole" best captures the fear and loathing that I have for these nasty people.

And most of us, unfortunately, have to deal with assholes in our workplaces at one time or another.

Who deserves to be branded an asshole? I like to use two tests before passing judgment. First, after talking to the alleged asshole, do you feel oppressed, humiliated, de-energized, or belittled? In general, do you feel worse about yourself? Second, does the alleged asshole aim his or her venom at people who are less powerful rather than at those people who are more powerful?

I can assure you that after that interaction with my colleague—which lasted less than a minute—I felt worse about myself. I went from being the happiest I'd ever been about my work performance to worrying that my teaching award would be taken as a sign that I wasn't serious enough about research (the main standard used for evaluating Stanford professors).

My colleague's behavior also passes the second test because when the episode occurred, this person was further up the ladder than I was. I learned a lot about her from the way she treated one of her subordinates—in this case, me.

I believe the best test of a person's character is how he or she treats those with less power. The brief nasty stares, the teasing and jokes that are really camouflaged public shaming and insults, the exclusion from minor and major gatherings—they're all exercises of power, and they don't just hurt for a moment. They have cumulative effects on our mental health and our commitment to our bosses, peers, and organizations.

Georgia State University professor Bennett Tepper's research on abusive supervision, for example, examined a cross section of 712 adults in a midwestern city who worked in the private, nonprofit, and public sectors. He found that many of these employees had bosses who used ridicule, put-downs, the silent treatment, and insults. These demeaning acts drove people to quit their jobs at higher rates and sapped the effectiveness of those who remained. A six-month follow-up found that those still trapped in their jobs suffered from less work and life satisfaction, reduced commitment to employers, and heightened depression, anxiety, and burnout. Similar findings have been uncovered in dozens of other studies. They all suggest that assholes can severely undermine an organization's productivity.

Given the psychological and financial harm done by assholes, you'd think that most organizations would refrain from hiring them or be quick to expel these creeps once their true selves are exposed. But it's not so simple. Although I suspect that some people are genetically predisposed to be nasty, years of research has suggested that under certain circumstances, almost any of us is susceptible to becoming an asshole. This is especially true of people who assume positions of power. Study after study has found that giving people even a little bit of power over others can induce them to abuse that power. It isn't just a myth: power can turn any of us into assholes.

Fortunately, there's also evidence that we can limit the negative influences of power and keep our offices civil, supportive, and even inspiring places to work. I've identified several strategies for combating assholes—and preventing ourselves from becoming one of them.

ARE ASSHOLES BORN OR MADE?

Yes, some assholes are born that way. But there is also strong evidence that no matter what our "personality" is, we all can turn into assholes under the wrong conditions. This happens frequently and with shocking speed and intensity when people assume powerful positions. A huge body of research—hundreds of studies—shows that when people are put in positions of power, they start talking more, taking what they want for themselves, ignoring what other people say or want, ignoring how less powerful people react to their behavior, acting more rudely, and generally treating any situation or person as a means for satisfying their own needs. What's more, being put in positions of power often blinds them to the fact that they are acting like jerks.

One of my Stanford colleagues, Deborah Gruenfeld, has spent years studying and cataloging the effects of putting people in positions where they can lord power over others. She's found that even tiny and trivial power advantages can rapidly change how people think and act, and usually for the worse. In one experiment, student groups of three discussed a long list of contentious social issues, things like abortion and pollution. One member was randomly assigned to the more powerful position of evaluating the recommendations made by the other two. After 30 minutes, the experimenter brought in a plate of five cookies. The more powerful students were more likely to take a second cookie, chew with their mouths open, and get crumbs on their faces and the table.

This study might sound silly, but it scares me because it shows how having just a slight power edge causes regular people to grab the goodies for themselves and act like rude pigs. I was on the receiving end of such boorish behavior a few years ago. It was at a lunch with the CEO of a profitable company who had just been ranked as one of the top corporate leaders by a famous business magazine. He treated our little group of four or five professors (all 50-plus-year-old professionals) as if we were naive and rather stupid children. Although, in theory, he was our guest, he told us where to sit and when we could talk. He interrupted several of us in mid-sentence to tell us he had heard enough or didn't care about what we were saying. He even criticized the food we ordered, saying things like "That will make you fat." He generally conveyed that he was our master and commander and that our job was to focus our efforts on satisfying his every whim.

The most striking part was that he seemed completely oblivious to the fact that he was bullying us and that we were offended. This is consistent with research showing that power makes it harder for people to see the world from the perspectives of others. In one recent study, Adam Galinksy of Northwestern University and his colleagues divided participants into two groups: members of one group were made to feel powerful by recalling and writing about an incident when they had power over others; the other group was asked to write about an incident in which someone had power over them. Then all the participants were told to draw the letter E on their forehead. If a person drew the E so it seemed backward to himself but legible to the rest of the world, this indicated that he had considered how others would see the letter. If the E seemed correct to himself but backward to everyone else, this suggested a failure to take other people's perspectives into account.

Sure enough, Galinsky and his colleagues found that people who had been primed to feel powerful were nearly three times as likely to draw the E so it seemed legible to themselves but backward to others. In other words, power made them much less likely to see the world through other people's eyes.

FIGHT THE POWER

These findings may seem discouraging, but they don't mean we're condemned to working with assholes. I've spent much of the last few years thinking about how to sustain a humane workplace and how employees can deal with nasty bosses and peers. Based on research and stories that I hear, I've developed a few tips for victims of workplace assholes.

My first tip is in a class by itself: Escape if you can. The best thing to do if you are stuck under the thumb of an asshole (or a bunch of them) is to get out as fast as possible. Not only are you at great emotional risk; you're also at risk of emulating the behavior of the jerks around you, catching it like a disease—what I call "asshole poisoning."

Indeed, experiments by psychologists Leigh Thompson and Cameron Anderson have shown that even when compassionate people join a group with a leader who is "high-energy, aggressive, mean, the classic bully type," they are "temporarily transformed into carbon copies of the alpha dog." Despite the risk of asshole poisoning, escape isn't always possible. As one woman wrote me in response to this advice, "I have to feed my family and pay my mortgage, and there aren't a lot of jobs that pay well enough to do that around here."

In those cases where a victim can't escape (at least for now), I suggest starting with polite confrontation. Some people really don't mean to be jerks. They might be surprised if you gently let them know that they are leaving you feeling belittled and demeaned. Other jerks are demeaning on purpose, but may stop if you stand up to them in a civil but firm manner. For example, an office worker wrote me that her boss was "a major jerk," but she found that he left her alone after she gave him "a hard stare" and told him his behavior was "absolutely unacceptable and I simply won't tolerate it."

Next, if a bully keeps spewing venom at you, limit your contact with the creep as much as possible. Try to avoid any meetings you can with him or her and try to talk by phone rather than in person. Keep conversations short; be polite, but don't provide a lot of personal information during meetings of any kind, including e-mail exchanges. If the bully says or writes something nasty, try to avoid snapping back, as that can fuel a vicious cycle of asshole poisoning. Also, recent research suggests that stand-up meetings are just as effective as sit-down meetings, but are shorter. So if you have to meet with jerks, try to meet in places without chairs and avoid sitting down whenever possible. This will limit your exposure to their abuse.

I also recommend keeping an "asshole diary," in which you carefully document what the jerk does and when it happens. A government employee wrote me a detailed e-mail about how she used a diary to get rid of a nasty, racist coworker:

> I documented the many harmful things she did with dates and times. I encouraged her other victims to do so too and these written and signed statements were presented to our supervisors. Our supervisors knew this worker was an asshole but didn't really seem to be doing anything to stop her harmful behaviors until they received these statements. The jerk went on a mysterious leave that no supervisor was permitted to discuss, and she never returned.

If all else fails, try to practice indifference. Management gurus and executives are constantly ranting about the importance of commitment, passion, and giving all you have to a job. That is good advice when your bosses and peers treat you with dignity. But if you work with people who treat you like dirt, they have not earned your passion and commitment. Don't let their vicious words and deeds touch your soul: learn to be comfortably numb until the day comes when you find a workplace that deserves your full commitment. Until then, direct your passion elsewhere, like your family, your hobbies, or perhaps a volunteer organization.

ASSHOLES ARE US

I want to stress again that being an asshole isn't just something that only happens to others and can't possibly happen to wonderful people like you and me. All of us are at risk. As I like to say, assholes are us.

But I have identified some strategies for handling the jerk within. One way to do that, as I've mentioned, is to stay away from assholes as much as possible and thus avoid asshole poisoning. But, especially if you take a position of power, there are several additional things you can do to stop yourself from turning into an asshole.

One is to eliminate as many unnecessary power differences between yourself and others. For instance, when Frank Blake became CEO of Home Depot last year, he eliminated the executive dining room, cut his own pay, and, according to the *New York Times*, distributed an image called the inverted pyramid, which places customers and employees above the chief executive.

Pay is an especially vivid sign of power differences, and many studies suggest that when the difference between the highest- and lowest-paid people in a company or team is reduced, a host of good things happen, including improved financial performance, better product quality, enhanced research productivity, and, for baseball teams, a better won-lost record.

In the United States and other Western countries, we are always pressing to create bigger differences between winners and losers. To be sure, some people are more important to an organization than others because they are more difficult to replace or have more essential skills. Status differences will always be with us. But Frank Blake and other like-minded leaders build organizations with fewer assholes and spark better performance by embracing what I call the "power-performance paradox." They realize that their company has and should have a pecking order, but they do everything they can to downplay and reduce status and power differences among members.

Another step you can take to avoid becoming an asshole is to get some friends and colleagues who will tell you when you are acting like one. Better yet, hold others responsible for telling you when you're being an asshole—make it safe for them to do so. And when they tell you, listen to them. Remember, power will blind you to all the ways you are acting like a jerk and hurting other people. If people tell you that you're acting like an asshole and your reaction is that they're wrong, odds are that you're fooling yourself.

I've learned that competition breeds assholes, so it's essential to try not to foster an overly competitive workplace. Many organizations constantly rate and rank people, giving the spoils to a few stars and treating the rest as second- and third-class citizens. The unfortunate result is that people who ought to be friends become enemies—ruthless jerks who run wild as they scramble to push themselves up the ladder and push their rivals down. They act on the dangerous and widespread assumption that professional life requires cutthroat competition. In truth, it is nearly always a blend of cooperation and competition, and organizations that forbid extreme internal competition not only are more civilized but perform better as well, despite societal myths to the contrary.

Research on "framing" by social psychologists suggests a few tricks you can use to avoid being overly competitive. The assumptions and language we use—the lenses through which we see the world—can have big effects on how we treat others. Even seemingly small differences in language that we hear and use can determine whether we cooperate or compete. Stanford researcher Lee Ross and his colleagues have run experiments in which they had pairs of students play a game. If the students cooperated, they'd share a reward equally, but if they competed, one player would take the lion's share of the goodies.

Ross and his colleagues told some players that the game was called the "Community Game" (conjuring up images of shared fate and collaboration); they told others they'd be playing the "Wall Street Game" (conjuring up images of a dog-eat-dog world). People who played the Community Game were dramatically more cooperative and honest about their intentions than those who believed they were playing the Wall Street Game. These findings were later replicated with U.S. Air Force Academy cadets. Related experiments show that when people are first exposed to words like *enemy, battle, inconsiderate, vicious, lawyer,* and *capitalist*, they are far less likely to cooperate than when first exposed to words like *helped, fair, warm, mutual,* and *share.*

The implication is that if you want to quell your inner jerk, use ideas and language that frame life in ways that will make you focus on cooperation. For instance, make a conscious effort to use the word *we* rather than *I* and *me.* Tape-record and listen to yourself and colleagues at a couple of meetings; if they are nearly all about "me, myself, and I" and "us versus them," it might be time to start changing the way you talk.

Taken together, these steps can help you enforce a No Asshole rule. If you manage your organization so that you address the disturbing influences of power and manage yourself to avoid catching and spreading asshole poisoning, you can fuel a virtuous cycle and help sustain a civilized workplace.

A FEELING FOR FICTION

Keith Oatley

"You be that one," I remember my daughter saying to a companion. "And I'll be this one." My daughter was about 5 at the time, and, as in the imaginary games played by children of that age, she and her friend were arranging roles. But they weren't about to play a game. They were preparing to watch a movie.

We tend to think of movie watching or book reading as passive activities. That may be true physically, but it's not true emotionally. When we watch a film or read a novel, we join ourselves to a character's trajectory through the story world. We see things from their point of view—feel scared when they are threatened, wounded when they are hurt, pleased when they succeed. These feelings are familiar to us as readers or viewers. But our propensity to identify with characters is actually a remarkable demonstration of our ability to empathize with others.

When we examine this process of identification in fiction, we appreciate the importance of empathy—not only in enjoying works of literature, but in helping us form connections with those around us in the real world. The feelings elicited by fiction go beyond the words on a page or the images on a screen. Far from being solitary activities, reading books or watching movies or plays actually can help train us in the art of being human. These effects derive from our cognitive capacity for empathy, and there are indications that they can help shape our relationships with friends, family, and fellow citizens.

THE STUFF DREAMS ARE MADE ON

In the West, the tradition of understanding literature derives from Aristotle, who, nearly 2,400 years ago, wrote a book called *Poetics*. The subject matter of his book was not just poetry. More broadly, it was what we now call fiction, which, like poetry, means "something made." Aristotle said that whereas history lets us know what has happened, poetry (fiction) is more important because it is about what can happen.

The central term in *Poetics* is *mimesis*, the relation of the story to the way the world works. This term can be interpreted in two ways. If you read an English translation, you will find the Greek word *mimesis* translated to mean "copying," "imitation," or "representation." These translations get it half right. While literary art can serve to imitate the world—what Hamlet called holding "the mirror up to nature"—it can also create new worlds. In other words, Aristotle thought that great plays, such as the tragedies of Sophocles, which he discussed in *Poetics*, created worlds of the imagination. Shakespeare likened this to the way we dream, such as when Prospero, the protagonist in Shakespeare's *The Tempest*, says that humans "are such stuff as dreams are made on." Dream is an apt metaphor because when we dream, without any input from eyes or ears, we create worlds of places, people, and emotions. What a good story does, by means of black marks on the white pages of a novel, or by the actions of a small group of people several yards away on a stage, or by the flickering images on a screen, is to offer the materials—a kind of kit—to start up and run the dream of the story world on your mind. A story is a partnership. The author writes it, and the reader or audience member brings it alive.

The emotions that you experience as you breathe life into a story are related to the characters, but they are not the characters' emotions. They are yours. How does this happen? How can an artificial world conjure up such real emotions, and what mental capacities do we engage in order to feel those emotions? Brilliant though Aristotle was, his *Poetics* is curiously silent on this question, as is much of the canon of Western literary theory that followed him.

But other traditions—one of Western psychology, one of Eastern literature—can help shed light on how fiction elicits such empathic responses from us.

MOVING PICTURES

Empathy can be thought of as feeling with someone, or for them. In a recent study using functional magnetic resonance imaging (fMRI) scans of brain activity, Tania Singer and her colleagues showed that a basis for empathy can be identified in the brain. Singer and her colleagues administered electric shocks to volunteers and also gave these volunteers signals when a loved one, present in the next room, was being shocked. In some parts of the volunteers' brains, activation occurred only when they themselves received a shock, but other parts associated with feeling pain were activated both when the volunteers received a shock and when they knew their loved one was getting a shock. Singer and her colleagues describe this dual activation as the emotional aspect of pain. They argue that their results show that the empathic response that we feel for someone we know and like is the same as the emotional aspect we feel ourselves.

That will ring true for anyone who's ever been caught up in a play, book, or movie—anyone who has wept for the young lovers in William Shakespeare's *Romeo and Juliet*, or with the Joad family in John Steinbeck's *The Grapes of Wrath*, or with those who have suffered in Steven Spielberg's *Schindler's List*.

Our fondness for fiction shows that we enjoy feeling with other people, even when sometimes the feelings are negative. In another recent psychological study, Tom Trabasso and Jennifer Chung asked 20 viewers to watch two films, *Blade Runner* and *Vertigo*. Each film was stopped at 12 different times. Soon after the beginning of each movie, and again at the end, all the viewers rated their liking for the protagonist and for the antagonist. One set of 10 viewers had the job of saying, at each of the film's 12 stopping points, how well or how poorly things were going for the protagonist and for the antagonist. These ratings agreed with the experimenters' own analysis of the characters' goals and actions. The job of the other set of 10 viewers was to rate what emotions, and of what intensity, they themselves were experiencing at each point where the film was stopped. These viewers experienced more positive emotions at points where things went well for the liked protagonist or badly for the disliked antagonist (as rated by the first set of 10 viewers); they also felt negative emotions when things went badly for the protagonist or well for the antagonist.

So, whenever we read a novel, look at a movie, or even watch a sports match, we tend to cast our lot with someone we find likable. When a favored character in a story does well, we feel pleased; when a disliked character succeeds, we are displeased.

This process seems rather basic. It is rather basic. If this liking for a protagonist were all there was to it, reading fiction and watching dramas would not be much different from going on a roller-coaster ride. Indeed, some books and movies do little more than offer just such an experience. They are called thrillers. But in some books and films, much more can occur. Along with the basic process of empathic identification, we can start to extend ourselves into situations we have never experienced, feel for people very different from ourselves, and begin to understand such people in ways we may have never thought possible. George Eliot, a novelist whose books offer such effects, put it like this:

> The greatest benefit we owe to the artist, whether painter, poet, or novelist, is the extension of our sympathies. Appeals founded

on generalizations and statistics require a sympathy ready-made, a moral sentiment already in activity; but a picture of human life such as a great artist can give, surprises even the trivial and the selfish into that attention to what is apart from themselves, which may be called the raw material of moral sentiment. . . . Art is the nearest thing to life; it is a mode of amplifying experience and extending our contact with our fellow-men beyond the bounds of our personal lot.

What Eliot is implying is that art is capable of inducing one of the most profound aspects of empathy: the ability to sensitize us to the emotions of other people, transcending the limits of our own experiences and perspective. This wasn't territory that Aristotle covered.

In India, there has been a literary tradition parallel to that of the West that does address this topic. In this Eastern tradition, readers' and audience members' emotions have had a more central role. The idea in Indian poetics is that fictional characters and fictional situations have to be created in the minds of readers and audience members by suggestion. The Sanskrit term for this suggestion is *dhvani*. This aspect of the tradition is not so different from Aristotle's idea of the world-creating aspect of *mimesis*. But the Eastern notion, for which there is no Aristotelian parallel, is that what is suggested to readers or audience members in their empathically imagined worlds are special literary emotions, called *rasas*.

The job of writers or actors is to write or act in such a way that the reader/audience experiences these *rasas*. The Indian theorists thought that we experienced *rasas* because, by means of the suggestiveness of the poetry and the actors' skills, memories would be brought to mind from the whole range of past lives. We moderns would probably now say that we experience emotions even from outside our own experience because of our kinship with the rest of humanity. But here is the important point that was stressed by the Indian theorists: *rasas* are like everyday emotions, except that we experience these literary emotions without the thick crust of egotism that often blinds us to the implications of our ordinary emotions in our daily lives. For instance, if we are sexually attracted to someone in ordinary life, we can become rather selfish. Indeed in the West, falling in love is often given as a reason for suspending other social obligations. In a play or novel, however, we not only feel empathically with the character in love, but can feel with other characters as well. The idea of a *rasa* is that we can feel the emotion, but also understand its social implications without our usual, often self-interested, involvement. We can experience the energizing aspects of love, but also—depending on the context— understand its potential effects on others.

You may be surprised to learn that in the West, the person who seems to have been the first to write about empathic processes in literature was Adam Smith, who became famous for his ideas about how the market regulated itself as if by an "invisible hand." Smith's abiding interest was in the glue that holds society together. His first book was *The Theory of Moral Sentiments*. In it he argued that an important component of this glue is what I am here calling empathy, which he called sympathy or compassion. Reading, he argued, draws on sympathy, because we necessarily become an interested but "impartial spectator" in other lives. We become involved in what is going on in the story, but not as if it were happening to us directly. We might become angry in sympathy with a protagonist, but without the narrow-minded vindictiveness that can occur when injustices affect us directly. The argument is the same as that of the *rasa* theorists, although it seems unlikely that Smith knew about them.

Reading certain kinds of fiction, then, is the very model of how we might properly view events in our social world. It is right that they engage our emotions, as if they were happening to someone with whom we are closely involved, but not directly to us. In literature we feel the pain of the downtrodden, the anguish of defeat, or the joy of victory—but in a safe space. In this space, we can, as it were, practice empathy. We can refine our human capacities of emotional understanding. We can hone our ability to feel with other people who, in ordinary life, might seem too foreign—or too threatening—to elicit our sympathies. Perhaps, then, when we return to our real lives, we can better understand why people act the way they do, and react with caution, even compassion, toward them.

In her book *Poetic Justice*, philosopher Martha Nussbaum has taken Adam Smith's argument further and claimed that reading, particularly of certain novels, not only uses our faculties as sympathetic spectators, but exercises them in such a way as to make us better citizens when it comes to social issues such as justice. Nussbaum points out that what we really mean by justice is not just mechanically applying a rule book. It involves being able to understand imaginatively and deeply what is going on both for perpetrators and for victims. It is hard to think how this can be better achieved than through certain kinds of literature. Even some television shows, such as *Law and Order*, are written to enable the viewer to enter imaginatively into both sides of issues such as racism, women's rights, and questions about whether people who are seriously mentally ill can act voluntarily.

Reading can be an escape—a ride on an emotional roller coaster. But we can also read and go to the theater to extend our sympathies. In *Romeo and Juliet*, we can feel for the adolescent Juliet as she finds herself in love with someone her parents hate because he belongs to the wrong family. In *The Tempest*, we can feel for the aging Prospero as he nears the end of his career. Our feelings are for these characters, but they are our own feelings. In the hands of writers like William Shakespeare or George Eliot, we can perhaps understand these feelings better than if they were caused by events in our own lives. Works of fiction draw on our skills of empathy and allow us to practice these skills. Then not only do they extend our individual experience, but they can become topics of discussion with others, who can show us even further implications of our emotions than what we had perceived ourselves.

A DIFFERENT VIEW

Alfie Kohn

FRANZ KAFKA once described war as a "monstrous failure of imagination." In order to kill, one must cease to see individual human beings and instead reduce them to an abstraction: "the enemy." Even in popular entertainment, the bad guys are never shown at home with their children. It's easy to cheer the death of a caricature, not of a three-dimensional person.

But to step outside one's own viewpoint and consider how the world looks to another person is one of the most remarkable capabilities of the human mind. Psychologists call this skill "perspective taking," and it offers a foundation for morality. People who can—and do—think about how others experience the world are more likely to reach out and help those people—or at a minimum are less likely to harm them.

Taking another person's perspective means realizing that in war, each person underneath our bombs is the center of his universe, just as you are the center of yours: he gets the flu, worries about his aged mother, likes sweets, falls in love—even though he lives half a world away and speaks a different language. To see things from his point of view is to recognize all the particulars that make him human, and ultimately it is to understand that his life is no less valuable than yours.

Less dramatically, many of the social problems we encounter on a daily basis can be understood as a failure of perspective taking. People who litter, block traffic by double-parking, or rip pages out of library books seem to be locked into themselves, unable or unwilling to imagine how others will have to deal with their thoughtlessness.

Developing the skill of perspective taking is a challenge; it's something people need to practice from the time they're young. So it's imperative that we try to cultivate it in our kids.

There are different levels of perspective taking, of course, and more sophisticated versions may elude very young children. The best we may be able to hope for in the case of a 4-year-old is the rather primitive ethics of the Golden Rule. We might say (in a tone that sounds like an invitation to reflect, rather than a reprimand), "I notice you finished all the juice and didn't leave any for Amy. How do you think you would feel if Amy did that?" The premise of this question, probably correct, is that both kids like juice and would be disappointed to find none available.

But George Bernard Shaw reminded us that this sort of assumption doesn't always make sense. "Do not do unto others as you expect they should do unto you," he advised. "Their tastes may not be the same." And, we might add, their needs or values or backgrounds might not be the same either. Older children and adults can realize that it's not enough to imagine ourselves in someone else's situation: we have to imagine what they're feeling in that situation. We have to see with their eyes rather than just with our own. We have to—if I may switch metaphors—ask not just what it's like to be in their shoes, but what it's like to have their feet.

So how can we promote perspective taking in our children? How can we help them to develop an increasingly sophisticated understanding of how things look from points of view other than their own? First, we can set an example. After a supermarket cashier says something rude to us, we can comment to our child who has witnessed this: "Huh. He didn't seem to be in a very good mood today, did he? What do you think might have happened to that man that made him so grouchy? Do you think someone might have hurt his feelings?"

It is enormously powerful to say things like this to our kids, to teach them that we need not respond to an individual who acts unpleasantly by getting angry—or, for that matter, by blaming ourselves. Rather, we can attempt to enter the world of that other person. It's our choice: Every day our children can watch us as we imagine someone else's point of view—or they can watch us remain self-centered. Every day they can witness our efforts to see strangers as human beings—or they can witness our failure to do so.

Besides setting an example, we can also encourage perspective taking by discussing books and television shows with our kids in a way that highlights the characters' diverse perspectives. ("We're seeing all of this through the eyes of the doctor, aren't we? But what do you think the little girl is feeling about what just happened?") We can even use perspective taking as a tool to help siblings resolve their conflicts. "Okay," we might say, after a blowup. "Tell me what just happened, but pretend you're your brother and describe how things might have seemed to him."

Finally, we can help younger children become more sensitive to others' emotions by gently directing their attention to someone's tone of voice, posture, or facial expression and by inviting them to reflect on what that person might be thinking and how he or she might be feeling. The point here is to build a skill (learning how to read other people), but also to promote a disposition (wanting to know how others are feeling and being willing to figure it out): "I know Grandma said it would be okay to go on another walk with you, but I noticed that she paused a few seconds before agreeing. And did you see how tired she seemed when she sat down just now?"

The very act of teaching kids to pick up on such cues can help them to develop the habit of seeing more deeply into others. It will encourage them to experience the world as another person does and perhaps to get a feel for what it's like to be that other person. This is a major step toward wanting to help rather than to hurt—and, ultimately, toward becoming a better person oneself.

CAN I TRUST YOU?
A CONVERSATION BETWEEN
PAUL EKMAN AND HIS DAUGHTER EVE

Jason Marsh

GROWING UP IN SAN FRANCISCO, a city renowned for its hedonism, Eve Ekman faced more than her fair share of temptations, especially when she got involved in the local punk scene as a teenager. Like most adolescents, she felt the urge to do some things she knew her parents wouldn't approve of—go to clubs on weeknights, dabble with alcohol and marijuana—and which would require lying about where she was going and what she planned to do once she got there.

But unlike those other kids, Eve has a father who is one of the world's leading experts on detecting lies. Paul Ekman, a professor emeritus at the University of California, San Francisco, pioneered the scientific study of facial expressions and body language. For more than 50 years, his research has identified how emotions are subtly expressed through nonverbal cues; for much of that time, he has devoted special attention to how and why people tell lies and how others can catch those lies. His work has been used by police departments, teachers, and even the U.S. Department of Homeland Security. In 2001, the American Psychological Association named Ekman one of the most influential psychologists of the twentieth century.

What's it like to be raised by a leading expert on
trust and deception? Psychologist Paul Ekman
extended a great deal of trust to his now
28-year-old daughter, Eve.

It sounds like every kid's worst nightmare: the parent who
always knows whether you're telling the truth. But when it came
down to it, Paul Ekman's scientific expertise on lying was of limited
usefulness to Paul Ekman the parent.

"I have been studying lying professionally for more than 20
years, but it was not easy to deal with it as a parent," he wrote in
his 1989 book, *Why Kids Lie: How Parents Can Encourage Truthfulness*, which includes chapters by his wife, Mary Ann Mason, a
professor and former dean at the University of California, Berkeley,
and his son Tom, Eve's older brother. Indeed, as that book makes
clear, it is one thing to be able to catch a kid in a lie; it's something
very different to be able to raise a trustworthy child.

So how does an expert on lying, deception, and truthfulness
try to foster trust and trustworthiness? Paul and Eve, who is
now 28, recently sat down with *Greater Good*'s editor-in-chief,
Jason Marsh, to discuss the benefits of trusting your kids (even
when it's nerve-wracking to do so), how to encourage trustworthy behavior, and what it takes to build trust between parents
and children.

EVE EKMAN: Do you ever remember catching me for anything when I broke your trust, or a time you caught me dead in a lie?

PAUL EKMAN: Nope. When I suspected that you had done something wrong, I went to some length to avoid putting you in a position where you would have to lie. Instead, when I was worried about you, I would ask leading questions like, "Is there something on your mind? Is there something you want to talk about?"

In that way, you had the opportunity to disclose on your own. I did not want to ask you every day if you had gotten into trouble, but there was a rule of disclosure. There were very few things I expected, but if you did not tell me, it was a lie.

I remember once, when I had heard you come in after curfew, I asked you, "What happened the other night? I heard you come in late." So I was already telling you, "I know you did that," without trying to catch you in a lie.

The issue clearly arises in every generation. I lied to my parents all the time. They were very restrictive, invading my privacy continuously. The challenge of my adolescence was learning how to outwit them, which I did. I had an entirely secret life.

EVE: So you are saying it is the nature of the relationship with the child that determines the role of trust and lying?

PAUL: Yes, certainly so. The role of the parent is an extremely difficult one because you have to keep moving backward. When parents start out, they are completely responsible for their child, who is totally helpless. As that child grows, you have to roll back, you have to grant control; otherwise, your child can't grow. You have to be able to live with the fact that as you grant the child more autonomy, they will get into all sorts of trouble. But you ultimately have to leave it up to them.

JASON MARSH: It seems like this could be difficult advice to follow, to trust that much. What was it from your research, or personal experience, that motivated you to take this approach?

PAUL: It wasn't based on research, mine or anyone else's. It was based on my own experience with parents who did just the opposite. They did everything they could to try to interfere with my life, and they were the last people I would have ever turned to when I was a child. I wanted to be the first people my kids would turn to.

It took some restraint, because worry was my middle name, way before I ever had a child. But I think, for children, the most important thing is to feel they can trust that their parents, whether they approve or disapprove, will always be available for help and support. If that's not the case, then I think you've really failed as a parent.

JASON MARSH: Eve, what kind of effect do you think this kind of parenting style had on your behavior growing up, and on your feelings of trust toward your parents?

EVE: I was not your conventional good girl. But I definitely did not want to disappoint the trust they gave me, because I thought they were cool, and I liked them. They weren't just authority figures; they were very open and available and accessible. And if I challenged what they did, they would explain it to me. It wasn't like, "Because I said so." There was always an explanation of why, and I guess that helped build trust. I always felt like, even in the worst-case scenarios, they would be the first person I would call. Still, to this day, I call them first when I have trouble.

PAUL: I remember the call from jail.

EVE: That was when I was arrested for protesting the war in Iraq.

JASON MARSH: Paul, do you think that by being so trusting, you not only earned the trust of your kids but also actually helped make them more trustworthy?

PAUL: Yes. I didn't want them to get started on my path of lying to my parents. Because I do believe that it's a slippery slope: you start lying once, you lie another time, you lie about more things, and you've crossed the threshold. And I didn't want to put them in a position where they would cross that threshold.

E V E : What kinds of difficulties do parents encounter even when they want to put this kind of trust in their kids?

P A U L : A major difficulty is that so much changes from generation to generation. What was normative in one generation can shift greatly—changing sexual morality, recreational drugs. Parents have a hard time trusting that their kids are prepared to deal with these things that are so new to the parents.

Beyond that, there is the difficulty of giving up control. Many parents are control freaks, and that is in part because they do not want to worry. And in ways they are right to worry—adolescents take risks that are very dangerous.

E V E : But it starts before adolescence, right?

P A U L : It stars at 3 to 5 years of age, and it gets really strong in adolescence.

The Dalai Lama asked me once, "What is destructive compassion?" And I said that destructive compassion is when you are so worried about your child that you overcontrol them.

Since I work in this area and think about this area, I try to be very explicit and never put anyone in the position where they feel they have to lie to me. If they think that I am going to be a strict disciplinarian, that will change the relationship as well. The major research I have done shows that the main reason people lie is to avoid being punished.

J A S O N   M A R S H : But it seems that a lot of parents feel caught in a catch-22. They may understand why it's important to trust their kids, but they may not feel that their kid is worthy of that trust. What can parents do to help encourage the kind of truthfulness in their kids that makes them more comfortable trusting those kids?

P A U L : They can do things all the time—over the dining room table, with stories, when they're playing Chutes and Ladders and kids get tempted to cheat in the game. I really think up to the age of 10 or 11, children are zealots for the truth—they really don't want to mislead or be misled. So you can build on that.

You can do it by example. When Eve was born, I quit smoking after I had smoked for 30 years. And I also decided I was going to try to see if I could lead my life without lying to anyone about anything. It was much harder to do that—to figure out ways to be truthful without being harmful or insulting, to stay polite but be truthful. And it became a real challenge. But I also thought, "I'm going to try to do this because that's the example I want to be showing. I want my kids to see that there's a way to be truthful." It was very deliberate.

Parents also need to establish the rules of disclosure and the obligations that come with their trust. For instance, we always made very clear to both of our kids that if they got into trouble in school, they were obliged to tell us. So if they didn't tell us, then they were lying to us. That meant we had to define "trouble." Trouble meant they were held after school or called to the principal's office. That's a rule of disclosure.

We need to spell out these rules and obligations in any relationship. In the business world, do you have to tell your employer if you're looking for another job? Does your employer need to tell you if they're thinking of cutting your position? What are the rules of disclosure? They're never revealed. They're kept ambiguous. That just makes for a lot of distrust and bad work relationships. Same in marriages. I have one colleague who told me, "My rule is that anything I do out of town is okay." I said, "Does your spouse know that?" He never felt he needed to tell his spouse about it. There was no disclosure. It's just the basis for misunderstanding and distrust.

JASON MARSH: Eve, do you think that growing up with those rules has affected your relationships with others?

EVE: It's funny because as my dad was speaking, I was thinking about how I really do respect authority. Even though I think I'm a dissenter at heart, I definitely respect authority.

You know, I'm afraid of getting caught, and that helps me not do things wrong. I was arrested once, but that was simply because I was protesting. Other than that, I've never broken the law. I've only gotten one ticket.

In general, I hope that when punishment is exacted, it's fair and just, and I do think that was modeled to me from my family relationships. I think if there's an inconsistent message, I could imagine feeling like, "Well, those laws don't apply to me."

And in my personal relationships with friends, as well as romantic relationships, I definitely think trust is core. I definitely know I'm someone people depend on. I'm a social worker, that's my profession, but I also feel I'm the person who people call when things are really hard and they need someone they can trust. And I feel really respectful of that role, and I appreciate it.

I think you experience people's family life through how they interact with you, and I feel like I've been the beneficiary of a great deal of trust, and I myself am trusting. But I've been burned. I remember talking with my dad about it at one point, like, "Why do I feel disappointed? I feel like I'm trusting, and I'm not sure that's always met." Like, in my early 20s, when I first started to have really meaningful and important relationships outside of family, I found there were some people for whom family wasn't a model of trust and for whom learning trust was new. And so they would maybe play people off each other, do those kinds of things that ultimately will burn you.

JASON MARSH: So Paul, when you hear Eve talk about her ability to trust others and instill trust in others toward her, I wonder if you could step back and, putting on your psychologist's hat, draw on some research to explain why that may be. How might the particular parenting style that you've practiced foster that trustworthiness over time? And perhaps even more importantly, what could be the negative consequences of not fostering that sense of trust and trustworthiness?

PAUL: There are a lot of clinical reports of people who are commitment adverse and can't trust others. Based on their reports of their childhood, it seems that this is often a result of how they were brought up. They found they couldn't trust their parents because their parents broke their promises or their commitments. And unreliability can be very damaging.

When I was 13, I spent five weeks rehearsing to play a role in a Gilbert and Sullivan show, *The Mikado*, for one performance, which my parents missed by 2 hours. I never forgave them for that. That was very decisive for me, that unreliability. Something like that can make it quite a struggle for you to trust others. Quite a struggle.

But there's been much less scientific attention given to the positive side: What does positive parental behavior that earns trust look like? What are its benefits? Psychologists study problems; we don't study success. But I would expect just the reverse—that people who were trusting as children grow up being able to be trustworthy.

JASON MARSH: Some parents might try to earn their kids' trust, but they might not exhibit trust toward their kids in return. What could be the consequences of not demonstrating trust toward your kids?

PAUL: You have children who are either crippled by the overcontrolling, micromanaging parent or who become devious in order to get their freedom. They've got to grow, and they are increasingly capable of acting independently. So they're going to find a way to do so, or you're going to destroy them.

If they find a way to gain autonomy through deviousness, through gaming the system, that's really a bad way to learn it because once you learn how to do it with your parents, there's a lot of temptation to do it with everybody else. That brings short-term gains and long-term losses. But if you're the type who just goes from one relationship to another, then you may never realize what you're losing—until you get late in your life and you feel you haven't built anything.

JASON MARSH: Based on research and your own

experience, is it possible for you to sum up what you believe is most important to raising kids who are both trusting and trustworthy?

PAUL: The two are related. People who are distrustful are usually not very trustworthy themselves, and difficult to deal with.

You have a fundamental choice to make about how you're going to lead your life: Are you going to be suspicious and risk disbelieving people who are truthful? Or are you going to be trusting and risk being misled? As a parent, you always need to be trusting and risk being misled. Being wrongly accused is terrible. And it is less pleasant to live your life being suspicious all the time, unless you are a police investigator. And you do not need to be an investigator in your home.

EVE: Is there such as thing as too much trust?

PAUL: No.

EVE: Really? Even when your kids are lying to you, and you know they're lying to you?

PAUL: There is no general rule.

EVE: I imagine people who read your book *Why Kids Lie* would want to be able to better catch their kids in lies.

PAUL: But that absolutely was not my intention; my intention was to explain to parents why kids lie, not how to catch them in lies. There is nothing in the book that teaches how to detect lies. That is not your job as a parent to be the cop, to be the interrogator. You must be the teacher, or the model. You want to talk to your kids about the real costs of lying. The real cost is not being trusted. If you are not trusted, it makes all intimate relationships impossible.

EVE: I did trust you and always felt you had my best intention in mind. I sometimes felt that I knew how to take care of myself more than you could give me credit for, but I think that is a pretty natural part of growing up and wanting full freedom.

To this day, I think that trust is present in my everyday thinking. When I am making a hard or risky decision, I think, "What would my parents think?"

PAUL: Having had parents who made every mistake you could make—they were good models of what not to do.

EVE: So, do you trust me?

PAUL: Of course.

HOT TO HELP

Daniel Goleman

WE OFTEN EMPHASIZE the importance of keeping cool in a crisis. But sometimes coolness can give way to detachment and apathy.

We saw a perfect example of this in the response to Hurricane Katrina, whose devastation was amplified enormously by the lackadaisical response from the agencies charged with managing the emergency. As we all witnessed, leaders at the highest levels were weirdly detached, despite the abundant evidence on our TV screens that they needed to snap to action. The victims' pain was exacerbated by such indifference to their suffering. So as we prepare for the next Katrina-like disaster, what can the science of social intelligence—especially research into empathy—teach policy makers and first responders about the best way to handle themselves during such a crisis?

This brings me to psychologist Paul Ekman, an expert on our ability to read and respond to others' emotions. When I recently spoke with Ekman, he discussed three main ways we can empathize with others, understanding their emotions as our own. The differences between these forms of empathy highlight the challenges we face in responding to other people's pain. But they also make clear how the right approach can move us to compassionate action.

A woman begs for help in the aftermath of
Hurricane Katrina.

The first form is "cognitive empathy," simply knowing how the
other person feels and what they might be thinking. Sometimes
called perspective taking, this kind of empathy can help in, say, a
negotiation or in motivating people. A study at the University of
Birmingham found, for example, that managers who are good at
perspective taking were able to move workers to give their best
efforts.

But cognitive empathy can illustrate the "too cold to care" phenomenon: when people try to understand another person's point
of view without internalizing his or her emotions, they can be so
detached that they're not motivated to do anything to actually
help that person.

In fact, those who fall within psychology's "dark triad"—narcis-
sists, Machiavellians, and sociopaths—can actually put cognitive
empathy to use in hurting people. As Ekman told me, a torturer
needs this ability, if only to better calibrate his cruelty. Talented
political operatives can read people's emotions to their own advantage, without necessarily caring about those people very much.

And so cognitive empathy alone is not enough. We also need
what Ekman calls "emotional empathy"—when you physically feel
what other people feel, as though their emotions were contagious.

This emotional contagion depends in large part on cells in the brain called mirror neurons, which fire when we sense another's emotional state, creating an echo of that state inside our own minds. Emotional empathy attunes us to another person's inner emotional world, a plus for a wide range of professions, from sales to nursing—not to mention for any parent or lover.

But wait: emotional empathy has a downside, too, especially for first responders. In a state of emotional empathy, people sometimes lack the ability to manage their own distressing emotions, which can lead to paralysis and psychological exhaustion. Medical professionals often inoculate themselves against this kind of burnout by developing a sense of detachment from their patients.

Cultivated detachment in rescue, medical, and social workers can actually help the victims of disaster. Ekman told me about his daughter, a social worker at a large city hospital. In her situation, he said, she can't afford to let emotional empathy overwhelm her. "My daughter's clients don't want her to cry when they're crying," he says.

The danger arises when detachment leads to indifference, rather than to well-calibrated caring. Today, we face this problem on a global level. "One of the problems of living in a television society is that every bit of suffering and misery that occurs anywhere in the world is shown to us," says Ekman—and generally, we can't do anything about it, at least not directly.

This can make emotional empathy seem futile and hinder the growth of the third kind of empathy, which Ekman calls "compassionate empathy." With this kind of empathy, we not only understand a person's predicament and feel with them, but are spontaneously moved to help, if needed.

Compassionate empathy was the vital ingredient missing from the top-level response to Hurricane Katrina—and in responses to many other disasters around the world, including the slow-burning disaster of global warming. Ekman calls compassionate empathy a skill, the acquired knowledge "that we're all connected."

This can lead to outbursts of what he calls "constructive anger."

In other words, reacting negatively to injustice or suffering can motivate us to work with others to make the world a better place. Just as empathy has its downsides, negative emotions like anger can have upsides. Staying cool in a crisis might bring some benefits. But sometimes we must let ourselves get hot in order to help.

PART THREE:
HOW TO CULTIVATE GOODNESS
IN SOCIETY AND POLITICS

INTRODUCTION

Dacher Keltner, Jason Marsh,
and Jeremy Adam Smith

CULTIVATING GOODNESS in ourselves is not just an end in itself; it is also a pathway to cultivating goodness in society at large. In fact, the main mission of *Greater Good* magazine is to show how the great potential for human goodness extends outward from the individual psyche to the larger society.

As research reveals, the ability to act on behalf of the greater good can not only improve our personal health and our relationships with other others—it can practically or symbolically promote peace in our society and between cultures. As Robert Reich, Steven Pinker, Dacher Keltner, Jan Egeland, and others argue in the following essays, empathy, compassion, generosity, and heroism are not luxuries, "discarded in disaster as one might shed a gold bar while trying to escape a sinking ship" (to quote sociologist Lee Clarke in an essay he wrote for the Summer 2008 issue of *Greater Good*). They are intrinsic to human nature and essential to our survival as a species.

Reading these essays cannot guarantee that you'll spring to action the next time you see a pedestrian collapse on the sidewalk or that you will immediately seek solutions to global warming. The inhibitions to action can be overwhelming, and are sometimes justified.

But these essays provide scientific insight into why we so readily, and at times unconsciously, assume the role of the bystander. In the process, they help to displace the shame and confusion we sometimes feel when we don't demonstrate the courage of our convictions.

Just as it takes practice to cultivate some of the other behaviors and emotions we've examined in this book—forgiveness, compassion, empathy—we may have to work to overcome our tendency to sit on the sidelines. But as Zeno Franco and Philip Zimbardo argue in their essay, our capacity for heroism is as natural to us as our inclinations toward apathy; nurturing heroism requires education, inspiration, and opportunities for reflection.

Of course, no cure exists for all the problems that plague this planet, just as there's no easy fix for a damaged relationship. But the science and stories featured in this book convey that we can always take steps in the right direction. They show us again and again how true political and social progress often stems from changes we can all learn to make in the way we relate to ourselves and others.

WE ARE ALL BYSTANDERS

Dacher Keltner and Jason Marsh

For MORE THAN 40 YEARS, Peggy Kirihara has felt guilty about Stewart.

Peggy liked Stewart. They went to high school together. Their fathers were friends, both farmers in California's Central Valley, and Peggy would always say hi when she passed Stewart in the hall.

Yet every day when Stewart boarded their school bus, a couple of boys would tease him mercilessly. And every day, Peggy would just sit in her seat, silent.

"I was dying inside for him," she says. "There were enough of us on the bus who were feeling awful. We could have done something. But none of us said anything."

Peggy still can't explain why she didn't stick up for Stewart. She had known his tormentors since they were all little kids, and she didn't find them threatening. She thinks if she had spoken up on his behalf, other kids might have chimed in to make the teasing stop.

But perhaps most surprising and distressing to Peggy is that she considers herself an assertive and moral person, yet those convictions weren't backed up by her conduct on the bus.

"I think I would say something now, but I don't know for sure,"

she says. "Maybe if I saw someone being beaten up and killed, I'd just stand there. That still worries me."

Many of us share Peggy's concern. We've all found ourselves in similar situations: the times we've seen someone harassed on the street and didn't intervene; when we've driven past a car stranded by the side of the road, assuming another driver would pull over to help; even when we've noticed litter on the sidewalk and left it for someone else to pick up. We witness a problem, consider some kind of positive action, then respond by doing . . . nothing. Something holds us back. We remain bystanders.

Why don't we help in these situations? Why do we sometimes put our moral instincts in shackles? These are questions that haunt all of us, and they apply well beyond the fleeting scenarios described above. Every day we serve as bystanders to the world around us—not just to people in need on the street but to larger social, political, and environmental problems that concern us, but which we feel powerless to address on our own. Indeed, the bystander phenomenon pervades the history of the past century.

"The bystander is a modern archetype, from the Holocaust to the genocide in Rwanda to the current environmental crisis," says Charles Garfield, a clinical professor of psychology at the University of California, San Francisco, School of Medicine who is writing a book about the psychological differences between bystanders and people who display moral courage.

"Why," asks Garfield, "do some people respond to these crises while others don't?"

In the shadow of these crises, researchers have spent the past few decades trying to answer Garfield's question. Their findings reveal a valuable story about human nature. Often, only subtle differences separate the bystanders from the morally courageous people of the world. Most of us, it seems, have the potential to fall into either category. It is the slight, seemingly insignificant details in a situation that can push us one way or the other.

Researchers have identified some of the invisible forces that restrain us from acting on our own moral instincts while also suggesting how we might fight back against these unseen inhibitors of altruism. Taken together, these results offer a scientific understanding for what spurs us to everyday altruism and a lifetime of activism, and what induces us to remain bystanders.

ALTRUISTIC INERTIA

Among the most infamous bystanders are 38 people in Queens, New York, who in 1964 witnessed the murder of one of their neighbors, a young woman named Kitty Genovese.

A serial killer attacked and stabbed Genovese late one night outside her apartment house, and these 38 neighbors later admitted to hearing her screams; at least 3 said they saw part of the attack take place. Yet no one intervened.

While the Genovese murder shocked the American public, it also moved several social psychologists to try to understand the behavior of people like Genovese's neighbors.

One of those psychologists was John Darley, who was living in New York at the time. Ten days after the Genovese murder, Darley had lunch with another psychologist, Bibb Latané, and they discussed the incident.

"The newspaper explanations were focusing on the appalling personalities of those who saw the murder but didn't intervene, saying they had been dehumanized by living in an urban environment," says Darley, now a professor at Princeton University. "We wanted to see if we could explain the incident by drawing on the social psychological principles that we knew."

A main goal of their research was to determine whether the presence of other people inhibits someone from intervening in an emergency, as had seemed to be the case in the Genovese murder. In one of their studies, college students sat in a cubicle and were instructed to talk with fellow students through an intercom. They were told that they would be speaking with one, two, or five other students, and only one person could use the intercom at a time.

There was actually only one other person in the study—a confederate (someone working with the researchers). Early in the study, the confederate mentioned that he sometimes suffered from seizures. The next time he spoke, he became increasingly loud and incoherent; he pretended to choke and gasp. Before falling silent, he stammered:

> If someone could help me out it would it would er er s-s-sure
> be sure be good . . . because er there er er a cause I er I uh I've
> got a a one of the er sei-er-er things coming on and and and I
> could really er use some help . . . I'm gonna die er er I'm gonna
> die er help er er seizure er . . .

Eighty-five percent of the participants who were in the two-person situation—and hence believed they were the only witness to the victim's seizure—left their cubicles to help. In contrast, only 62 percent of the participants who were in the three-person situation and 31 percent of the participants in the six-person situation tried to help.

Darley and Latané attributed their results to a "diffusion of responsibility": when study participants thought there were other witnesses to the emergency, they felt less personal responsibility to intervene. Similarly, the witnesses of the Kitty Genovese murder may have seen other apartment lights go on or seen each other in the windows and assumed someone else would help. The end result is altruistic inertia. Other researchers have also suggested the effects of a "confusion of responsibility," where bystanders fail to help someone in distress because they don't want to be mistaken for the cause of that distress.

Darley and Latané also suspected that bystanders don't intervene in an emergency because they're misled by the reactions of the people around them. To test this hypothesis, they ran an experiment in which they asked participants to fill out questionnaires in a laboratory room. After the participants had gotten to work, smoke filtered into the room—a clear signal of danger.

When participants were alone, 75 percent of them left the room and reported the smoke to the experimenter. With three participants in the room, only 38 percent left to report the smoke. And quite remarkably, when a participant was joined by two confederates instructed not to show any concern, only 10 percent of the participants reported the smoke to the experimenter.

The passive bystanders in this study succumbed to what's known as "pluralistic ignorance"—the tendency to mistake one another's calm demeanor as a sign that no emergency is actually taking place. There are strong social norms that reinforce pluralistic ignorance. It is somewhat embarrassing, after all, to be the one who loses his cool when no danger actually exists. Such an effect was likely acting on the people who witnessed the Kitty Genovese incident; indeed, many said they didn't realize what was going on beneath their windows and assumed it was a lover's quarrel. That interpretation was reinforced by the fact that no one else was responding either.

A few years later, Darley ran a study with psychologist Daniel Batson that had seminary students at Princeton walk across campus to give a talk. Along the way, the students passed a study confederate, slumped over and groaning in a passageway. Their response depended largely on a single variable: whether or not they were late. Only 10 percent of the students stopped to help when they were in a hurry; more than six times as many helped when they had plenty of time before their talk.

Lateness, the presence of other people—these are some of the factors that can turn us all into bystanders in an emergency. Yet another important factor is the characteristics of the victim. Research has shown that people are more likely to help those they perceive to be similar to themselves, including others from their own racial or ethnic group. In general, women tend to receive more help than men. But this varies according to appearance: more attractive and femininely dressed women tend to receive more help from passersby, perhaps because they fit the gender stereotype of the vulnerable female.

We don't like to discover that our propensity for altruism can depend on prejudice or the details of a particular situation—details that seem beyond our control. But these scientific findings force us to consider how we'd perform under pressure; they reveal that Kitty Genovese's neighbors might have been just like us. Even more frightening, it becomes easier to understand how good people in Rwanda or Nazi Germany remained silent against the horrors around them. Afraid, confused, coerced, or willfully unaware, they could convince themselves that it wasn't their responsibility to intervene.

But still, some did assume this responsibility, and this is the other half of the bystander story. Some researchers refer to the "active bystander," that person who witnesses an emergency, recognizes it as such, and takes it upon herself to do something about it.

Who are these people? Are they inspired to action because they receive strong cues in a situation indicating it's an emergency? Or is there a particular set of characteristics—a personality type—that makes some people more likely to be active bystanders while others remain passive?

WHY PEOPLE HELP

A leader in the study of the differences between active and passive bystanders is psychologist Ervin Staub, whose research interests were shaped by his experiences as a young Jewish child in Hungary during World War II.

"I was to be killed in the Holocaust," he says. "And there were important bystanders in my life who showed me that people don't have to be passive in the face of evil."

One of these people was his family's maid, Maria, a Christian woman who risked her life to shelter Staub and his sister while 75 percent of Hungary's 600,000 Jews were killed by the Nazis.

Staub has tried to understand what motivates the Marias of the world. Some of his research has put a spin on the experimental studies pioneered by Darley and Latané, exploring what makes people more likely to intervene rather than serve as passive bystanders.

In one experiment, a study participant and a confederate were placed in a room together, instructed to work on a joint task. Soon afterward, they heard a crash and cries of distress. When the confederate dismissed the sounds, saying something like, "That sounds like a tape" or "I guess it could be part of another experiment," only 25 percent of the participants went into the next room to try to help. But when the confederate said, "That sounds bad. Maybe we should do something," 66 percent of the participants took action. And when the confederate added that participants should go into the next room to check out the sounds, every single one of them tried to help.

In another study, Staub found that kindergarten and first-grade children were actually more likely to respond to sounds of distress from an adjoining room when they were placed in pairs rather than alone. That seemed to be the case because, unlike the adults in Darley and Latané's studies, the young children talked openly about their fears and concerns and together tried to help.

These findings suggest the positive influence we can exert as bystanders. Just as passive bystanders reinforce a sense that nothing is wrong in a situation, the active bystander can, in fact, get people to focus on a problem and motivate them to take action.

John Darley has also identified actions a victim can take to get others to help him. One is to make his need clear—"I've twisted my ankle and I can't walk; I need help"—and the other is to select a specific person for help—"You there, can you help me?" By doing this, the victim overcomes the two biggest obstacles to intervention. He prevents people from concluding there is no real emergency (thereby eliminating the effect of pluralistic ignorance) and prevents them from thinking that someone else will help (thereby overcoming diffusion of responsibility).

But Staub has tried to take this research one step further. He has developed a questionnaire meant to identify people with a predisposition toward becoming active bystanders. People who score well on this survey express a heightened concern for the welfare of others, greater feelings of social responsibility, and a commitment to moral values—and they also prove more likely to help others when an opportunity arises.

Similar research has been conducted by sociologist Samuel Oliner. Like Staub, Oliner is a Holocaust survivor whose work has been inspired by the people who helped him escape the Nazis. With his wife Pearl, a professor of education, he conducted an extensive study into the altruistic personality, interviewing more than 400 people who rescued Jews during the Holocaust, as well as more than 100 nonrescuers and Holocaust survivors alike. In their book *The Altruistic Personality*, the Oliners explain that rescuers shared some deep personality traits, which they described as their capacity for extensive relationships—their stronger sense of attachment to others and their feelings of responsibility for the welfare of others. They also found that these tendencies had been instilled in many rescuers from the time they were young children, often stemming from parents who displayed more tolerance, care, and empathy toward their children and toward people different from themselves.

"I would claim there is a predisposition in some people to help whenever the opportunity arises," says Oliner, who contrasts this group to bystanders. "A bystander is less concerned with the outside world, beyond his own immediate community. A bystander might be less tolerant of differences, thinking, 'Why should I get involved? These are not my people. Maybe they deserve it?' They don't see helping as a choice. But rescuers see tragedy and feel no choice but to get involved. How could they stand by and let another person perish?'"

Kristen Monroe, a political scientist at the University of California, Irvine, has reached a similar conclusion from her own set of interviews with various kinds of altruists. In her book *The Heart of Altruism*, she writes of the "altruistic perspective," a common perception among altruists "that they are strongly linked to others through a shared humanity."

But Monroe cautions that differences are often not so clear-cut between bystanders, perpetrators, and altruists. "We know that perpetrators can be rescuers and some rescuers I've interviewed have killed people," she says. "It's hard to see someone as one or the other because they cross categories. Academics like to think in categories. But the truth is that it's not so easy."

Indeed, much of the bystander research suggests that one's personality only determines so much. To offer the right kind of help, one also needs the relevant skills or knowledge demanded by a particular situation.

As an example, John Darley referred to his study in which smoke was pumped into a room to see whether people would react to that sign of danger. One of the participants in this study had been in the navy, where his ship had once caught on fire. "So when this man saw the smoke," says Darley, "he got the hell out and did something, because of his past experiences."

There's an encouraging implication of these findings: if given the proper tools and primed to respond positively in a crisis, most of us have the ability to transcend our identities as bystanders.

"I think that altruism, caring, social responsibility is not only doable, it's teachable," says Oliner.

And in recent years, there have been many efforts to translate research like Oliner's into programs that encourage more people to avoid the traps of becoming a bystander.

ANTI-BYSTANDER EDUCATION

Ervin Staub has been at the fore of this anti-bystander education. In the 1990s, in the wake of the Rodney King beating, he worked with California's Department of Justice to develop a training program for police officers. The goal of the program was to teach officers how they could intervene when they feared a fellow officer was about to use too much force.

"The police have a conception, as part of their culture, that the way you police a fellow officer is to support whatever they're doing, and that can lead to tragedy, both for the citizens and the police themselves," says Staub. "So here the notion was to make police officers positive active bystanders, getting them engaged early enough so that they didn't have to confront their fellow officer."

More recently, Staub helped schools in Massachusetts develop an anti–bystander curriculum, intended to encourage children to intervene against bullying. The program draws on earlier research that identified the causes of bystander behavior. For instance, older students are reluctant to discuss their fears about bullying, so each student tacitly accepts it, afraid to make waves, and no one identifies the problem—a form of pluralistic ignorance. Staub wants to change the culture of the classroom by giving these students opportunities to air their fears.

"If you can get people to express their concern, then already a whole different situation exists," he says.

This echoes a point that John Darley makes: more people need to learn about the subtle pressures that can cause bystander behavior, such as diffusion of responsibility and pluralistic ignorance. That way they'll be better prepared the next time they encounter a crisis situation. "We want to explode one particular view that people have: 'Were I in that situation, I would behave in an altruistic, wonderful way,'" says Darley. "What I say is, 'No, you're misreading what's happening. I want to teach you about the pressures [that can cause bystander behavior]. Then when you feel those pressures, I want that to be a cue that you might be getting things wrong.'"

Research suggests that this kind of education is possible. One set of studies even found that people who attended social psychology lectures about the causes of bystander behavior were less susceptible to those influences.

But of course, not even this form of education is a guarantee against becoming a bystander. We're always subject to the complicated interaction between our personal disposition and the demands of circumstance. And we may never know how we'll act until we find ourselves in a crisis.

To illustrate this point, Samuel Oliner tells the story of a Polish bricklayer who was interviewed for *The Altruistic Personality*. During World War II, a Jewish man who had escaped from a concentration camp came to the bricklayer and pleaded for help. The bricklayer turned him away, saying he didn't want to put his own family at risk. "So is he evil?" asks Oliner. "I wouldn't say he's evil. He couldn't act quickly enough, I suppose, to say, 'Hide in my kiln,' or 'Hide in my barn.' He didn't think that way."

"If I was the bricklayer and you came to me, and the Nazis were behind you and the Gestapo was chasing you—would I be willing to help? Would I be willing to risk my family? I don't know. I don't know if I would be."

THE COST OF APATHY:
AN INTERVIEW WITH ROBERT REICH

Jason Marsh

THE WEALTHIEST 1 PERCENT of Americans now make 70 times more in after-tax income than the bottom one-fifth of households. Since 2002, the average inflation-adjusted income of the wealthiest 1 percent has risen 42 percent, while the income of the bottom 90 percent of households has risen about 4.7 percent.

Robert Reich has been one of the most prominent critics of these growing inequities. Reich, who is now a professor of public policy at the University of California Berkeley, has served in three national administrations, most recently as secretary of labor under President Bill Clinton, where he implemented the Family and Medical Leave Act and led a national fight against sweatshops in the United States and illegal child labor around the world. He has also written 11 books, including *The Work of Nations*, *Locked in the Cabinet*, and most recently, *Supercapitalism*.

Reich's writings and lectures stand apart from those of other critics who focus on inequality. He doesn't settle for easy condemnations of outsourcing or offshoring, nor does he think such effects of globalization can be easily undone. At the same time, he rejects the idea that these changes need result in greater disparities of wealth.

Robert Reich.

Instead, Reich attributes rising inequality not only to structural economic changes but to how Americans, and their policy makers, have failed to meet the social challenges posed by the new economy. While others point fingers at the government or big corporations, Reich also holds a mirror up to American society.

To Reich, rising inequality is intertwined with a breakdown of Americans' social contract—the norms, mores, and values that dictate their mutual commitments and responsibilities to one another. In this fall 2004 interview with *Greater Good*, Reich explored the political implications of our emotions and values.

GREATER GOOD: What does empathy have to do with inequality?

ROBERT REICH: Any society depends upon empathy in order for people to be able to answer the question, What do we owe one another as members of the same society?

Indeed, without empathy, the very meaning of a society is up for grabs. Margaret Thatcher famously declared that there was no such thing as a society. There might be a nation, for strictly political purposes, there might be a culture, in terms of tradition, but a society, she felt, was a construct without meaning. I disagree. I think that we have all sorts of societies. Some of them are very tight: clubs, religious affiliations, friendships, neighborhoods. Some are much larger, extending outward in concentric circles from us as individuals. And we are bound by feelings of empathy and affiliation. Those feelings inspire us to come to the aid of those within these concentric circles.

G G : It's easy to point to indicators of rising inequality. What do you see as the indicators of dwindling empathy?

R R : Rising inequality itself is an indicator of a breakdown in the social contract. It means that for a variety of reasons, those who have resources—and political power—are not taking steps to ensure that large numbers of others in the same society have opportunities to better themselves and have the resources they need to become full-fledged members of that society. Wide inequality suggests that we may not be living in the same society any longer. In fact, it could be argued that we're drifting into separate societies: one very rich, one very poor, and one a middle class that's increasingly anxious and frustrated.

G G : How did this happen? Is it a new phenomenon?

R R : It's happened before in the United States in the 1880s and 1890s, the so-called Gilded Age. Inequality of wealth and opportunity were extreme. In happened again in the 1920s—not quite to the same degree as the 1880s and 1890s, but inequality was very wide in the '20s. It is happening now for a third time. Now we can have an interesting debate about cause and effect—that is, is inequality the effect of dwindling empathy and a reduction in social solidarity? Or is inequality somehow causing it, to the extent that people who are very wealthy no longer come in contact with people who are poor and no longer feel the empathy that comes from contact? It's probably both.

G G : So what are some of the broader factors contributing to widening inequality today?

R R : Well, technology and globalization are the two major structural causes. The more technologically sophisticated our economy becomes, and the more globalized, those people who are well educated can take advantage of technology and globalization to do continuously better. Those who are not well educated and lack social connections find that technology and globalization reduce their economic security, replace their jobs, and condemn them to a fairly menial existence.

G G : If we're not part of that group, why should we care about inequality?

R R : In very narrow, selfish terms, we might care because those of us who are well positioned might not want to bring up our children in a society that is sharply divided between rich and poor. That kind of society has a very difficult time coming to decisions, because the winners and the losers are so clearly differentiated. Democracy itself can be undermined. Violence, crime, and demagoguery can result. The experience of living in a country with a lot of disparities of wealth, income, and opportunity may be unpleasant. And that society as a democracy may be increasingly dysfunctional.

G G : With changes in wealth resulting from broad technological shifts and globalization, what can people do on a local or individual level to address growing inequality?

R R : Many things. There are many public policies at the federal, state, and local levels that can reduce inequality without necessarily reducing the benefits of technology and globalization. I teach an entire course about these policy areas. They range from improved education, job training, and early-childhood education all the way through the earned income tax credit, minimum wage, macroeconomic policies, and many others. There's no magic bullet. But it is important that the United State becomes more aware of what is happening and why widening inequality poses a danger. We don't have to be economic determinists and throw up our hands and assume it's inevitable. There are steps that can be taken.

G G : Are there policy steps that can be taken to address dwindling empathy in particular that would in some ways motivate people to care more about inequality in the first place?

R R: Yes. We know from history in this country and elsewhere that empathy is related to facing common challenges. The more people feel that they are in the same boat, the more they empathize with one another. Do we face a common challenge today? Of course. Terrorism. Global warming. An aging population. All of these and many others are common problems we face. The art of leadership is the art of enabling people to understand their commonalities and to build empathy upon that sense of commonality.

G G: And do you see that art practiced by our public leaders today?

R R: Not nearly enough. Public leaders today—that is, elected officials—tend to be too dependent on public opinion polls. And public opinion polls only register where people are right now. You can't lead people to where they already are, because they're already there. The essence of leadership is leading them to where they're not, but where they could be.

G G: So if people aren't in a position right away to be public leaders or effect policy change, what do you hope will change in their consciousness? What could they start to do tomorrow?

R R: I hope they have a sense of their own power and their capacity to inspire others. Too many people in this country today are discouraged, if not cynical, about the possibilities for reform and progressive change. And yet the climate is ripe for it. People are waking up to some of the large problems—the social inequities in this country and around the world—that are beginning to haunt us. If we do nothing, they will simply get worse. An individual working alone has limited capacity, obviously. But individuals coming together—in their communities, in their neighborhoods, in their small societies—and linking up with others in other communities and neighborhoods can accomplish a huge amount.

THE ACTIVISM CURE

Meredith Maran

PHILOSOPHER-PHYSICIAN ALBERT SCHWEITZER once said, "The only ones among you who will be really happy are those who have sought and found how to serve."

Kate Hanni, 48, a real estate broker in Napa, California, is living proof—emphasis on *living*. On June 21, 2006, she was lured to a million-dollar home by a man who'd posed as a home buyer, then attacked her when she arrived. For 25 minutes he beat, stabbed, and tortured her, then left her on the floor to die. "My hair was torn out," Kate says. "The skin on my hands and knees was gone. But worst of all, so was my dignity and my sense of safety in the world."

Kate's physical injuries healed over time, but the psychic damage she suffered was lasting and profound. "After six months of intensive therapy," she says, "I was still afraid to be alone. If no one else was home, I had a panic attack every time I opened my own front door."

In December of that year, Kate and her husband and sons were en route to a family vacation when their plane was stranded on the tarmac for 9 hours, leaving them and their fellow passengers without food, water, or working toilets. "Being trapped on that plane triggered the victimized feeling I'd had since the assault," Kate says.

"All of a sudden I thought, 'Enough is enough.'" Within weeks Kate launched a Web site, flyersrights.com, to spearhead the swelling movement for airline passengers' rights. Within months she'd quit her job and become the executive director of the Coalition for an Airline Passengers' Bill of Rights—appearing on national TV, being interviewed by every major newspaper in the United States.

"When I took on this issue," Kate says, "I'd tried everything therapy had to offer, but I was still a prisoner of my fears. Then I was invited to fly to New York to appear on *Good Morning America*. Either I was going to face my fears and go, or I was going to miss an opportunity to spread the word."

"I went," she says. "And I forgot to be afraid. Since then, my terror has been *gone*." Kate exhales a long, jagged breath. "Taking on this cause has done me more good than any therapy ever could."

VOLUNTEER FOR HEALTH

Kate Hanni's experience illustrates what doctors and psychotherapists have long observed and scientists can now explain. People who give to others give healthier, happier lives to themselves.

Whether a person has experienced a life-altering trauma like Kate's or suffers from anxiety or depression or is grappling with a garden-variety case of the blues, research shows that those who take "the activism cure" find personal healing in their efforts to heal the world.

The first major study to observe this phenomenon began in 1986, when the National Institute on Aging undertook an ambitious long-term research project. The Americans' Changing Lives Studies divided 3,617 respondents into two groups: those who did volunteer work and those who didn't. The researchers surveyed each member of the two groups in 1986, 1989, 1994, and 2006, comparing their levels of happiness, life satisfaction, self-esteem, sense of control over life, physical health, and depression.

"People who were in better physical and mental health were

more likely to volunteer," reported the study's leader, Peggy Thoits, professor of sociology at Vanderbilt University. "And conversely, volunteer work was good for both mental and physical health. People of all ages who volunteered were happier and experienced better physical health and less depression."

Building on that study, researchers Marc Musick and John Wilson at the University of Texas used the same data but focused in on mental health. They, too, found that over time, volunteering lowered depression. "Some of the protection came from the social integration of volunteering," Musick found. "Volunteer work improves access to social and psychological resources, which are known to counter negative moods."

Is the "activism cure" all in our heads, or does it work on our bodies, too? Paul Arnstein of Boston College evaluated the effects of volunteering on chronic pain—and found that volunteering reduced pain and disability. The participants named "making a connection" and "having a sense of purpose" as the sources of their improved health. When they were polled again several months later, the participants reported that their well-being had continued to improve.

"The narrow thinking that medications are the only way to control persistent pain," Dr. Arnstein concluded, "has resulted in a lot of suffering."

Researchers have discovered a physiological basis for the warm glow that often seems to accompany giving. "The benefits of giving back are definitely biological," says bioethicist Stephen G. Post, coauthor of *Why Good Things Happen to Good People.* "Contemporary neuroscience has confirmed the connection between the physiological and psychological. We know now that the stress response, hormones, and even the immune system are impacted by, and impact, the pathways in the brain. MRI studies of the participants' brains revealed that making a donation activated the mesolimbic pathway—the brain's reward center."

Citing the findings of an ongoing study sponsored by the National Institute on Mental Health, Post reports, "The mesolimbic pathway of the emotional part of the brain releases feel-good chemicals, triggering a feeling of physical energy. Thirteen percent of people also report alleviation of physical pain. So there really is joy in giving."

Chief among those chemicals is dopamine, the hormone and neurotransmitter that plays important roles in motor activity, learning, motivation, sleep, attention, and mood. Dopamine reinforces the human urge to do whatever feels good—for better and for worse. On the upside, dopamine encourages us to hang out with people who are nice to us, savor a great meal, head for the hammock on a hot summer day, and do nice things for others.

"When we do good deeds," Post says, "we're rewarded by a dopamine pulse. Giving a donation or volunteering in a food bank tweaks the same source of pleasure that lights up when we eat or have sex. It's clear that helping others, even at low thresholds of several hours of volunteerism a week, creates mood elevation."

On the downside, dopamine has been implicated in addiction, serving as a flashing neon "pleasure" sign that keeps the addict coming back for more. But addicts, too, can benefit from giving back. "Alcoholics who work the 12th step of Alcoholics Anonymous, bringing the message to other addicts," Post says, "have twice the recovery rate of those who don't."

Who needs heroin when volunteering can give you what researchers call "the helper's high"? Based on brain scans of his research subjects, National Institutes of Health cognitive neuroscientist Jordan Grafman reports, "Those brain structures that are activated when you get a reward are the same ones that are activated when you give. In fact, they're activated more when you give."

THE RESILIENCE FACTOR

If you or anyone you know has ever gone through a hard time— in other words, if you or anyone you know are human—you've undoubtedly observed that people respond as differently to adversity as they do to flavors of ice cream. Some sail through with confident, optimistic flags unfurled. Others facing a similar situation spend weeks, months, or years flailing in the quicksand of despair.

Experts call this variable the "resilience factor." Endless research dollars have been spent attempting to unlock its mysteries in hopes of allowing more of us to sail and fewer of us to get stuck in the muck. It's still not clear what combination of genetics, upbringing, and circumstance makes one person more resilient than the next. But most experts agree that feeling powerless doesn't help— and that feeling competent and in control does. That's why Jerilyn Ross, president and CEO of the Anxiety Disorders Association of America and author of *One Less Thing to Worry About*, is a proponent of the activism cure.

"When we give back, it shifts the focus outside ourselves," Ross says. "It creates a sense of satisfaction that increases endorphins and therefore, a sense of well-being." "When we're feeling down," she continues, "the instinct is often to vent to friends. It's good to have a support system, but if that's all there is, it's hard to get distance from what's bothering you. Doing things for other people, thinking about other people, is like giving your brain a break from despair."

SHARING STORIES

In 1991, when her husband, Mike, was killed in a collision with a drunk driver, Laura Dean-Mooney was overwhelmed by despair. "In one instant," she says, "a complete stranger turned me into a widow and a single mom."

Over the next several months, Laura sought help from a grief counselor and "prayed like crazy." But as time passed and her anguish didn't, she felt the need to do more. She became a speaker for MADD (Mothers Against Drunk Driving), telling her story to offenders in DUI programs, testifying before victim impact panels. "I could see their attitudes change as they listened," she recalls. "One offender told me he'd never again start his car without thinking of me and Mike, and he vowed he'd never drive drunk again."

"For the first time since the accident," Laura says, "I felt that I had a mission in life. If I could keep even one person from experiencing the same loss, I could change the world in a positive way."

Laura was surprised to find that her activism also changed *her*. "Sharing my story was an extremely cathartic process," she says.

Karen Gleason, of Orinda, California, also found relief in activism. In 2000, at age 58, she was diagnosed with breast cancer. When her treatment ended, Karen decided to live out a dream deferred. She'd always wanted to visit Africa, and finally, she did. "In a small community called Ruinzoree," Karen recalls, "I discovered a program that was fighting AIDS very effectively, but the program had no money. So I started a nonprofit organization to raise the funds that were needed."

Today Friends of Ruinzoree raises $130,000 a year and serves 800 families. The program's grateful clients credit Karen's work with saving their lives, and she credits her volunteerism with helping to save hers. Karen is now cancer free and happier than she's ever been.

"I believe that my immune system got stronger because I had emotional health," Karen says. "And for me, emotional health comes from feeling like I'm needed, and being part of a group of like-minded people. . . . When I start to worry about cancer or anything else, I just focus on the joy I get from knowing I'm making a difference. That's what feeds me."

SOMETHING GREATER THAN YOU

Kate Hanni and Laura Dean-Mooney turned to activism in response to some of the harshest blows that life has to offer. The activist cure works for them and for the people their organizations serve. But can activism also help ordinary people deal with the ordinary challenges that render so many of us so unhappy, unsettled, and unglued these days?

Stephen Post is certain that it can. Citing the findings of the Musick-Wilson study, he says, "Even volunteering for 2 or 3 hours a week has been found to lower situational depression. One can't expect this in severe cases, but it doesn't take a whole lot of activity to create an emotional shift in people who are mildly depressed."

Chia Hamilton is a case in point. In 2005, she was newly retired from 25 years as a human resources coordinator. She'd looked forward to retirement with great anticipation, but once she'd read all the books on her nightstand, taught herself some new computer programs, and turned her front yard into a prolific vegetable garden, she found herself facing days that suddenly felt long and empty, wondering what she'd do with the rest of her life.

A creeping depression started to infiltrate her normally upbeat temperament. Friends were worried about her. She was worried about herself. And then one day while she was grocery shopping, a notice on the bulletin board caught her eye. A few weeks later, Chia was sitting with a roomful of inmates at San Quentin Prison, facilitating a conflict resolution workshop. For the next six years, Chia traveled the country, bringing the mission of nonviolent communication to hundreds of prisoners.

At age 63, 45 years after she finished high school, Chia decided to go to college and get her degree. "My whole life, I'd never known what I wanted to do," she says. "Volunteering helped me uncover who I was and gave me the confidence to figure it out—and go get it."

Maybe someday, physicians and psychiatrists will write prescriptions for charitable donations and citizen action instead of scrips for pills and psychotherapy. But for now, women like Kate Hanni, Laura Dean-Mooney, Karen Gleason, and Chia Hamilton will go on prescribing activism for themselves—and offering sustenance to others in the process.

"Helping others is the best medicine for anyone who has been traumatized," Kate Hanni says. "I got to face my fears much more effectively than I would have if I'd stayed at home and kept going to therapy. Activism gets you out of yourself and into action. It makes you feel like you're part of something greater than you."

For Kate, it's more than a feeling. Two years ago she was a traumatized victim, unable to work, sleep, eat, or be alone, even in her own home. Today she's the spokesperson for the national movement of outraged air travelers, named one of the nation's 25 Most Influential Executive Women in Travel by *Forbes* in 2008. Once too terrified to travel, Kate has organized events in every major city, founded a rock group called The Toasted Heads (whose signature tune is a version of "We Gotta Get Outta This Place," suitable for singing while stranded on a plane), and stormed the halls of Congress on a regular basis.

"This cause gave me a purpose for living that's so exciting," Kate says. "I wake up and jump out of bed to get started every day. I've never felt better."

Kate pauses. When she speaks again, her voice is somber. "And it wouldn't have happened if it weren't for the horrifying events of the past."

AMERICA'S TRUST FALL

Jeremy Adam Smith and Pamela Paxton

"TRUST NO ONE."
That was the slogan of the TV series *The X-Files*, which followed two FBI agents in their quest to uncover "the truth" about a government conspiracy. Perhaps the most defining series of the 1990s, *The X-Files* touched a cultural nerve and captured a mood of growing distrust in America.

Since the series ended in 2002, however, our trust in each other has declined even further, despite a brief rebound after September 11. The mood of cynicism and distrust captured by *The X-Files* in the '90s seems just as relevant today—indeed, a new *X-Files* movie was released in 2008, and a Leonardo DiCaprio movie released the following month took the slogan one step further: "Trust no one. Deceive everyone." The decline or absence of trust also figures prominently in more recent hit TV series like *Mad Men*, *Survivor*, and *The Sopranos*. In fact, "Trust no one" has essentially served as Americans' motto over the last two generations: For 40 years— the years of Vietnam, Watergate, junk bonds, Monica Lewinsky, Enron, the Catholic Church sex scandals, and the Iraq war—our trust in each other has been dropping steadily, while trust in many institutions has been seriously shaken in response to scandals.

This trend is documented in a variety of national surveys. The

General Social Survey, a periodic assessment of Americans' moods and values, shows a 10-point decline from 1976 to 2006 in the number of Americans who believe that other people can generally be trusted. The General Social Survey also shows declines in trust in our institutions, although these declines are often closely linked to specific events. From the 1970s to today, trust has declined in the press (from 24 percent to 11 percent), education (from 36 percent to 28 percent), banks (from 35 percent to 31 percent), corporations (from 26 percent to 17 percent), and even organized religion (from 35 percent to 25 percent). And Gallup's annual Governance survey shows that trust in the government is even lower today than it was during the Watergate era, when the Nixon administration had been caught engaging in criminal acts. It's no wonder popular culture is so preoccupied with questions of trust.

But research on trust isn't all doom and gloom; it also offers reason for hope. A growing body of research hints that humans are hardwired to trust. Indeed, a closer examination of surveys shows that trust is resilient: major events can stoke our trust in institutions, just as other events can inhibit them. The science of trust suggests that humans want to trust, even need to trust, but they won't trust blindly or foolishly. They need solid evidence that their trust is warranted. Using this research as a guide, we can begin to understand why trust has been declining, and how we might rebuild it.

WHY TRUST MATTERS

Trust is an intrinsic part of human nature—the foundation of healthy psychological development, established in the bond between infant and caregiver, a process facilitated by the hormone oxytocin.

Trust is most simply defined as the expectation that other people's future actions will safeguard our interests. It is the magic ingredient that makes social life possible. We trust others when we take a chance, yielding them some control over our money, secrets, safety, or other things we value.

People trust other people when they hire a babysitter, drive their cars, or leave the house unarmed. And we must also trust large organizations, like schools and businesses, for modern society to function. People trust institutions when they dial 911, take prescription medicines, and deposit money in the bank. Without trust, we would be paralyzed, and social life would grind to a halt.

When honored, trust promotes feelings of goodwill between individuals, which in turn benefits community. Researchers Robert Sampson, Steve Raudenbush, and Felton Earls have shown, in a study based on interviews with thousands of people across hundreds of Chicago neighborhoods, that, other things being equal, neighborhoods where residents trust one another have less violence than those where neighbors are suspicious of one another. A 2008 Pew Research Center study discovered that in nations where "trust is high, crime and corruption are low."

Trust helps the economy. Economists Armin Falk and Michael Kosfeld have shown that when performing tasks for others, an atmosphere of distrust hurts individuals' motivation and accomplishments and probably increases the cost of doing business.

Other research by Stephen Knack and Philip Keefer has found that countries whose citizens trust each other experience stronger economic growth.

Trust is also essential to democracy, where people must be willing to place political power in the hands of their elected representatives and fellow citizens. Without trust, individuals would be unwilling to relinquish political power to those with opposing viewpoints, even for a short time. They would not believe that others will follow the rules and procedures of governance or voluntarily hand over power after losing an election. If that trust declines, so does democracy.

Community, economy, democracy: once we recognize the role of trust in each of them, we can appreciate why declines in trust can be so damaging to society.

WHAT DRIVES MISTRUST?

From that perspective, falling levels of trust are an ominous sign for American society. But why has trust been declining in the United States for so long?

Some researchers, such as *Bowling Alone* author Robert Putnam, have argued that this rise of distrust reflects profound generational shifts. Americans born roughly between 1910 and 1940 were a particularly civic and trusting generation, these researchers claim, forged in the crises of the Great Depression and World War II—crises that required people to rely on one another and band together. Government dealt with these crises effectively through New Deal programs and military victory over the Axis powers, winning the confidence of its citizens.

That generation is now dying out, replaced by younger people who, according to this theory, are progressively less trusting (starting with baby boomers, whose slogan allegedly was, "Don't trust anyone over 30"). In fact, a series of focus groups, conducted in 2001 by Harvard University's GoodWorks Project, revealed an "overwhelming" distrust of politicians, the political process, and the media among the teenagers they interviewed. This generational decline implies that America's waning trust in others will not easily recover.

But why have succeeding generations become progressively less trusting? There are a number of possible explanations, none of them definitive.

For starters, trust in others depends on how much contact people have with other people—and Americans today are measurably more isolated than previous generations. They have become less likely, for example, to have close friends or to be members of voluntary associations such as bird-watching groups and church choirs.

This is important, because people who belong to such associations tend to become more trusting as a consequence. Experiments, as well as experience, show that people trust people they know before they trust strangers—and so the more people you know, the more you trust. Researchers Nancy Buchan, Rachel Croson, and Robyn Dawes found that even when they created pseudo-groups by randomly giving study participants instructions on differently colored pieces of paper, the participants trusted members of their color "group" more than the others. The more memberships we have in groups—almost any group—the more trust we have in our lives.

The rise of television and electronic media as a major source of entertainment and news may exacerbate isolation and thus play a role in the decline of trust. When the GoodWorks Project ran another series of focus groups with adults in 2004, researchers "found that individuals typically blame the media for loss of trust."

Again, the effect appears to be generational. "Most of the young people we interviewed have a default stance of distrust towards the media," says Carrie James, research director of GoodWorks. According to James, young people simply feel less tied to larger institutions and American culture—they might trust family and close friends, but "they don't have good mental models" of how to trust more distant figures.

Of course, the most civic and trusting generation that survived the Depression and World War II grew up without TV or the Internet. Successive generations have watched more TV, in different ways, and with different program content than the older generation. Today's young people also spend a great deal of time surfing the Internet. Both media have the effect of isolating us during leisure time and repetitively highlighting the most dangerous and corrupt aspects of our society. For better and for worse, the seemingly boundless supply and demand for voracious media coverage of scandals means that Americans are painfully aware of our shortcomings and the shortcomings of our leaders.

It's also likely that growing economic inequality is contributing to our crisis of trust. Inequality in America declined during the mid-twentieth century, when our most trusting generation came of age, but the gap between rich and poor has widened dramatically since then: since 1979, for example, the after-tax income of the richest 1 percent of Americans increased by 176 percent, but it only increased by about 20 percent for everyone else, with the poorest Americans earning just 6 percent more than they did at the end of the 1970s. As many studies and surveys reveal, most recently a 2007 report from the Pew Research Center, people feel more vulnerable when they're at a social disadvantage, making it more risky to trust others. Thus, those of lower income and racial minorities tend to answer more often that people will "take advantage" of them.

It may also be true that America's growing diversity hurts social trust. Many researchers have found that diverse neighborhoods and nations are less trusting than homogenous ones, though diversity is also linked to a high degree of economic vitality and cultural creativity. When Robert Putnam analyzed data from his Social Capital Community Benchmark Survey—which covered 41 communities across the United States—he found that cross-group trust was high in rural, homogeneous South Dakota and relatively low in heterogeneous urban areas like San Francisco. As America urbanizes and diversifies, trust is declining—at least in the short run.

FALLING AND RISING

The news is not all bad. Trust in institutions hasn't fallen in a straight line; instead, it rises and falls in response to specific events.

Consider how people answered the question about their confidence in religion between 1987 and 2006. In early 1987, 30 percent of the population said they had a "great deal" of confidence in organized religion. In 1987, however, several televangelist scandals erupted, including that of Jim Bakker. By 1988, confidence in organized religion had dropped to 21 percent. Americans' confidence then rebounded from 1988 to 2000, eventually climbing back to pre-scandal levels. Then in 2002, as a result of the Catholic Church's sex scandals, confidence in religious institutions dropped dramatically again, to 19 percent. Since 2002, confidence in organized religion has again rebounded—to 25 percent in 2006.

Similarly, the stock market crash of 1987 and the S&L bailout of 1989 hurt trust in banks and financial institutions. But public trust in finance gradually recovered (helped along by the boom years of the '90s) until it received another shock, the accounting scandals of 2002. We see a similar dip in Americans' trust in business: In 2000, 29 percent of respondents said they had a great deal of confidence in major companies. In 2002 (after the Firestone tires recall, Enron, and the wider accounting scandals), that number had dropped to 18 percent. It is too early to say what precise effect the current mortgage crisis will have on trust in banks and business, but based on past patterns, we can predict that trust in both institutions will decline significantly.

So the pattern with institutions is less of general decline than of negative responses to scandals, followed by gradual recoveries. These scandals often focus public attention on a few fallible individuals—the embezzlers or child molesters. But once the shock of the scandal fades, the public returns to trusting the institution as a whole, rather than judging it by its most untrustworthy members.

Unfortunately, Americans' trust in one another does not generally react to historical events the way their trust in institutions does. In fact, according to the General Social Survey, trust in each other has declined much more steadily and consistently than has our trust in institutions. Since there are few, if any, scandals that seem to impugn the "average person," it takes a major event to influence America's trust in individuals in the way that their trust in institutions is routinely influenced.

WE WANT TO BELIEVE

While it may be difficult, if not impossible, to control interpersonal trust—you cannot *tell* people to trust each other—we can take steps to make our institutions more trustworthy. Indeed, it may be Americans' more resilient trust in institutions that is our best hope of restoring mutual trust. Institutions help facilitate social, political, and economic transactions of all kinds by reducing uncertainty for individuals. Experiments show that when individuals successfully engage in an exchange that involves trust, it creates more trust and positive emotions.

For instance, sociologist Peter Kollock reports that at the end of a series of lab experiments involving trusting exchanges, study participants who trusted one another and reciprocated the trust sought each other out, greeted each other as old friends, and, in one case, made plans to meet for lunch the next day. Since many of our daily transactions with one another—for instance, in church or at work—are mediated by larger institutions, making these institutions more trustworthy seems like a vital first step toward cultivating trust in society at large.

Research has identified steps that institutions can take to promote trust and help reduce distrust. For example, by protecting minority rights (through voting protections and antidiscrimination policies), a government can facilitate trust and cooperation among individuals who might otherwise be wary of each other. Indeed, looking at 46 countries over a 10-year period, one of us (Pamela Paxton) found that more democratic countries—countries that safeguard these kinds of rights—produce more trusting citizens.

This result is echoed in other studies. For example, a team of researchers led by University of Michigan political scientist Ronald Inglehart found that countries that had embraced democracy, gender equality, multiculturalism, and tolerance for gays and lesbians saw big jumps in happiness over a 17-year period. And according to Robert Putnam, we can build cross-group trust by promoting meaningful interaction across ethnic lines and expanding social support for new immigrants.

Part of our effort to rebuild trust should involve providing a quality education to all Americans, for study after study shows that people with more education express more trust. Working toward equality is another possible step. Several studies have found that citizens of the most egalitarian societies are most likely to trust each other and their institutions.

There may be little that the government or other institutions can do to increase individual sociability, but individual citizens can help rebuild trust by joining community groups, connecting with neighbors, and talking to others about important issues in their lives. And if the leaders of national and local voluntary associations work to build better connections across different groups, they will help to rebuild community and a sense of trust.

Of course, we cannot *blindly* trust institutions, or each other. While America may want to be a trusting nation, it certainly doesn't want to be a nation of chumps. In an age when institutions have been shown to betray our trust—and those betrayals are amplified over and over through the media—many more people might logically and understandably see *The X-Files* slogan—"Trust no one"—as good advice.

This is why vague, unsupported calls for increased trust in institutions like banks or the office of the president are not viable solutions to the decline in trust. Instead, Americans need to see concrete steps to improve institutional transparency and accountability and to reduce fraud.

The exact steps vary from institution to institution, but all must be supported by an underlying commitment to honesty and reliability. Banks, for example, should implement policies to prevent the kind of deceptive lending practices that contributed to the fall 2008 financial meltdown. Government should open records, investigate abuses of power, and hew to constitutional principles. For institutions to be able to promote interpersonal trust, Americans must be able to trust that leaders and institutions will do what they say they are going to do—keep our money safe, protect our freedoms, advance our health, and so on—even when we are disappointed by particular individuals.

In the end, it is our natural drive to trust that offers our best hope of rebuilding trust in America. That drive was summed up by this tagline for a 2008 summer film: "I want to believe." The film? The new *X-Files* movie. As the switch suggests, even in the worst of times, lurking under our suspicious gaze lies a need to trust in each other.

THE POWER PARADOX

Dacher Keltner

IT IS MUCH SAFER to be feared than loved, wrote Niccolò Machiavelli in *The Prince*, his classic sixteenth-century treatise advocating manipulation and occasional cruelty as the best means to power. Almost 500 years later, Robert Greene's national best seller, *The 48 Laws of Power*, would have made Machiavelli's chest swell with pride. Greene's book, bedside reading of foreign policy analysts and hip-hop stars alike, is pure Machiavelli.

Here are a few of his 48 laws:

LAW 3:   Conceal your intentions.
LAW 6:   Court attention at all costs.
LAW 12:   Use selective honesty and generosity to
          disarm your victims.
LAW 15:   Crush your enemy totally.
LAW 18:   Keep others in suspended terror.

You get the picture.

Guided by centuries of advice like Machiavelli's and Greene's, we tend to believe that attaining power requires force, deception, manipulation, and coercion. Indeed, we might even assume that positions of power demand this kind of conduct—that to run

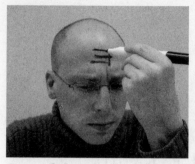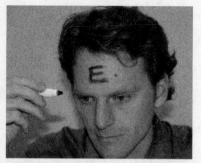

In a study by Adam Galinsky and colleagues, participants made to feel
powerful were three times more likely than others to write an E on
their forehead so that it was forwards to themselves but backwards to
others (left), suggesting they were less likely to consider
other people's points of view.

smoothly, society needs leaders who are willing and able to use
power this way.

As seductive as these notions are, they are dead wrong. Instead,
a new science of power has revealed that power is wielded most
effectively when it's used responsibly, by people who are attuned
to and engaged with the needs and interests of others. Years of
research suggests that empathy and social intelligence are vastly
more important to acquiring and exercising power than are force,
deception, and terror.

This research debunks long-standing myths about what constitutes true power, how people obtain it, and how they should use it.
But studies also show that once people assume positions of power,
they're likely to act more selfishly, impulsively, and aggressively,
and they have a harder time seeing the world from other people's
points of view. This presents us with the paradox of power: the
skills most important to obtaining power and leading effectively
are the very skills that deteriorate once we have power.

The power paradox requires that we be ever vigilant against the
corruptive influences of power and its ability to distort the way
we see ourselves and treat others. But this paradox also makes
clear how important it is to challenge myths about power, which

persuade us to choose the wrong kinds of leaders and to tolerate gross abuses of power. Instead of succumbing to the Machiavellian worldview—which unfortunately leads us to select Machiavellian leaders—we must promote a different model of power, one rooted in social intelligence, responsibility, and cooperation.

MYTH #1: POWER EQUALS CASH, VOTES, AND MUSCLE

The term *power* often evokes images of force and coercion. Many people assume that power is most evident on the floor of the United States Congress or in corporate boardrooms. Treatments of power in the social sciences have followed suit, zeroing in on clashes over cash (financial wealth), votes (participation in the political decision-making process), and muscle (military might).

But there are innumerable exceptions to this definition of power: a penniless 2-year-old pleading for (and getting) candy in the checkout line at the grocery store, one spouse manipulating another for sex, or the success of nonviolent political movements in places like India or South Africa. Viewing power as cash, votes, and muscle blinds us to the ways power pervades our daily lives.

New psychological research has redefined power, and this definition makes clear just how prevalent and integral power is in all of our lives. In psychological science, power is defined as one's capacity to alter another person's condition or state of mind by providing or withholding resources—such as food, money, knowledge, and affection—or administering punishments, such as physical harm, job termination, or social ostracism. This definition de-emphasizes how a person actually acts and instead stresses the individual's capacity to affect others. Perhaps most importantly, this definition applies across relationships, contexts, and cultures. It helps us understand how children can wield power over their parents from the time they're born or how someone—say, a religious leader—can be powerful in one context (on the pulpit during a Sunday sermon) but not another (on a mind-numbingly slow line at the DMV come Monday morning). By this definition, one can be powerful without needing to try to control, coerce, or dominate. Indeed, when people resort to trying to control others, it's often a sign that their power is slipping.

This definition complicates our understanding of power. Power is not something limited to power-hungry individuals or organizations; it is part of every social interaction where people have the capacity to influence one another's states, which is really every moment of life. Claims that power is simply a product of male biology miss the degree to which women have obtained and wielded power in many social situations. In fact, studies I've conducted find that people grant power to women as readily as men, and in informal social hierarchies, women achieve similar levels of power as men.

So power is not something we should (or can) avoid, nor is it something that necessarily involves domination and submission. We are negotiating power every waking instant of our social lives (and in our dreams as well, Freud argued). When we seek equality, we are seeking an effective balance of power, not the absence of power. We use it to win consent and social cohesion, not just compliance. To be human is to be immersed in power dynamics.

MYTH #2: MACHIAVELLIANS WIN
IN THE GAME OF POWER

One of the central questions concerning power is who gets it. Researchers have confronted this question for years, and their results offer a sharp rebuke to the Machiavellian view of power. It is not the manipulative, strategic Machiavellian who rises in power. Instead, social science reveals that one's ability to get or maintain power, even in small-group situations, depends on one's ability to understand and advance the goals of other group members. When it comes to power, social intelligence—reconciling conflicts, negotiating, smoothing over group tensions—prevails over social Darwinism.

For instance, highly detailed studies of "chimpanzee politics" have found that social power among nonhuman primates is based less on sheer strength, coercion, and the unbridled assertion of self-interest and more on the ability to negotiate conflicts, to enforce group norms, and to allocate resources fairly. More often than not, this research shows, primates who try to wield their power by dominating others and prioritizing their own interests will find themselves challenged and, in time, deposed by subordinates.

In my own research on human social hierarchies, I have consistently found that it is the more dynamic, playful, engaging members of the group who quickly garner and maintain the respect of their peers. Such outgoing, energetic, socially engaged individuals quickly rise through the ranks of emerging hierarchies.

Why social intelligence? Because of our ultrasociability. We accomplish most tasks related to survival and reproduction socially, from caring for our children to producing food and shelter. We give power to those who can best serve the interests of the group. Time and time again, empirical studies find that leaders who treat their subordinates with respect, share power, and generate a sense of camaraderie and trust are considered more just and fair.

Social intelligence is essential not only to rising to power, but to keeping it. My colleague Cameron Anderson and I have studied the structure of social hierarchies in college dormitories over the course of a year, examining who is at the top and remains there, who falls in status, and who is less respected by their peers. We've consistently found that it is the socially engaged individuals who keep their power over time. In more recent work, Anderson has made the remarkable discovery that modesty may be critical to maintaining power. Individuals who are modest about their own power actually rise in hierarchies and maintain the status and respect of their peers, while individuals with an inflated, grandiose sense of power quickly fall to the bottom rungs. So what is the fate of Machiavellian group members, avid practitioners of Greene's 48 laws, who are willing to deceive, backstab, intimidate, and undermine others in their pursuit of power? We've found that these individuals do not actually rise to positions of power. Instead, their peers quickly recognize that they will harm others in the pursuit of their own self-interest, and tag them with a reputation of being harmful to the group and not worthy of leadership.

Cooperation and modesty aren't just ethical ways to use power, and they don't only serve the interests of a group; they're also valuable skills for people who seek positions of power and want to hold onto them.

MYTH #3: POWER IS STRATEGICALLY ACQUIRED, NOT GIVEN

A major reason why Machiavellians fail is that they fall victim to a third myth about power. They mistakenly believe that power is acquired strategically in deceptive gamesmanship and by pitting others against one another. Here Machiavelli failed to appreciate an important fact in the evolution of human hierarchies: that with increasing social intelligence, subordinates can form powerful alliances and constrain the actions of those in power. Power increasingly has come to rest on the actions and judgments of other group members. A person's power is only as strong as the status given to that person by others.

The sociologist Erving Goffman wrote with brilliant insight about deference—the manner in which we afford power to others with honorifics, formal prose, indirectness, and modest nonverbal displays of embarrassment. We can give power to others simply by being respectfully polite.

My own research has found that people instinctively identify individuals who might undermine the interests of the group, and prevent those people from rising in power through what we call "reputational discourse." In our research on different groups, we have asked group members to talk openly about other members' reputations and to engage in gossip. We've found that Machiavellians quickly acquire reputations as individuals who act in ways that are inimical to the interests of others, and these reputations act like a glass ceiling, preventing their rise in power. In fact, this aspect of their behavior affected their reputations even more than their sexual morality, recreational habits, or their willingness to abide by group social conventions.

In *The Prince*, Machiavelli observes: "Any man who tries to be good all the time is bound to come to ruin among the great number who are not good. Hence a prince who wants to keep his authority must learn how not to be good, and use that knowledge, or refrain from using it, as necessity requires."

He adds, "A prince ought, above all things, always to endeavor in every action to gain for himself the reputation of being a great and remarkable man." By contrast, several Eastern traditions, such as Taoism and Confucianism, exalt the modest leader, one who engages with the followers and practices social intelligence. In the words of the Taoist philosopher Lao-tzu, "To lead the people, walk behind them." Compare this advice to Machiavelli's, and judge them both against years of scientific research. Science gives the nod to Lao-tzu.

THE POWER PARADOX

"Power tends to corrupt; absolute power corrupts absolutely," said the British historian Lord Acton. Unfortunately, this is not entirely a myth, as the actions of Europe's monarchs, Enron's executives, and out-of-control pop stars reveal. A great deal of research—especially from social psychology—lends support to Acton's claim, albeit with a twist: power leads people to act in impulsive fashion, both good and bad, and to fail to understand other people's feelings and desires.

For instance, studies have found that people given power in experiments are more likely to rely on stereotypes when judging others, and they pay less attention to the characteristics that define those other people as individuals. Predisposed to stereotype, they also judge others' attitudes, interests, and needs less accurately. One survey found that high-power professors made less accurate judgments about the attitudes of low-power professors than those low-power professors made about the attitudes of their more powerful colleagues. Power imbalances may even help explain the finding that older siblings don't perform as well as their younger siblings on theory-of-mind tasks, which assess one's ability to construe the intentions and beliefs of others.

Power even prompts less complex legal reasoning in Supreme Court justices. A study led by Stanford psychologist Deborah Gruenfeld compared the decisions of U.S. Supreme Court justices when they wrote opinions endorsing either the position of a majority of justices on the bench—a position of power—or the position of the vanquished, less powerful minority. Sure enough, when Gruenfeld analyzed the complexity of justices' opinions on a vast array of cases, she found that justices writing from a position of power crafted less complex arguments than those writing from a low-power position.

A great deal of research has also found that power encourages individuals to act on their own whims, desires, and impulses. When researchers give people power in scientific experiments, those people are more likely to physically touch others in potentially inappropriate ways, to flirt in more direct fashion, to make risky choices and gambles, to make first offers in negotiations, to speak their mind, and to eat cookies like the Cookie Monster, with crumbs all over their chin and chest.

Perhaps more unsettling is the wealth of evidence that having power makes people more likely to act like sociopaths. High-power individuals are more likely to interrupt others, to speak out of turn, and to fail to look at others who are speaking. They are also more likely to tease friends and colleagues in hostile, humiliating fashion. Surveys of organizations find that most rude behaviors—

shouting, profanities, bald critiques—emanate from the offices and cubicles of individuals in positions of power. My own research has found that people with power tend to behave like patients who have damaged their brain's orbitofrontal lobes (the region of the frontal lobes right behind the eye sockets), a condition that seems to cause overly impulsive and insensitive behavior. Thus, the experience of power might be thought of as having someone open up your skull and take out that part of your brain so critical to empathy and socially appropriate behavior.

Power may induce more harmful forms of aggression as well. In the famed Stanford Prison Experiment, psychologist Philip Zimbardo randomly assigned Stanford undergraduates to act as prison guards or prisoners—an extreme kind of power relation. The prison guards quickly descended into the purest forms of power abuse, psychologically torturing their peers, the prisoners. Similarly, anthropologists have found that cultures where rape is prevalent and accepted tend to be cultures with deeply entrenched beliefs in the supremacy of men over women.

This leaves us with a power paradox. Power is given to those individuals, groups, or nations who advance the interests of the greater good in socially intelligent fashion. Yet unfortunately, having power renders many individuals as impulsive and poorly attuned to others as your garden-variety frontal lobe patient, making them prone to act abusively and lose the esteem of their peers. What people want from leaders—social intelligence—is what is damaged by the experience of power.

When we recognize this paradox and all the destructive behaviors that flow from it, we can appreciate the importance of promoting a more socially intelligent model of power. Social behaviors are dictated by social expectations. As we debunk long-standing myths and misconceptions about power, we can better identify the qualities powerful people should have and better understand how they should wield their power. As a result, we'll have much less tolerance for people who lead by deception, coercion, or undue force. No longer will we expect these kinds of antisocial behaviors from our leaders and silently accept them when they come to pass.

We'll also start to demand something more from our colleagues, our neighbors, and ourselves. When we appreciate the distinctions between responsible and irresponsible uses of power—and the importance of practicing the responsible, socially intelligent form of it—we take a vital step toward promoting healthy marriages, peaceful playgrounds, and societies built on cooperation and trust.

EDIBLE ETHICS:
AN INTERVIEW WITH MICHAEL POLLAN

Jason Marsh

It's not uncommon these days to find yourself stranded in a supermarket aisle, paralyzed by the choices before you. How do you decide between the organic eggs laid by cage-free hens and the eggs laid by free-range hens fed on omega-3 fatty acids? Should you really buy that tomato, even though it's well out of season? Is it worth paying an extra $5 for the sustainably farmed, antibiotic-free chicken breast?

Before trying to answer any of these questions, it would help to read Michael Pollan's books. For years, eaters have turned to Pollan, a regular contributor to the *New York Times Magazine* and a professor of journalism at the University of California, Berkeley, for some of the most thoughtful, provocative, and practical contemporary writing on food.

In his 2007 bestseller *The Omnivore's Dilemma: A Natural History of Four Meals*, Pollan attempts to navigate the seemingly endless food choices available to Americans today. Getting past marketing slogans, dietary fads, and cryptic ingredients—what exactly are sodium aluminum sulfate and xanthan gum, and why are they in our food?—he traces our food's journey from farms and factories, through the marketplace, and onto our plates.

Michael Pollan.

The Omnivore's Dilemma was a logical successor to Pollan's previous book, *The Botany of Desire*, which chronicled the history of humans' relationship with four common plants. But it might be more appropriately grouped with other books, such as Eric Schlosser's *Fast Food Nation* and Marion Nestle's *Food Politics*, which try to explain the social and political forces that shape our food's production, and shed light on the impact our food choices have on our health, our communities, and our planet.

What makes many of these choices so hard is that they're personal, everyday decisions fraught with vast ethical implications. As Pollan makes clear in his book, every food purchase we make, whether it's at a McDonald's or a Whole Foods supermarket, supports a certain set of environmental and economic values. But we can't be sure of which values we're supporting when the labels on our food make it hard to understand where this food actually came from—and that's where Pollan comes in.

GREATER GOOD: In *The Omnivore's Dilemma*, you investigate the stories we're not being told about where our food comes from. But it's also hard to understand the stories we are being told, as they often rely on words like "sustainable farming," "free range," and, especially, "organic"—words that we may have encountered in the supermarket, but we may not know exactly what they mean.

MICHAEL POLLAN: I think that's true. In doing this research, I tried to look behind some of those stories to the reality, and sometimes the reality was not at all what the story suggested.

For instance, I think consumers assume that when they spend the extra money to support an organic dairy, they're supporting a small farmer, they're supporting dairies where cows get to eat grass, as cows evolved to do. But in fact, while that is true of many dairies, there are also now huge organic feedlot dairies, where cows live in groups of several thousand, where they do not get to graze in a pasture, and they eat corn all the time, which isn't very good for the cows to eat.

That's not deceptive, exactly. There's nowhere on the package that says, "We graze our cattle on pastures on small family farms." But there's a lot of suggestiveness going on—there are pictures of cows that are on grass, and that kind of thing.

GG: But what's interesting is that ethics is even part of the marketing strategy in the first place. It's not just about what tastes the best or is best for your health.

MP: Yeah, exactly. That's what Whole Foods is doing. Whole Foods, very cleverly, figured out how to combine two things that are very hard to combine in American culture: pleasure and virtue. Right? They've made shopping a pleasurable experience and eating their food a very pleasurable experience, and they combine it with this implication, and it's often very true, that you're making an ethical choice when you buy their food. You may spend a little bit more—or in the case of Whole Foods, a lot more—but by buying this apple and not that one, or this steak and not that one, you're contributing to a better environment, and you're voting with your dollars for a better world. They hold themselves up as the supermarket of ethical choices.

But there are some real questions about that. There are a

lot of foods at Whole Foods that aren't whole, that are highly processed. It's a mixed bag—it's not all organic, either. And I think that their marketing strategy, which is very clever, is that by having a few things that are organic and humane, they create an aura over all of it. So you feel that you enter that store and you're in the realm of virtuous shopping, and any decision you make within that store is not going to compromise your ethical sensibility.

I'm afraid it's not true. I'll give you one example. I was just in a Whole Foods in Berkeley, and they have farmed Atlantic salmon. Now I've never been to a salmon farm, but by and large, from everything I've read, farmed salmon is ethically dubious at best. There's an enormous environmental footprint made by those farms. And the fish they produce is not as healthy as wild salmon. So I'm surprised that's there.

You can't go into Whole Foods and assume that all the work has been taken care of and that everything has been vetted to your satisfaction. And that's a key issue: your satisfaction. There are so many different ethical decisions you can make, and sometimes they collide. It's not the case that there's virtuous food and nonvirtuous food.

GG: So what's an example of one of those collisions of virtues?

MP: Well, some people are really concerned about their health, or their children's health. And for them, perhaps organic is a good choice because it has no pesticides. Some people really care about the welfare of the animals. Well, organic is a better choice, but it doesn't really solve that problem. Organic animals can live on feedlots. They can be fed diets they shouldn't be eating. I did visit farms that sell free-range organic chicken. Those are not chickens running around in little farmyards. They're in a huge confinement operation. They don't go outside, in fact. They have the option of going outside, but they don't take it.

Or some people care about energy. The food system is a tremendous chunk of our energy use—20 percent. I think driving consumes around 18 percent of the energy we use. People don't think of food that way, but the choices you make about food have a huge impact on global warming and our dependence on foreign oil.

But you can grow and consume food in a way that doesn't consume as much energy. The interesting thing is that it's not organic. Organic is a little bit better on energy consumption, in that you're not spreading fossil fuel fertilizer, you're using compost. But it's still processed the same way now, and it's still transported all over the country the same way. So if energy is what you're really worried about, you should be buying locally grown food, even if it's not organic. So you see how it gets a little bit more complicated.

G G : This movement to buy more locally grown food is something you discuss in your book. Other than reducing our energy usage, what other cases can be made for buying locally?

M P : Again, it's a question of what you care about. But local underwrites the continuing existence of local farms. Now why is that a value? Well, because local farms give us a certain kind of local landscape. Where I come from, in New England, there is this undulating patchwork of fields and forests, outlined by stone walls. You look at that landscape, and it's picturesque; it's a really precious American landscape. Where did it come from? Well, it came from farmers and their animals and the people who ate those animals or drank their milk. And without that system, it's a museum that has to be mowed to keep it like that. So keeping those farms alive is really the way to keep those landscapes alive. And that's why I would argue that buying locally in a place like New England is a more valuable, ethical act than writing a check to a land trust or land conservation group. It is an environmental decision. It's an aesthetic decision, too.

But there are also virtues in having farmers in your community. These people understand something about nature that a lot of the rest of us don't—about water, about weather. If there were no farms in my town in New England, there would be no farmers. These are people who are artists or craftsmen of nature. The best ones have developed models to teach us how to get along better in nature than we do. And to lose that whole encyclopedia of knowledge would be a terrible loss.

And another thing about supporting local farms is that you can ask farmers what they're doing. All these supermarket stories—labels—are really just substitutes for being able to ask the farmer yourself.

G G: But if we commit to supporting local farms, are we hurting farmers in other countries who might need our dollars more?

M P: Yeah, well, you could argue that. Although on the ground I think that argument looks a little different. I mean, now lots of our produce comes from Mexico. But that's no small farmer growing those blackberries. Chances are that's an American company who had bought land from a former subsistence farmer who's going broke because our exports of corn have essentially put him out of business. He sold his good farmland to the con-solidator, who's growing for export, and he's moved on to more marginal land, or he's moved to the city, where he's joining the impoverished.

So that idea that you're supporting small farmers in the Third World when you buy that product—I don't think so. There may be cases where that's true, but by and large you're supporting an export agriculture that's highly mechanized, supports very few people, and, odds are, has displaced a lot of subsistence farmers.

G G: I think a lot of people get frustrated or confused when they realize that some of these ethical choices conflict. What can you tell them?

M P: Yeah, there are a certain number of people who, when you apprise them of the complexities of these choices, throw up their hands and just turn off. They're like, "It's so complicated, I'm going to McDonalds." And it is and it isn't complicated. If you put it in the starkest terms, there are good and bad choices.

There are choices that are basically building a new food system, and there are many struts underneath that food system: humane, organic, pastured, etc. And you do have a lot of votes; you have three votes a day, at least. And even if you just cast one or two of them in an ethical way every day, you've made a contribution to building this alternative. And that's not a small thing.

It's not all or nothing. People shouldn't feel because they can't go whole hog, and make all their eating choices completely consistent with their personal affect, that they shouldn't go at all. If you're conscious, the odds are your instincts will then tell you what to do. If you just give it a little thought, eat with some more consciousness, I have enough confidence in human nature that you will then make choices that are better than the ones you make in ignorance. But you have to be informed.

THE HOT SPOT

Lisa Bennett

THREE YEARS AGO, I became obsessed with global warming. Practically overnight, my worries about its potential effects outstripped my worries about so many other national and global issues, even personal ones.

Indeed, as the mother of two young boys, I began to think it a bit crazy that I attended to every bump and scrape of my children's little bodies and budding egos, but largely ignored the threat likely to put sizable areas of the world, including parts of the coastal city where we live, underwater within their lifetime.

That year, 2005, marked a turning point for many people. After decades of observation, speculation, and analysis, the world's climate scientists had reached a consensus, and increasingly the general public was accepting it. As *USA Today* reported, "The Debate Is Over: Globe Is Warming."

The next step, scientists advised, was action. We needed to take significant and urgent steps to cut our dependence on fossil fuels by 25 percent or more, something NASA's top climate scientist, James Hansen, said we had only a decade to do if we were to avoid the great global warming tipping point—that level at which increased temperatures would unleash unprecedented global disasters.

So how are we doing?

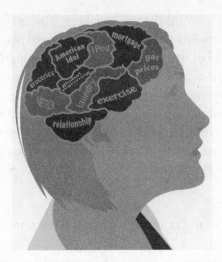

Surely, some things have changed. Sales of the Toyota Prius and other hybrids have skyrocketed. Many of us have converted to the new energy-saving compact fluorescent light bulbs. A flood of books are hitting the market offering tips about how to save the earth. And there is a frenzy of advertising about everything from "eco-friendly" houses to "green" hair salons, showing just how widespread Americans' desire is to do the right thing for the environment.

Yet none of this adds up to the significant and urgent action scientists have called for. The question is why: Why don't more of us respond more seriously to the most serious threat to the planet in human history?

"Many climate scientists find the response to global warming completely baffling," says Elke Weber, a Columbia University psychologist and the chair of the Global Roundtable on Climate Change's Public Attitudes/Ethical Issues Working Group. According to Weber, climate scientists just can't understand why government and the public have been so slow to act on the extraordinary information these scientists have provided.

But now a growing number of social scientists are offering their expertise in behavioral decision making, risk analysis, and evolutionary influences on human behavior to explain our limited responses to global warming. Among the most significant factors they point to: the way we're psychologically wired and socially conditioned to respond to crises makes us ill suited to react passionately to the abstract and seemingly remote threat posed by global warming. Their insights are also leading to some intriguing recommendations about how to get people to take action—including the potentially dangerous prospect of playing on people's fears.

OUR MISLEADING EMOTIONS

There are a significant number of researchers now devoted to studying how people decide that something is truly bad for them. They are called "risk-analysis scholars," and they believe there are, in general, two ways we may assess a risk such as global warming. One is through our analytical abilities, by which we examine the scientific evidence and make logical decisions about how to respond. This is the process that was used by climate scientists to reach the strong and clear conclusion that the risks of global warming are momentous and require immediate and significant action.

But most of us do not rely on our analytical abilities to evaluate the risk of global warming—or any risk, for that matter. Instead, we rely on the second and more common way of perceiving risk: our emotions.

"For most of us, most of the time, risk is not a statistic. Risk is a feeling," says Weber. We are swayed by our feelings, and those feelings—while an essential part of the decision-making process—can be misleading guides, depending on the type of risk involved.

For example, in a recent paper on how emotion shapes risk perception, Weber cites the growing number of parents who choose to forego having their children vaccinated against diphtheria, tetanus, and pertussis. To most physicians, this is a highly irrational decision, since vaccinations help prevent serious illnesses and pose very slight risks. So why do parents make such decisions? Because when they learn that roughly one child out of 1,000 will suffer from high fever and one out of 14,000 will suffer seizures as a result of vaccinations, their emotions lead them to imagine that *their* child will be the one to suffer.

"If I feel scared," says Weber, "that overshadows any amount of pallid statistical information."

And, perhaps most importantly, emotions, more than anything else, are what motivate us to act. As decades of behavioral decision research has shown, most people have to *feel* a risk before they do something about it.

In this way, our limited response to global warming is similar to our limited response to mass murder or genocide, according to Paul Slovic, a professor of psychology at the University of Oregon and the president of Decision Research, a nonprofit that studies human judgment, decision making, and risk.

In a series of research papers, Slovic has explored why reports of genocide so often fail to stir us to action. These reports, he writes, usually stress the thousands or even millions of people who have been killed. In doing so, they speak to our analytical abilities but not our feelings. Slovic has found that people are much more likely to donate money to a cause after reading the story of a single victim than after reading a statistic citing a million victims.

Like genocide, the long-term consequences of global warming are so enormous that we can't wrap our heads around them. Scientists predict in 40 years global warming will displace 20 million people from Beijing, 40 million from Shanghai and surrounding areas, and 60 million from Calcutta and Bangladesh. These statistics are daunting, but they're abstract; they don't inspire us to feel for the one individual whose life will be put at risk. As a result, we fail to take appropriate action.

And as with others, so with ourselves: it is emotions, such as fear or worry, that motivate us to protect ourselves from risk. With global warming, this presents an even more challenging situation because, says Weber, our emotions are shaped by two forms of past experience: either direct personal experience or evolutionary experience that still guides human behavior.

We feel the hairs stand up on the back of our necks if someone in a dark alley appears dangerous. This happens because, from an evolutionary perspective, deep in our psyches we know what it feels like to have another human being physically threaten us. There's also the chance that we've been threatened or assaulted personally.

But we have no innate experience of global warming that tells us, from personal or evolutionary experience, that when we burn too many fossil fuels, it causes the buildup of greenhouse gases that trap warm air within the earth's atmosphere, which in turn melts ice caps and glaciers, raises ocean levels, and causes hurricanes to intensify, floods to worsen, droughts to increase, lakes and water supplies to disappear, and, as in any such dire and threatening circumstances, famine and warfare to spread. As dramatic as these scenarios are, we can't feel them because we haven't experienced them (yet). Human-driven climate change is simply unprecedented.

"Global warming doesn't make evolutionary sense to us," says Weber. "Our minds haven't adjusted to the much more complex technological risks that are removed in space and time."

TIMING IS EVERYTHING

Our lack of past experience with global warming is also exacerbated by the fact that global warming is not a clear and present danger but, rather, something that is projected to reveal its most dramatic consequences decades from now.

"It's a very well established fact about human behavior," says Slovic, "that we discount future negative outcomes a great deal, especially if it means having to postpone some immediate positive benefit, such as the convenience of driving our car." He likens our attitudes toward the future risks of global warming to how teenagers discount the risk of smoking, despite abundant evidence of its risks.

"Young people tend not to be quite clear about whether there will be consequences from their smoking, what they would be, and what it would be like for them," he says. "The future risk is not imaginable, and that tends to make people more complacent."

The fact that global warming appears to represent a hazard of nature also leads people to underestimate the risk. "People don't respect nature and what it can do," says Slovic. "They feel nature is benign, even though it really isn't."

Case in point: He contrasts the response to Hurricane Katrina with the response to September 11: "After Katrina, people started to pay more attention to strengthening the levies even though the information was available in advance. There was a short period of time when there was a heightened response; then it dampened."

The response to September 11, in contrast, has been far more significant and long-lasting, even though, he says, "from a physical damage standpoint, 9/11 was relatively smaller." The difference was that Katrina, which many scientists believe was fueled by human-driven global warming, seemed like an act of nature, and that failed to trigger our millennia-old fears of having our homes and lives invaded by a stranger—fears evoked by September 11.

REALITY VERSUS WORLDVIEW

A third obstacle that limits people's response to global warming—and even their willingness to believe in it—is also one of the most intractable. In a series of recent studies, a group of scholars from Yale and other universities have been studying how cultural values shape our perceptions of risk. Based on the premise that Americans are culturally polarized on a range of societal risks, from global warming to gun control, Paul Slovic, Yale Law School professor Dan Kahan, and others analyzed the results of surveys and experiments that matched the risk perceptions of some 5,000 Americans to the worldviews of those Americans. Their finding: People may simply reject evidence that clashes with their worldview.

"To a certain extent our attitude toward risk and behaviors are conditioned not just by the raw facts of the matter, but by the orientation that we have to the world," says Slovic.

In the case of global warming, researchers found two general worldviews that seemed to have the most significant influence on perception and action. One group consists of egalitarians, or people who prefer a society where wealth, power, and opportunity are broadly distributed. Researchers called the other group the hierarchists, those who prefer a society that is linear in its structure, with leaders on top and followers below.

"What we've seen through this research is that egalitarians are generally more concerned about environmental risks over a range of hazards, including global warming. Hierarchists tend to be less concerned," says Slovic. In fact, he says, when it comes to perceptions of risk, one's worldview is vastly more influential than other individual characteristics, such as race or political ideology.

The researchers also found that when proposed solutions to global warming clash with people's worldviews, those people are more likely to reject evidence of the problem altogether. For example, in one experiment, Kahan and his colleagues gave two groups of people two contrasting newspaper articles about global warming. Both reported the problem in similar terms: temperatures were rising, human behavior was the cause of climate change, and global warming could lead to disastrous environmental and economic consequences if left unaddressed. But the articles then went on to offer different solutions: one called for increased regulation of pollution emissions, while the other called for revitalization of nuclear power.

When people with a hierarchical worldview received the article that called for increased regulation—policies currently associated with a more egalitarian and liberal worldview—they were more likely to reject that global warming was a problem than when they received the article that called for a revitalization of nuclear power.

This research helps explain the attitudes and behaviors of global warming skeptics. Slovic says it also shows how difficult it is to communicate persuasively when people feel their worldview is challenged. "The truly disconcerting thing about this work is that it shows how difficult it is to change people's views and behaviors with factual information," says Slovic. "People spin the information to keep their worldview intact." They do their best to hold onto their worldview, says Slovic, because so much of their personal identity and social networks are tied up in maintaining it.

FEARFUL FUTURES, HOPEFUL ACTIONS

With such significant obstacles to spurring action on global warming, what can social scientists recommend about how to inspire the necessary response?

First, communication about global warming needs to reach people's emotions and trigger fear, and that means emphasizing the dramatic consequences to come. "It is only the potentially catastrophic nature of (rapid) climate change (of the kind graphically depicted in the 2004 film *Day After Tomorrow*) and the global dimension of adverse effects, which may create hardships for future generations, that have the potential for raising a visceral reaction to the risk," Elke Weber writes in a recent paper on why global warming doesn't scare us yet.

This means making future hardships vivid, imaginable, personalized, and credible, says Slovic. For example, he suggests that people communicating about global warming answer the questions, How will it change the whole economy and whole quality of life in a particular region? Will the forests die out? Will the summers be so hot and dry that the earth will be uninhabitable?

In setting out to evoke fear, however, one must tread judiciously. "If people are being scared without seeing a way out, it makes them dysfunctional and freeze," says Weber. "They will switch channels and watch Britney Spears instead."

And that leads to a second recommendation: people need to be offered a set of actions they can take to combat global warming. "In general, a good guide is: Where does most of our energy get used?" says Susanne C. Moser, coeditor of the 2007 anthology *Creating a Climate for Change.* The top three categories of energy consumption for individuals are transportation, home energy use, and food consumption. Already, plenty of books and Web sites offer tips on how to reduce energy use in all these areas. Reports on global warming need to draw on these resources so that people feel there is something concrete they can do about it.

Finally, beyond the many small energy-saving solutions people can take, combating global warming will require making people more aware of the large-scale lifestyle changes that will really make a difference. "I don't want to have to make a zillion little decisions," says Baruch Fischoff, a professor at Carnegie Mellon University and the former president of the Society for Risk Analysis. "Rather, I'd like to see people working out for me some alternative ways of organizing my life where it will really be a sustainable way to live."

Indeed, figuring out these big lifestyles changes, Fischoff suggests, is the practical work that now lies ahead for climate and social scientists.

As for ordinary Americans like myself, I believe that significant collective action on global warming will come from a very personal place—such as love for our kids, who will, after all, be among those most likely to experience its greatest consequences. But perhaps even more significantly, I'm finding hope in knowing that the drive to protect our children is another universal desire for which most of us are, in fact, hardwired.

IN SEARCH OF THE MORAL VOICE

Jason Marsh

IN THE SUMMER OF 2000, the International Committee of the Red Cross (ICRC) asked Harvard University researchers Nancy Briton and Jennifer Leaning to analyze some of the most comprehensive data ever collected about human suffering in war. Over the previous year, the ICRC had held thousands of hours of interviews with residents of 12 of the most war-torn areas on earth. The interviews were part of its People on War project, an attempt to document the varied human experiences of war in order to build greater support for international humanitarian principles. From Afghanistan to Colombia, combatants, refugees, doctors, housewives, and many others discussed the impact war had made on their lives. Briton and Leaning found the interviews almost unbearably powerful.

But they also found something else. Amid heart-wrenching accounts of humiliation and loss were unsolicited expressions of compassion and memories of altruistic acts. This surprised Briton and Leaning, particularly because interviewers for the People on War project didn't ask about experiences of compassion. For the most part, says Briton, the interviewers asked the subjects "about terrible things that happened to them in war," yet some subjects "spontaneously gave examples of people who had helped them." There was the Abkhazian farmer who remembered how his Georgian neighbors had interceded on his behalf, even lying before tanks that approached his village; a Nigerian community leader who recalled how Nigerian and Biafran enemy combatants shared food at the war front.

After months of being immersed in stories of "unending woe," says Leaning, these "little instances of resistance" stood out. By no means did Briton and Leaning think these cases negated the horrors of warfare, but they did see them as evidence that war doesn't always wipe out moral consciousness.

"There was a cumulative sense of how horrible these events had been for people, how completely their lives had been destroyed and their physical circumstances upended," says Leaning. "We're dealing with populations that are enmeshed in a terribly ugly social setting for months or for years, and they all are aware of feeling degraded as they continue to be degraded. They're ashamed of what they're doing, but they're still doing it." When people can break free of this violence and degradation, their behavior provides "an indication of what might be called up in greater number, in greater consistency, if we understood its origins," she says.

After completing an initial analysis of the ICRC's data, Briton and Leaning obtained funding for a new analysis from the Fetzer Institute, a private foundation that supports scientific research. They sorted by hand through hundreds of pages of interview transcriptions, looking for mentions of compassion or altruism.

By finding and categorizing these behaviors, Briton and Leaning write in their report on their project, they hoped to suggest "possible ways of encouraging the expression of positive other-centered behavior in wartime conditions." In other words, if their research could indicate why some people exhibit the better qualities of human nature, especially in brutal circumstances, perhaps it could help societies deliberately promote altruism and compassion in the future—during war and potentially in everyday life as well.

Briton and Leaning were not the first to examine such questions about altruistic and compassionate behavior; indeed, their project is the latest in a series of research on the topic. Perhaps the most notable work on the subject is Samuel and Pearl Oliner's 1988 book *The Altruistic Personality*, a study of people who rescued Jews from the Nazis during the Holocaust. Occasionally, Briton and Leaning's report highlights similarly heroic deeds that meant the difference between life and death. But for the most part, their project has focused on the significance of everyday acts of altruism in the context of war, not necessarily the heroism of moral exemplars. To them, when one's sense of morality is embedded in a world of hate and murder, some of the simplest acts—sharing a glass of water or temporary shelter with the enemy, for instance—take on extraordinary significance. These altruistic acts enable people on the giving and the receiving ends to reclaim their humanity and moral dignity at a time when both are usually obscured by the fog of war. Sometimes, even doing nothing—simply not committing violent acts—can be compassionate, according to Briton and Leaning, who call such (non)actions "compassionate restraint."

What could motivate such acts? Briton and Leaning say it will take much more research on the topic before we know for sure. But they have identified four main factors: feelings of self-efficacy, a desire for reciprocity, a sense of group affiliation, and a wish to reclaim one's moral identity.

Examples of self-efficacy can take different forms. The report quotes a Palestinian ambulance driver who said that because of his profession, he would rescue a wounded Israeli soldier, even if that soldier had killed a relative of his. It also cites a Christian Lebanese journalist who used his press ID to rescue Muslims from danger. These stories echo a point made often in psychological literature: people are more likely to try to help someone if they think they're capable of succeeding. A sense of personal usefulness can trigger altruistic impulses that might otherwise remain dormant.

According to Leaning, this is key to why the ICRC trains soldiers in the principles of international humanitarian law. She thinks it is extremely important that governments and nongovernmental organizations (NGOs) like the ICRC "drill into soldiers that there is a moral decision process that they are responsible for." These tools of moral reasoning usually don't come instinctively, she says. Instead, soldiers must be made to feel that ethical decision making is a part of their job, and they must receive thorough instruction in making these decisions—something most governments haven't been proactive about, she says.

Those combatants who performed altruistic acts often attributed their behavior to reciprocity—the idea being that they treated their enemies the same way they wanted to be treated in return. Briton admits that this idea might not sound too "touchy feely." But she theorizes that combatants may have cited reciprocity as their motive as a "face-saving device": rather than seeming soft, they could present themselves as tough-minded, pragmatic soldiers, even when their actions were motivated largely by compassion. Other interview subjects explained reciprocity not as a calculated means to be rewarded for positive behavior, but as a way to stop violence by treating others with the kindness they would want to experience themselves. For instance, an Afghani housewife remembered how her father spared the life of a man who had killed her brother, saying that revenge only causes more bloodshed; a tribal elder in Somalia said he would "treat civilians of my enemies just as I am treating my own civilians. I will be kind to them."

Subjects' tendency to exhibit altruism toward members of their own group might not seem surprising. But, as Briton points out, "we're all members of lots of different groups at any given time." Some people, she and Leaning found, were able to find common ground with people they could have easily dismissed as enemies. They seemed capable of transcending the ethnic or political divisions usually imposed by war: a Somali man said he rejected tribalism, choosing instead to identify with "the party of peace maintenance"; a Bosnian journalist remembered how she could not hold hostilities against her Serbian neighbor because their children had grown up together.

Briton says she believes that the implications of this finding go far beyond the arena of war. "I think they extend to everyday behavior," she said. "I think that if anyone can find that thread of similarity with another person, for whatever reason, they're going to treat them as an in-group member rather than an out-group member. They're little threads, but there are so many that are available to us."

Finally, there were some people, Briton and Leaning report, who simply seemed sick and tired of war and sought to regain their moral identity that war had eclipsed. The authors found this group especially inspiring. "It's nice when people can reach back into their psyches, into their pasts, and believe that they are moral beings, and be happier with that than being violent," said Briton. For instance, one Christian ex-combatant from Lebanon said she never forgot her core values, because she had come from a decent family. When she once encountered a Muslim at a checkpoint, she helped him escape rather than hand him over to certain execution. After a former military official in Cambodia had given a displaced woman half his ration bag of rice, he was struck by her claim that she had never met a "good soldier" like him. He said he never forgot this statement, and he started to understand the tragedy of what he and other combatants in Cambodia were perpetuating.

But how can people be consistently reminded of their moral identities when they are stuck in the moral vacuum of war? Briton and Leaning say they noticed that the People on War interviews actually served an important function to this end. This is an observation echoed by Gilbert Holleufer, a communication advisor with the ICRC who was instrumental in launching the People on War project and later worked with Briton and Leaning analyzing the data.

To Holleufer, one anecdote sums up the effect of the People on War project. In South Africa, the ICRC conducted an interview with about a dozen members of a paramilitary group—"really dangerous people, violent men," he said. They trusted the Red Cross enough to do the interview, but kept their weapons at their sides. After a while, they opened up and discussed how they had been swept up in combat, how they had killed women and children. At the end of the discussion, the group's leader approached the ICRC delegate, patted him on the back, and told him, "You know, the outside world considers us as wild animals. My hands are stained with blood. But your discussion here has given me back part of my dignity."

This story resonates deeply with Jennifer Leaning. From reading the People on War interviews, and through her own previous work in war zones, she learned to recognize that "people in these places are grateful for contact with the outside world. It makes them feel like human beings." She says she feels strongly that one of the greatest services the ICRC and other NGOs can provide is "the external eye of the moral observer." The mere presence of these groups can remind people of their own humanity, spurring them to recapture their moral identity through acts of compassion and altruism. If people in warfare have lost touch with their own moral voice, she says, "perhaps they'll have a shock of recognition when they see someone coming out of a Land Rover and holding a white flag."

This is one of several hypotheses that Briton and Leaning want to test in a follow-up study. They said their work so far provides a solid platform from which to launch further investigations, but they stressed that they have yet to prove definite connections between any of these factors and altruistic behavior. They're currently seeking more funding to revisit many of the questions spawned by the People on War project, but want to conduct interviews that ask subjects explicitly about altruistic or compassionate motivations. Down the line, they hope that some of their research will inform intervention efforts.

Though they have no illusions that such research can ever stop wars, they think it could at least make conflicts less ugly. The key, says Leaning, lies in finding ways to strengthen people's "moral musculature" before they ever find themselves in the midst of conflict, an objective she thinks "should be part of a common educational agenda across the world."

After undertaking this initial project, Nancy Briton says she is optimistic that such a goal can be achieved: "To know that there is just a little glimmer of humanity and of hope even in the most demoralizing, traumatic, horrible situations in the world—it really does give me a bit of hope for the future."

MAKING PEACE THROUGH APOLOGY

Aaron Lazare

IN APRIL OF 2004, televised photographs revealed to the world the abuse of Iraqi prisoners held by the United States military in the Abu Ghraib prison. These photos, and many other images that followed, showed soldiers taking pleasure in torturing and mocking naked Iraqi prisoners. The prisoners' treatment drew criticism from around the world; it was described as cruel, humiliating, appalling, and unacceptable. Iraqis, understandably, were enraged. As details unfolded, Americans, including government and military officials, expressed shame that their country's democratic and humanitarian values were being undermined.

The U.S. government, as the responsible party, sought forgiveness-—not only from the Iraqis, but also from the American public. Toward this end, President George W. Bush, Secretary of Defense Donald Rumsfeld, and National Security Advisor Condoleezza Rice offered public comments, including what some might call apologies. President Bush told the American public how he had apologized to King Abdullah II of Jordan. "I was sorry for the humiliation suffered by the Iraqi prisoners and the humiliation suffered by their families," he said. "I told him I was as equally sorry that people seeing those pictures didn't understand the true nature and heart of America. . . . I am sickened that people got the wrong impression." In an appeal on an Arabic-language television station, the president said that Iraqis "must understand that I view these practices as abhorrent. They must also understand that what took place . . . does not represent the America that I know. . . . Mistakes will be investigated." Speaking on the same television channel, Condoleezza Rice said, "We are deeply sorry for what has happened to these people and what the families must be feeling. It's just not right. And we will get to the bottom of what happened." Secretary of Defense Rumsfeld told the Senate Armed Services Committee, "These events occurred on my watch. As secretary of defense, I am accountable for them and I take full responsibility."

These attempted apologies and expressions of consolation failed to elicit forgiveness from the Iraqi people or the Arab world in general. In fact, the words may have aggravated feelings of hostility and resentment. What was missing from these so-called apologies? Why were they flawed?

WHAT MAKES AN APOLOGY WORK?

For the past 10 years, I have studied the structure and function of public and private apologies. My goal has been to understand why certain apologies succeed or fail to elicit forgiveness and bring about reconciliation. During my analysis, I have been surprised that most writers and researchers overlook the relationship between forgiveness and apology. Forgiveness is often portrayed as a generous gift bestowed on us by someone we offended or as a gift we unconditionally extend to someone who offended us, regardless of an apology. Yet my own analysis has convinced me that forgiveness and apology are inextricably linked. Indeed, especially after a party has been humiliated, as in the case of Abu Ghraib, apology is a vital, often necessary, step toward assuaging feelings of humiliation, promoting forgiveness, and restoring balance to a relationship.

I believe there are up to four parts to the structure of an effective apology. (Not every apology requires all four parts.) These are: acknowledgment of the offense; explanation; expressions of remorse, shame, and humility; and reparation.

Of these four parts, the one most commonly defective in apologies is the acknowledgment. A valid acknowledgment must make clear who the offender is (or has the standing to speak on behalf of the offender) and who is the offended. The offender must clearly and completely acknowledge the offense. People fail the acknowledgment phase of the apology when they make vague and incomplete apologies ("for whatever I did"); use the passive voice ("mistakes were made"); make the apology conditional ("if mistakes have been made"); question whether the victim was damaged or minimize the offense ("to the degree you were hurt" or "only a few enlisted soldiers were guilty at Abu Ghraib"); use the empathic "sorry" instead of acknowledging responsibility; apologize to the wrong party; or apologize for the wrong offense.

The U.S. apology for Abu Ghraib contained several of these deficiencies. For a national offense of this magnitude, only the president has the standing to offer an apology. It appeared that other spokespersons were apologizing on behalf of President Bush, or even to shield him. That was the first deficiency. Second, the apology must be directed to the offended people, such as the Iraqis, the American public, and the American military. Instead, in President Bush's most widely publicized comments, he apologized to the king of Jordan and then reported his conversation secondhand to the offended parties. He never directly addressed the Iraqis, the American public, or the American military. Third, the person offering the apology must accept responsibility for the offense. Neither President Bush nor Condoleezza Rice accepted such responsibility. Instead, they extended their sorrow to the Iraqi people. Feeling sorry does not communicate acceptance of responsibility. The president also avoided taking responsibility as the commander-in-chief by using the passive voice when he said, "Mistakes will be investigated." In addition, he failed to acknowledge the magnitude of the offense, which is not only the immediate exposure of several humiliating incidents, but a likely pervasive and systematic pattern of prisoner abuse occurring over an extended period of time, as reported by the International Red Cross.

The next important phase of an apology is the explanation. An effective explanation may mitigate an offense by showing it was neither intentional nor personal and is unlikely to recur. An explanation will backfire when it seems fraudulent or shallow, as by saying, "The devil made me do it" or "I just snapped" or "I was not thinking." There is more dignity in admitting "There is no excuse" than in offering a fraudulent or shallow explanation.

President Bush, and others in his administration, tried to explain prisoner abuse at Abu Ghraib as the work of a few bad apples. Rather than discussing any broader explanation for the abuses—or outlining how he would make sure they did not happen again—he just stressed that they did not represent "the true nature and heart of America."

Remorse, shame, and humility are other important components of an apology. These attitudes and emotions show that the offender recognizes the suffering of the offended. They also help assure the offended party that the offense will not recur, and they allow the offender to make clear that he should have known better.

President Bush failed the humility test when he suggested that his critics did not know "the true nature and heart of America" and that he was as sickened by people getting the "wrong impression" of America as he was by the abuses at Abu Ghraib. In my opinion, he was implying that the United States was a victim in the incident.

Finally, reparation is a way for an apology to compensate, in a real or symbolic way, for the offender's transgression. When the offense causes damage or loss of a tangible object, the reparation is usually replacement or restoration of the object. When the offense is intangible, symbolic, or irreversible—ranging from an insult or humiliation to serious injury or death—the reparation may include a gift, an honor, a financial exchange, a commitment to change one's ways, or a tangible punishment of the guilty party.

Of the three attempted apologies, only Secretary Rumsfeld's apology accepted responsibility for the "events." But neither he nor President Bush recommended any reparations, including his possible resignation.

HOW APOLOGIES HEAL

Within the above structure of apology, an effective apology can generate forgiveness and reconciliation if it satisfies one or more of seven psychological needs in the offended party. The first and most common healing factor is the restoration of dignity, which is critical when the offense itself is an insult or a humiliation. Another healing factor is the affirmation that both parties have shared values and agree that the harm committed was wrong. Such apologies often follow racial or gender slurs because they help establish what kind of behavior is beyond the pale. A third healing factor is validation that the victim was not responsible for the offense. This is often necessary in rape and child abuse cases when the victim irrationally carries some of the blame. A fourth healing factor is the assurance that the offended party is safe from a repeat offense; such an assurance can come when an offender apologizes for threatening or committing physical or psychological harm to a victim. Reparative justice, the fifth healing factor, occurs when the offended sees the offending party suffer through some type of punishment. A sixth healing factor is reparation, when the victim receives some form of compensation for his or her pain. Finally, the seventh healing factor is a dialogue that allows the offended parties to express their feelings toward the offenders and even grieve over their losses. Examples of such exchanges occurred, with apologies offered, during the Truth and Reconciliation Commission hearings in South Africa.

In the U.S. government's apologies for the Abu Ghraib incident, there was not a full acknowledgement of the offense and an acceptance of responsibility, so there could be no affirmation of shared values. In addition, there was no restoration of dignity, no assurance of future safety for the prisoners, no reparative justice, no reparations, and no suggestion for dialogue with the Iraqis. So it should not come as a surprise that the Iraqi people—and the rest of the world—were reluctant to forgive the United States.

A causal relationship between apology and forgiveness is understandable based on this analysis of apology. The apology repairs the damage that was done. It heals the festering wound and commits the offender to a change in behavior. When the apology meets an offended person's needs, he does not have to work at forgiving. Forgiveness comes spontaneously; the victim feels like his offender has released him of a burden or offered him a gift. In response, he often wants to return the gift by downplaying the damage done to himself, sharing part of the blame for the offense, or complimenting the offender in some way. Commonly, the relationship becomes stronger with a bond forged out of the honesty and courage of the offending party.

GETTING IT RIGHT

For an example of this type of apology, it is useful to compare the Abu Ghraib incident with another case of prisoner abuse and its aftermath.

Eric Lomax, a Scotsman in the military during World War II, was captured in Singapore by the Japanese and held prisoner at Kanburi, Thailand, from 1940 to 1944. In his book *The Railway Man*, Lomax describes his experience of being caged like an animal in a tiny cell, beaten, starved, and tortured. His captors broke his bones. The interpreter, Nagasi Takashi, who appeared to be in command, became the focus of Lomax's hostility.

After his release from prison at the end of the war, Lomax was a broken man, behaving as if he were still in captivity, unable to show normal emotions or maintain important relationships. He frequently thought about exacting revenge on the translator and was unable to forgive, even though he knew his vengeance was consuming him. In 1989, Lomax discovered that his nemesis was alive and was writing about his repentance and his desire to be forgiven for his wartime activities. Lomax wanted revenge. He wanted to reconstruct his story of those war years. He wanted to see Takashi's sorrow. He wanted to have power over him.

Lomax and his wife wrote to Takashi, who then asked for a meeting. Both men and their wives met for two weeks near the site of the prison camp in Thailand and at Takashi's home in Japan. With Takashi's help, Lomax was able to piece together the story of his prison existence. Takashi acknowledged with sorrow and guilt the wrongs for which he and his county were responsible. He said he had never forgotten Lomax's face and admitted that he and others in the Japanese Imperial Army had treated Lomax and his countrymen "very, very badly." He explained how, since the war, he had argued against militarism and built memorials for the war dead. During their meetings, Lomax observed Takashi's suffering and grief.

Before they met, Lomax had been unable to forgive. He was controlled by his grudges and vengeance. It took a heartfelt and extended apology on the part of Takashi to meet Lomax's needs— the need to have his dignity restored, to feel safe, to understand that he and Takashi had shared values, to grieve, and to learn that Takashi suffered perhaps as much as he did. After the two weeks, Lomax said his anger was gone. Takashi was no longer a "hated enemy" but a "blood brother." Lomax wrote that he felt like "an honored guest of two good people."

Although apology and forgiveness between these men occurred in private, their story serves as a microcosm of what can happen after public apologies between groups or nations. Whether an offended party is an individual or a collection of individuals, an apology must meet the same basic psychological needs in order for it to bring about forgiveness and reconciliation.

EXCEPTIONS AND CONCLUSIONS

There are situations in which it is useful to forgive without an apology. One obvious example is where the offending party is deceased. Forgiveness then helps the aggrieved get on with his life. In other situations, where the unrepentant offender shows no signs of remorse or change of behavior, forgiveness can be useful, but reconciliation would be foolish and self-destructive. For example, a woman who has been abused by an unrepentant husband may forgive him but choose to live apart. Without an apology, it is difficult to imagine forgiveness accompanied by reconciliation or restoration of a trusting relationship. Such forgiveness is an abdication of our moral authority and our care for ourselves.

These situations aside, effective apologies are a tool for promoting cooperation among people, groups, and nations in a world plagued by war and conflict. Although the apologies of the U.S. government to the Iraqis for the abuses at Abu Ghraib fell short, we must keep in mind that it is rare for apologies to be offered and accepted during war. In such times, emotions run high, preserving face and an image of strength are critical, and it is all too easy to demonize the enemy. But in the decades since World War II, several nations (or individuals or groups within nations) from both sides have apologized for their actions during that war. In 1985, Richard von Weizsäcker, then the president of Germany, apologized to all of Germany's victims of the war. The U.S. government apologized to Japanese Americans who were interned during World War II. Additionally, in the wake of the Holocaust, Pope John XXIII eliminated all negative comments about Jews from the Roman Catholic liturgy. He followed this effort by convening the Second Vatican Council, or Vatican II, which marked a turning point in the church's relationship with Jews, Muslims, and others. These and many other successful apologies, both private and public, require honesty, generosity, humility, and courage.

We can only hope that current and subsequent administrations in the United States, Iraq, and other nations can, in the decades ahead, acknowledge their offenses, express their remorse, and offer reparations for acts committed during wartime. Without such apologies, we may be left with grudges and vengeance for decades to come.

TRUTH + RECONCILIATION

Desmond Tutu

MALUSI MPUMLWANA was a young enthusiastic antiapartheid activist and a close associate of Steve Biko in South Africa's crucial Black Consciousness Movement of the late 1970s and early 1980s. He was involved in vital community development and health projects with impoverished and often demoralized rural communities. As a result, he and his wife were under strict surveillance, constantly harassed by the ubiquitous security police. They were frequently held in detention without trial.

I remember well a day Malusi gave the security police the slip and came to my office in Johannesburg, where I was serving as general secretary of the South African Council of Churches. He told me that during his frequent stints in detention, when the security police routinely tortured him, he used to think, "These are God's children and yet they are behaving like animals. They need us to help them recover the humanity they have lost." For our struggle against apartheid to be successful, it required remarkable young people like Malusi.

All South Africans were less than whole because of apartheid. Blacks suffered years of cruelty and oppression, while many privileged whites became more uncaring, less compassionate, less humane, and therefore less human. Yet during these years of suffering and inequality, each South African's humanity was still tied to that of all others, white or black, friend or enemy. For our own dignity can only be measured in the way we treat others. This was Malusi's extraordinary insight.

I saw the power of this idea when I was serving as chairman of the Truth and Reconciliation Commission in South Africa. This was the commission that the postapartheid government, headed by our president, Nelson Mandela, had established to move us beyond the cycles of retribution and violence that had plagued so many other countries during their transitions from oppression to democracy. The commission granted perpetrators of political crimes the opportunity to appeal for amnesty by giving a full and truthful account of their actions and, if they so chose, an opportunity to ask for forgiveness—opportunities that some took and others did not. The commission also gave victims of political crimes a chance to tell their stories, hear confessions, and thus unburden themselves from the pain and suffering they had experienced.

For our nation to heal and become a more humane place, we had to embrace our enemies as well as our friends. The same is true the world over. True enduring peace—between countries, within a country, within a community, within a family—requires real reconciliation between former enemies and even between loved ones who have struggled with one another.

How could anyone really think that true reconciliation could avoid a proper confrontation? After a husband and wife or two friends have quarreled, if they merely seek to gloss over their differences or metaphorically paper over the cracks, they must not be surprised when they are soon at it again, perhaps more violently than before, because they have tried to heal their ailment lightly.

True reconciliation is based on forgiveness, and forgiveness is based on true confession, and confession is based on penitence, on contrition, on sorrow for what you have done. We know that when a husband and wife have quarreled, one of them must be ready to say the most difficult words in any language, "I'm sorry," and the other must be ready to forgive for there to be a future for their relationship. This is true between parents and children, between siblings, between neighbors, and between friends. Equally, confession, forgiveness, and reconciliation in the lives of nations are not just airy-fairy religious and spiritual things, nebulous and unrealistic. They are the stuff of practical politics.

Those who forget the past, as many have pointed out, are doomed to repeat it. Just in terms of human psychology, we in South Africa knew that to have blanket amnesty where no disclosure was made would not deal with our past. It is not dealing with the past to say glibly, "Let bygones be bygones," for then they will never be bygones. How can you forgive if you do not know what or whom to forgive? In our commission hearings, we required full disclosure for us to grant amnesty. Only then, we thought, would the process of requesting and receiving forgiveness be healing and transformative for all involved. The commission's record shows that its standards for disclosure and amnesty were high indeed: of the more than 7,000 applications submitted to the Truth and Reconciliation Commission, it granted amnesty to only 849 of them.

Unearthing the truth was necessary not only for the victims to heal, but for the perpetrators as well. Guilt, even unacknowledged guilt, has a negative effect on the guilty. One day it will come out in some form or another. We must be radical. We must go to the root, remove that which is festering, cleanse and cauterize, and then a new beginning is possible.

Forgiveness gives us the capacity to make a new start. That is the power, the rationale, of confession and forgiveness. It is to say, "I have fallen but I am not going to remain there. Please forgive me." And forgiveness is the grace by which you enable the other person to get up, and get up with dignity, to begin anew. Not to forgive leads to bitterness and hatred, which, just like self-hatred and self-contempt, gnaw away at the vitals of one's being. Whether hatred is projected out or projected in, it is always corrosive of the human spirit.

We have all experienced how much better we feel after apologies are made and accepted, but even still it is so hard for us to say that we are sorry. I often find it difficult to say these words to my wife in the intimacy and love of our bedroom. How much more difficult it is to say these words to our friends, our neighbors, and our coworkers. Asking for forgiveness requires that we take responsibility for our part in the rupture that has occurred in the relationship. We can always make excuses for ourselves and find justifications for our actions, however contorted, but we know that these keep us locked in the prison of blame and shame.

In the story of Adam and Eve, the Bible reminds us of how easy it is to blame others. When God confronted Adam about eating the forbidden fruit from the Tree of Knowledge of Good and Evil, Adam was less than forthcoming in accepting responsibility. Instead he shifted the blame to Eve, and when God turned to Eve, she, too, tried to pass the buck to the serpent. (The poor serpent had no one left to blame.) So we should not be surprised at how reluctant most people are to acknowledge their responsibility and to say they are sorry. We are behaving true to our ancestors when we blame everyone and everything except ourselves. It is the everyday heroic act that says, "It's my fault. I'm sorry." But without these simple words, forgiveness is much more difficult.

Forgiving and being reconciled to our enemies or our loved ones are not about pretending that things are other than they are. It is not about patting one another on the back and turning a blind eye to the wrong. True reconciliation exposes the awfulness, the abuse, the pain, the hurt, the truth. It could even sometimes make things worse. It is a risky undertaking, but in the end it is worthwhile, because in the end only an honest confrontation with reality can bring real healing. Superficial reconciliation can bring only superficial healing.

If the wrongdoer has come to the point of realizing his wrong, then one hopes there will be contrition, or at least some remorse or sorrow. This should lead him to confess the wrong he has done and ask for forgiveness. It obviously requires a fair measure of humility. But what happens when such contrition or confession is lacking? Must the victim be dependent on these before she can forgive?

There is no question that such a confession is a very great help to the one who wants to forgive, but it is not absolutely indispensable. If the victim could forgive only when the culprit confessed, then the victim would be locked into the culprit's whim, locked into victimhood, no matter her own attitude or intention. That would be palpably unjust.

In the act of forgiveness, we are declaring our faith in the future of a relationship and in the capacity of the wrongdoer to change. We are welcoming a chance to make a new beginning. Because we are not infallible, because we will hurt especially the ones we love by some wrong, we will always need a process of forgiveness and reconciliation to deal with those unfortunate yet all too human breaches in relationships. They are an inescapable characteristic of the human condition.

We have had a jurisprudence, a penology in Africa that was not retributive but restorative. Traditionally, when people quarreled, the main intention was not to punish the miscreant but to restore good relations. This was the animating principle of our Truth and Reconciliation Commission. For Africa is concerned, or has traditionally been concerned, about the wholeness of relationships. That is something we need in this world—a world that is polarized, a world that is fragmented, a world that destroys people. It is also something we need in our families and friendships. For retribution wounds and divides us from one another. Only restoration can heal us and make us whole. And only forgiveness enables us to restore trust and compassion to our relationships. If peace is our goal, there can be no future without forgiveness.

WHY IS THERE PEACE?

Steven Pinker

OVER THE PAST CENTURY, violent images from World War II concentration camps, Cambodia, Rwanda, Darfur, Iraq, and many other times and places have been seared into our collective consciousness. These images have led to a common understanding that technology, centralized nation-states, and modern values have brought about unprecedented violence.

Our seemingly troubled times are routinely contrasted with idyllic images of hunter-gatherer societies, which allegedly lived in a state of harmony with nature and each other. The doctrine of the noble savage—the idea that humans are peaceable by nature and corrupted by modern institutions—pops up frequently in the writing of public intellectuals like, for example, Spanish philosopher José Ortega y Gasset, who argued that "war is not an instinct but an invention."

But now that social scientists have started to count bodies in different historical periods, they have discovered that the romantic theory gets it backward: far from causing us to become more violent, something in modernity and its cultural institutions has made us nobler. In fact, our ancestors were far more violent than we are today. Indeed, violence has been in decline over long stretches

of history, and today we are probably living in the most peaceful moment of our species' time on earth.

A HISTORY OF VIOLENCE

In the decade of Darfur and Iraq, that statement might seem hallucinatory or even obscene. But if we consider the evidence, we find that the decline of violence is a fractal phenomenon: we can see the decline over millennia, centuries, decades, and years. When the archeologist Lawrence Keeley examined casualty rates among contemporary hunter-gatherers—which is the best picture we have of how people might have lived 10,000 years ago—he discovered that the likelihood that a man would die at the hands of another man ranged from a high of 60 percent in one tribe to 15 percent at the most peaceable end. In contrast, the chance that a European or American man would be killed by another man was less than 1 percent during the twentieth century, a period of time that includes both world wars. If the death rate of tribal warfare had prevailed in the twentieth century, there would have been 2 billion deaths rather than 100 million, horrible as that is.

Ancient texts reveal a stunning lack of regard for human life. In the Bible, the supposed source of all our moral values, the Hebrews are urged by God to slaughter every last resident of an invaded city. "Go and completely destroy those wicked people, the Amalekites," reads a typical passage in the book of Samuel. "Make war on them until you have wiped them out." The Bible also prescribes death by stoning as the penalty for a long list of nonviolent infractions, including idolatry, blasphemy, homosexuality, adultery, disrespecting one's parents, and picking up sticks on the Sabbath. The Hebrews, of course, were no more murderous than other tribes; one also finds frequent boasts of torture and genocide in the early histories of the Hindus, Christians, Muslims, and Chinese.

But from the Middle Ages to modern times, we can see a steady reduction in socially sanctioned forms of violence. Many conventional histories reveal that mutilation and torture were routine forms of punishment for infractions that today would result in a fine. In Europe before the Enlightenment, crimes like shoplifting or blocking the king's driveway with your oxcart might have resulted in your tongue being cut out, your hands being chopped off, and so on. Many of these punishments were administered publicly, and cruelty was a popular form of entertainment.

We also have very good statistics for the history of one-on-one murder, because for centuries many European municipalities have recorded causes of death. When the criminologist Manuel Eisner scoured the records of every village, city, county, and nation he could find, he discovered that homicide rates in Europe had declined from 100 killings per 100,000 people per year in the Middle Ages to less than 1 killing per 100,000 people in modern Europe.

And since 1945 in Europe and the Americas, we've seen steep declines in the number of deaths from interstate wars, ethnic riots, and military coups, even in South America. Worldwide, the number of battle deaths has fallen from 65,000 per conflict per year to less than 2,000 deaths per conflict in this decade. Since the end of the Cold War in the early 1990s, we have seen fewer civil wars, a 90 percent reduction in the number of deaths by genocide, and even a reversal in the 1960s-era uptick in violent crime.

Given these facts, why do so many people imagine that we live in an age of violence and killing? The first reason, I believe, is that we have better reporting. As political scientist James Payne once quipped, the Associated Press is a better chronicler of wars across the globe than were sixteenth-century monks. There's also a cognitive illusion at work. Cognitive psychologists know that the easier it is to recall an event, the more likely we are to believe it will happen again. Gory war zone images from TV are burned into memory, but we never see reports of many more people dying in their beds of old age. And in the realms of opinion and advocacy, no one ever attracted supporters and donors by saying that things just seem to be getting better and better. Taken together, all these factors help create an atmosphere of dread in the contemporary mind, one that does not stand the test of reality.

Finally, there is the fact that our behavior often falls short of our rising expectations. Violence has gone down in part because people got sick of carnage and cruelty. That's a psychological process that seems to be continuing, but it outpaces changes in behavior. So today some of us are outraged—rightly so—if a murderer is executed in Texas by lethal injection after a 15-year appeal process. We don't consider that a couple of hundred years ago, a person could be burned at the stake for criticizing the king after a trial that lasted 10 minutes. Today we should look at capital punishment as evidence of how high our standards have risen, rather than how low our behavior can sink.

EXPANDING THE CIRCLE

Why has violence declined? Social psychologists find that at least 80 percent of people have fantasized about killing someone they don't like. And modern humans still take pleasure in viewing violence, if we are to judge by the popularity of murder mysteries, Shakespearean dramas, Mel Gibson movies, video games, and hockey.

What has changed, of course, is people's willingness to act on these fantasies. The sociologist Norbert Elias suggested that European modernity accelerated a "civilizing process" marked by increases in self-control, long-term planning, and sensitivity to the thoughts and feelings of others. These are precisely the functions that today's cognitive neuroscientists attribute to the prefrontal cortex. But this only raises the question of why humans have increasingly exercised that part of their brains. No one knows why our behavior has come under the control of the better angels of our nature, but there are four plausible suggestions.

The first is that the seventeenth-century philosopher Thomas Hobbes got it right. Life in a state of nature is nasty, brutish, and short—not because of a primal thirst for blood but because of the inescapable logic of anarchy. Any beings with a modicum of self-interest may be tempted to invade their neighbors and steal their resources. The resulting fear of attack will tempt the neighbors to strike first in preemptive self-defense, which will in turn tempt the first group to strike against them preemptively, and so on. This danger can be defused by a policy of deterrence—don't strike first, retaliate if struck—but to guarantee its credibility, parties must avenge all insults and settle all scores, leading to cycles of bloody vendetta.

These tragedies can be averted by a state with a monopoly on violence. States can inflict disinterested penalties that eliminate the incentives for aggression, thereby defusing anxieties about preemptive attack and obviating the need to maintain a hair-trigger propensity for retaliation. Indeed, Manuel Eisner attributes the decline in European homicide to the transition from knightly warrior societies to the centralized governments of early modernity. And today, violence continues to fester in zones of anarchy, such as frontier regions, failed states, collapsed empires, and territories contested by mafias, gangs, and other dealers of contraband.

James Payne suggests another possibility: that the critical variable in the indulgence of violence is an overarching sense that life is cheap. When pain and early death are everyday features of one's own life, one feels less compunction about inflicting them on others. As technology and economic efficiency lengthen and improve our lives, we place a higher value on life in general.

A third theory, championed by journalist Robert Wright, invokes the logic of nonzero-sum games: scenarios in which two agents can each come out ahead if they cooperate, such as trading goods, dividing up labor, or sharing the peace dividend that comes from laying down their arms. As people acquire know-how that they can share cheaply with others and develop technologies that allow them to spread their goods and ideas over larger territories at lower cost, their incentive to cooperate steadily increases, because other people become more valuable alive than dead.

Then there is the scenario sketched by philosopher Peter Singer. Evolution, he suggests, bequeathed people a small kernel of empathy, which by default they apply only within a narrow circle of friends and relations. Over the millennia, people's moral circles have expanded to encompass larger and larger polities: the clan, the tribe, the nation, both sexes, other races, and even animals. The circle may have been pushed outward by expanding networks of reciprocity, à la Wright, but it might also be inflated by the inexorable logic of the Golden Rule: the more one knows and thinks about other living things, the harder it is to privilege one's own interests over theirs. The empathy escalator may also be powered by cosmopolitanism, in which journalism, memoir, and realistic fiction make the inner lives of other people, and the precariousness of one's own lot in life, more palpable—the feeling that "there but for fortune go I."

Whatever its causes, the decline of violence has profound implications. It is not a license for complacency: we enjoy the peace we find today because people in past generations were appalled by the violence in their time and worked to end it, and so we should work to end the appalling violence in our time. Nor is it necessarily grounds for optimism about the immediate future, since the world has never before had national leaders who combine premodern sensibilities with modern weapons.

But the phenomenon does force us to rethink our understanding of violence. Man's inhumanity to man has long been a subject for moralization. With the knowledge that something has driven it dramatically down, we can also treat it as a matter of cause and effect. Instead of asking, "Why is there war?" we might ask, "Why is there peace?" If our behavior has improved so much since the days of the Bible, we must be doing something right. And it would be nice to know what, exactly, that is.

THE MORALITY OF GLOBAL GIVING: AN INTERVIEW WITH JAN EGELAND

Jason Marsh

BEFORE DECEMBER 2004, few Americans had heard of Jan Egeland. But after the Indian Ocean earthquake and tsunami killed more than 225,000 people in 11 countries, all eyes were on the humanitarian response to the disaster, and this was Egeland's job. As the United Nations undersecretary-general for humanitarian affairs, he had to coordinate the international aid for the tsunami's victims.

But what launched Egeland's name into international headlines wasn't just his work for the U.N., but an offhand comment he made the day after the tsunami struck.

"It is beyond me why we are so stingy, really," Egeland told reporters. "Christmastime should remind many Western countries at least how rich we have become. And if—actually, the foreign assistance of many countries is now 0.1 or 0.2 percent of their gross national income. I think that is stingy, really. I don't think that is very generous."

At the time, the United States had pledged just $15 million in tsunami relief; later, it upped its pledge to $950 million. But Egeland later said he was criticizing levels of foreign aid from developed nations in general, not the international response to the tsunami or the response from the United States in particular.

Jan Egeland.

It was too late. American officials interpreted Egeland's comments as a jab at American generosity and shot back that the U.S. government leads the world in foreign aid donations. President Bush charged that Egeland was "very misguided and ill informed."

Except Egeland wasn't misinformed. While the United States does lead the world in the total amount of money it gives to developing countries, it ranks last among developed nations in the percentage of its national income—the total value of all the goods and services it produces—that it devotes to foreign aid. That figure is 0.18 of 1 percent in the United States, and the median among developed nations is about 0.4 of 1 percent. The country that gives the highest share of its national income, Sweden still gives less than 1 percent.

Some critics responded to Egeland by saying that private donations from U.S. citizens and corporations make up for its shortcomings in public aid. "We open our wallets for private groups that are better at targeting money where it's needed," said an editorial in the *Wall Street Journal*. "When it comes to this sort of giving, nobody beats Americans."

In fact, at the time the United States ranked second in the

percentage of its national income that went toward private charitable donations, and the combined amount of public and private
donations from the United States still placed it in the middle of
the international pack.

But no matter how much individuals and corporations give each
year, do these types of donations have the same practical effect or
symbolic significance as the aid that comes from governments?

Indeed, Egeland's comments may have put a lot of people on
the defensive, but they also raised some challenging questions. We
might be giving billions of dollars each year in foreign development
aid, but is that adequate? And why should we give more? Do we
really have such a great collective moral obligation to strangers
who live halfway around the world, especially when there are so
many people in need in our own country?

Social scientists have continually found that people are more
likely to demonstrate altruism toward members of their own social
group, with whom they share a sense of identity. While there might
be some fluctuations in the amount we give as a nation or as individuals, perhaps there's a limit to how much empathy we should
be expected to feel and how much money we should be expected
to give to other nations.

These aren't questions we usually like to confront, partly
because their answers seem so elusive. It's hard to say what would
constitute enough foreign aid. No leader or nation is capable of
fixing the world's inequities, so talking about them may seem only
to induce guilt and resentment.

But Egeland at least succeeded in instigating an international
conversation that was long overdue. (He also arguably incited governments to do more for the tsunami victims: donations shot up
shortly after he made his controversial remarks, in what Egeland
dubbed a display of "competitive compassion.")

In 2005, Egeland revisited some of these issues with *Greater
Good*, discussing the morality, and the possible limits, of global
altruism.

GREATER GOOD: It seems hard enough to convince people to donate money to the poor in their own countries, or even their own neighborhoods. What responsibility do nations have to strangers halfway around the world, when so many of their own people are in distress?

JAN EGELAND: The notion of meeting need regardless of where it occurs is one of the fundamental principles of humanitarianism.

If the need is within their own borders, nations have a responsibility to respond to that; if beyond national borders, they have a similar obligation. I believe that the rich countries are growing ever richer, and the poor are falling further behind. I also believe that both governments and individuals in rich countries spend billions on essentially discretionary spending, including on luxuries, pure and simple. Given this, we have no excuse for not alleviating the often truly dire suffering of families caught in circumstances beyond their control.

GG: And are the wealthier nations of the world doing enough to meet these responsibilities to people in need?

JE: Definitely not. The range of nonmilitary aid contributions varies tremendously, with the most generous nations giving over 0.8 percent of their national income and some giving as little as 0.15 percent. This means that rich countries are all keeping at least 99 percent for themselves.

GG: But after you implied in December 2004 that the wealthier nations of the world should have been donating more money to the tsunami relief effort, many public officials and private citizens, especially in the United States, pointed to the large donations given by individuals. Many Americans were saying they were happy to donate money, but they wanted to control who received that money and how much they gave. Do you see a problem in shifting foreign aid from being the responsibility of governments to being the charge of private individuals?

JE: I obviously do not see a problem with the outpouring of generosity by individuals in response to the tsunami. In fact, I would welcome increased individual donations to other natural disasters and to complex emergencies, most of which are chronically underfunded, especially those in Africa.

However, individual or corporate funding can never be a substitute for multilateral humanitarian aid on the part of governments. For one thing, donations by individuals are most frequently in response to well-publicized disasters or crises, which inevitably attract the lion's share of aid in the first place. This, then, begs the question of who will help those in more forgotten, lower-profile crises, who are often the neediest in the world. Moreover, by its very nature, individual donation is *ad hoc* and cannot be counted on, nor will it redress geographic gaps or gaps in the types of supplies or services provided for the people in need.

Donor governments, however, annually dedicate a proportion of their resources for humanitarian activities. While I would like this proportion to increase in absolute terms, and to be contributed in a more timely fashion, at least we know that we can count on regularly receiving some part of what we need from governments.

G G : And is there a broader statement made by government aid, as opposed to private donations?

J E : Aid by governments represents a collective national response by all members of a country to those most in need in poor countries. So it therefore carries added weight as a transnational symbol of support and concern.

G G : There has been a growing body of research into what inspires people to help others in distress, even at a cost to themselves. One thing that seems clear is that people are far more likely to demonstrate altruism when they recognize a shared identity between themselves and the person in need. How can you marshal international support for people who aren't bound by a common national or ethnic identity?

J E : I think human beings are virtually "hardwired" to reach out a helping hand when we witness people in need. The first responders are always those closest at hand—neighbors, towns-people, relatives, civic organizations, and local and national officials. In complex emergencies like Sudan, people fleeing violence turn to so-called "host communities," themselves living in poverty, who take them in. Neighboring countries—again sometimes often desperately poor—also lend a hand, giving asylum to masses of refugees, as did both Iran and Pakistan for Afghan refugees for many years, as Chad is doing now for its Sudanese neighbors.

I do think proximity can inspire altruism, especially when we see suffering up close and firsthand—for example, when people from developed countries find themselves in developing coun-tries or in countries in crisis. This can serve as a lifelong wake-up call for them. Moreover, in today's world, with the advance of communications, we can see situations happening live on television or through photographs instantly relayed through e-mail or satellite transmission, and this immediate proximity to crisis brings the story home to people.

G G : But even with those technological advances, can we really expect levels of foreign aid to rise significantly from their present levels? Perhaps it's an indication that human beings are really just self-interested animals?

J E : I am optimistic about this for several reasons. For one thing, the United Nations secretary-general has proposed the establishment of a fund for humanitarian emergencies that could jump-start operations where needed. This would be a useful improvement on what we currently have, the Central Emergency Revolving Fund, which at $50 million is simply too small for responding to major crises.

Second, I am heartened by the recent news that the Euro-pean Union has agreed on a proposal about how its members can meet the goal of pledging 0.7 percent of their gross national incomes on aid, thereby increasing their contributions by over $25 billion [in U.S. dollars] by 2010. This is not at all too much to ask.

I am also encouraged by the inspiring global generosity that we saw for the survivors of the tsunami. It showed humanity at its best, when life was at its worst for millions of people on the other side of this planet. In addition to the billions of dollars from individuals and corporations, a record number of governments also contributed. I refuse to believe that this response was a fluke.

Finally, we need to recognize that giving to the less privileged gives us a sense of satisfaction. This Christmas, I witnessed many dedicated volunteers standing in the cold, ringing the bell for the Salvation Army. The passersby who paused to put money in the kettle did not continue on their way with a look of regret, but with a smile.

GLOBAL COMPASSION:
A CONVERSATION BETWEEN
THE DALAI LAMA AND PAUL EKMAN

Paul Ekman

E MOTIONS UNITE AND DIVIDE the worlds, both personal and global, in which we live, motivating the best and the worst of our actions. Without emotions there would be no heroism, empathy, or compassion, but neither would there be cruelty, selfishness, or spite.

Bringing different perspectives to bear—Eastern and Western, spirituality and science, Buddhism and psychology—the Dalai Lama and I came together in conversation and sought to clarify these contradictions, in hopes of illuminating paths to a balanced emotional life and a feeling of compassion that can reach across the globe.

As the leader of a millennia-old spiritual tradition as well as a nation in exile, the Dalai Lama holds something resembling divine status among his fellow Tibetans. He is the world's principal living advocate of nonviolence and the winner, in 1989, of the Nobel Peace Prize and, in 2007, of the Congressional Gold Medal, the highest award given to a civilian by the U.S. government. He is denounced and at times publicly despised by the leaders of the People's Republic of China, which has occupied Tibet since 1950.

Yet he is also more than a religious and political leader: In the Western world his celebrity approaches that of a rock star. He has authored several best-selling books and is nearly always traveling, speaking, and inspiring audiences that number in the thousands. He is also strongly interested in integrating the findings of modern science into the Buddhist worldview.

I first met the Dalai Lama in 2000, when I attended a small conference on destructive emotions organized by the Mind and Life Institute, in Boulder, Colorado. Whether through a shared sense of playful and probing curiosity, our commitment to reducing human suffering, or a conviction that we were likely to learn from each other, the Dalai Lama and I immediately found an unexpectedly strong rapport across the wide gulf of the intellectual heritages we each represent.

During the weekend of April 22–23, 2006, the Dalai Lama and I sat down for the first of three dialogues, which were to total 39 hours of intimate exchange over a period of 15 months. In the following dialogue, adapted from our book *Emotional Awareness*, the Dalai Lama and I explore the nature and prospects of global compassion. To the Dalai Lama's right sat my ally in this endeavor, Thupten Jinpa, who served as the translator for the meeting.

THE LIMITS OF COMPASSION

EKMAN: The problem of our time, of our century, is to achieve a global compassion; otherwise we run the risk that we will destroy ourselves. We are talking about influencing all the people in the world, who are, to a large extent, brought up in exactly the opposite way, with a national—or even worse, a tribal—concern and nothing beyond that. We are not starting on neutral territory; we start with a need to counter tribal-bound compassion. How do we do this? What are the first steps?

DALAI LAMA: (*Translated.*) The first step is to be able to educate people to see the downside of a completely individualistic rather than a global concern, to recognize the pros and cons, the benefits and the disadvantages, of compassion for all living beings. (*Switching to English.*) Here, the narrow-mindedness to think of one's own nation, one's own country, one's own tract. Or only the West—America and Europe—not thinking about Africa, Latin America, Middle East, or Asia. And the Asians say, "Oh, we're Asia"; there is a sense of rivalry with the West. So, what is the benefit of that? For us to think globally is a positive benefit: the economy, the environment, and also the political system. I think with politics, there is, how do you say?

JINPA: Rivalry.

DALAI LAMA: Rivalry, based on the national feeling, policy commitments, and concern about power. (*Translated.*) The first step is to appreciate really and deeply the pros and cons, the benefits and the disadvantages of narrow-mindedness, nationalism, tribalism, provincialism, whatever it is, as opposed to a global consciousness, a unity of humanity. How do we do this on a global scale? Here it becomes very important to reflect deeply upon the interconnected nature of the modern economy, and how environmentally our fates are all intertwined.

This reality, I think, is totally different from the reality of the nineteenth century, eighteenth century, seventeenth century. At that time, the Western nations had more advanced technology than other people, and so they exploited some other countries. The reality was "we" and "them"—this was the basis. Today, the reality is much different. Everything is heavily interdependent.

EKMAN: So it would appear that the world has been changing in the last century to better fit a Buddhist view. In the sixteenth century, the Buddhists had the same view as they do today, but the world did not fit it. You could live your life without much regard for how other people on the planet were living their lives. Now it is a fact of life that what one person does has effects on others; we are all interdependent.

DALAI LAMA: A new reality. (*Translated*.) But the problem is that the politicians are not able to follow that trend. No.

EKMAN: I see what you are pointing to. There are two destructive forces to contend with.

One of them is historically grounded resentment. In areas like the Balkans, the hatred goes back for centuries; it is living your life now in terms of what happened to your father or your uncle. But facing realities today is not so easy to achieve. Much is based on equalizing the score for past resentments. Resentment—a long-term, harbored sense of injustice and unfairness—is a real obstacle.

Another obstacle is a concern with the short term rather than the long term. Politicians generally are only concerned with what happens in the short term, because that is what is going to affect them.

DALAI LAMA: Yes. (*Translated*.) On a global level, we need to have a deeper appreciation of how many of the conflicts and problems that we face today are really the consequence of an inadequate appreciation of the global dimension, and that this is the result of narrow-mindedness, of one form or another.

More than a century ago, Darwin had already pointed out the need for this kind of global sentiment. [*Earlier in their conversation, Ekman had described Darwin's views on the origin of compassion, which were remarkably similar to the Buddhist view.—Ed.*] Even on the individual level, it may be helpful to bring to people's attention the health dimensions of the more positive emotions, like compassion. How thinking more globally, thinking about others, provides an outlook within which the individual may no longer get caught up in the petty issues and problems that often become stumbling blocks.

To give an analogy, there is an admonition in the Buddhist texts to appreciate that basic existence itself is subject to personal dissatisfaction. This natural "unsatisfactoriness" is a fundamental condition of existence. This is like global awareness. When you have a better appreciation of global awareness, then, with relation to specific instances of pain (whether it is physical pain or emotional pain), you have a greater ability to deal with it. Whereas if your understanding of suffering is confined to a specific instance of the pain in the present, if you keep thinking about it and thinking about it, it could actually make you feel hopeless and helpless.

EKMAN: Yes. There is always some dissatisfaction with the nature of life. It is fundamental to life. It is not all honey and sweetness; there is difficulty.

CULTIVATING COMPASSION

EKMAN: Should the effort to generate global compassion be focused on an antidote to narrow-mindedness or on an intervention to bring about more compassion? To get one, you do have to get rid of the other.

DALAI LAMA: (*Translated.*) My approach is to bring light, powerfully, onto the downside of narrow-mindedness, which then provides a powerful rationale for having a more broad-minded, global perspective and concern for others. So they are related, a kind of a premise. (*Claps hands together.*)

In Buddhist meditation practice in order to practice compassion, first you reflect deeply upon the downside of narrow-minded self-centeredness. Then you reflect upon the positive consequences and the potential of more other-centered perspectives. On the basis of these reflections, you cultivate compassion. Otherwise, if you simply admonish others to cultivate compassion, and if you do not give them the resources—particularly the rationale for its need—it is just wishful thinking. Whereas, if you explain from the point of view of self-interest—it is for your own interest and well-being; it is essential—it makes a difference.

There are two kinds of self interest. (*Switching to English.*) Without self-interest, generally speaking, there is no basis for development of determination. But extreme self-centeredness is foolish, selfish interest.

E K M A N : If we put two advertisements in the newspaper, one stating that we are holding a weekend workshop, free of charge, to develop compassion and the other that we are going to have a weekend workshop, free of charge, to reduce your narrow-mindedness, I think the compassion advertisement would draw more people than the narrow-mindedness ad. Coming to a narrow-mindedness workshop requires you to acknowledge that you are narrow-minded, which most people would be reluctant to do.

D A L A I L A M A : (*Translated.*) Compassion is what we are aspiring for. The whole notion of narrow-mindedness, the downside of being narrow-minded, is part of the argument for the need for compassion.

When you advertise, if you talk about dealing with narrow-mindedness, people might think, "What is it for?" Whereas, if you say, "cultivation of compassion," people can relate to it. But the problem is that though most people may share the idea that it is a very valuable thing, a precious thing, sometimes people have a rather naive understanding of what compassion is. But people might also feel that it is a noble idea and it is a noble value. We need to give people a deeper understanding of compassion, grounded in a real appreciation of its need and value.

E K M A N : But there is the serious challenge of scale. How do we do this on a global level? For instance, we have to address the disproportionate use of the world's resources. Americans are not the majority of the world's population, but in terms of the world's oil consumption, they consume a disproportionate amount.

DALAI LAMA: (*Translated.*) It is partly because America has quite a large landmass, so you have to drive long distances. (*Ekman laughs.*) If it were a smaller country, there would be less scope for consumption.

EKMAN: We eat a lot of beef, which requires an enormous amount of energy to produce compared to diets that are more common in other parts of the world. If we were to make things more equitable worldwide, in order for the poorest to not be so poor, the richest might not be able to live so luxuriously as they now live.

Some economists argue that is not true. But some argue that it is very true, that people do not want to give up either their individualist aspirations or the fact that they can drive huge cars, go wherever they want, and eat steaks every night. "And you are telling me I have to maybe only have steak once a week? Or I have to drive a smaller car? Is that what compassion requires?"

I say this with a bit of a smile, but I think it is a serious problem to confront, how we share the world's resources equitably when we have an inequitable situation to begin with and a very powerful nation that is benefiting from the inequity—this may be a very large obstacle to achieving global compassion.

DALAI LAMA: (*Translated.*) One of the things that people can consider or have brought to their attention is the question of the sustainability of their current lifestyle. If we were to continue on this path of consumption, at this current level, how long could this last?

EKMAN: Some might think, "As long as it lasts for me and my children, why should I be concerned?" That is the problem, as I see it.

DALAI LAMA: Oh.

E K M A N : Matters are getting to the point where people are beginning to worry: "Maybe my children will have a burden if we do not change things now." For example, America is mortgaging itself with a deficit that may be a burden to our children. I believe that we should recognize this as bad selfishness.

D A L A I L A M A : Mm-hmm.

E K M A N : As a parent with children, I realize that if I give up a little bit of my standard of living, it will be better for my children and grandchildren. It will not benefit me, but if I make some reductions, it will benefit them. From a Buddhist view, giving up attachment—to material comfort or lifestyle or whatever—if accomplished freely, not begrudgingly, there will be psychological benefits in the state of the person's mind as a consequence of this compassionate act.

D A L A I L A M A : Yes.

E K M A N : So, it is the built-in compassion we have for our offspring that may help to save the world. It may be difficult to care about the children in Darfur, but worrying about my own children and grandchildren is easy. I better start reducing the inequity, for my own children's sake. So, it is building on what is already there.

D A L A I L A M A : Yes. That is how we start: family level. (*Translated.*) Part of the tension here may be arising from a fairly standard Western attitude for dealing with problems that you want to solve. The world has many problems, and the idea that all the problems can be solved is probably not very realistic. There were great teachers in the past, across many cultures, who have taught certain ways of being, but if you look carefully, it seems that none of these teachers premised their teaching on the assumption that everyone is going to listen or going to change themselves and follow them.

Similarly, Darwin expressed very powerful sentiments [about the need for the welfare of all sentient beings]. He probably did not expect that they would be achieved. (*Ekman laughs.*) He probably did not write them on the assumption that everybody was going to listen to him.

The same applies to us. Our responsibility is to try our best and do what we can. Then that will be a part of things that we may achieve. Ten people follow a practice—good. One hundred—better. A thousand—still better. Not all 6 billion.

E K M A N : Maybe over time.

D A L A I   L A M A : (*Switching to English.*) If the work is something that is worthwhile, then, regardless whether we can achieve it or not, make attempt. That is, I think, important. Courageous.

THE HEROINE WITH ONE THOUSAND FACES

Lisa Bennett

M Y SONS WERE BOUNCING on their beds before bedtime when I pulled out a new hand-me-down pair of pajamas for my youngest son, Julian. The top was covered with a bright blue-and-pink image of Kim Possible, Disney's teenage superhero.

Julian was thrilled. Aidan, my oldest, smiled indulgently: How could his little brother embrace a girl superhero? Then I reminded him that the pj's were once his, ones he had pleaded for. He reddened and stopped bouncing. "They were?" he said. It's true: Kim Possible, cheerleader and crime fighter, was once his hero.

But somewhere between the age of 3 and 8, all that changed, and the only form of hero for him now was a male one: Obi-Wan Kenobi, Anakin Skywalker, Han Solo, almost anyone of *Star Wars* fame—save, well, Princess Leia. When he and his best friend recently played a *Star Wars* computer game that required players to take on the role of Princess Leia, they laughed uncomfortably, as if partaking in something they'd best keep secret.

Not too long ago, female superheroes were scarce, mainly limited to Wonder Woman. But in recent years we've seen a rise in female heroes and superheroes—for both children and adults—on

The author's youngest son, Julian, has started to
reject playing with female action figures.

television, in comics, and in film. Among the more famous: Xena
the Warrior Princess, Buffy the Vampire Slayer, Jean Grey of the
X-Men, and, for the younger set, Powerpuff Girls. Yet the very idea
of a female hero remains complex. Challenge yourself right now to
think about a real-life hero. Who comes to mind? Chances are it is
a man in a dramatic situation, running into a burning building to
save someone or fighting in a war. Women do the same things, of
course. But our common archetype of modern-day heroes seems
to revolve around acts of dramatic male physical prowess and risk
taking.

Recent research, however, has started to challenge that narrow
conception of heroism. Alice H. Eagly, of Northwestern University,
and Selwyn W. Becker, of the University of Chicago, studied the
extent to which men and women participated in a variety of risky
and heroic situations, such as rescuing Jews during the Holocaust.
They also compared the number of men and women who had been
awarded a Carnegie Medal, which is given to people who risk
their lives trying to save someone else, and examined less dramatic
actions that still involved risk, such as donating a kidney or joining
the Peace Corps.

Their findings: Among those awarded a Carnegie Medal, men

vastly outnumbered women, comprising 92 percent of medalists. Yet in every other case Eagly and Becker studied, women were more likely to engage in heroic acts than men. For example, among those classified as "Righteous among the Nations"—non-Jews who risked their lives to save Jews during the Holocaust—women out-numbered men in France, Poland, and the Netherlands. In the situations that demanded less risky forms of heroism, women also outnumbered men. For example, women comprised 57 percent of kidney donors between 1988 and 2004, and 60 percent of Peace Corps volunteers in 2003.

Moreover, there are other, quieter—but still arguably heroic—kinds of risks that women assume for the good of others. In numer-ous surveys, for example, when people are asked to identify a female hero, they list their mother or some other female relative or neighbor who made great long-term sacrifices to help another in need.

"There is a cultural association of heroism with the military and emergency situations, but we really don't know the extent to which the public has a broader perception of heroism," says Eagly. "It may be that the public is broader than the scholars in their understanding of heroism."

So what would happen if the media image makers were to recognize and amplify that broader notion of heroism—if, for example, they were to honor the real-life stories of young women who give up their privileged circumstances to help people in the Middle East or in New Orleans? Or if they recognized the sac-rifices of midlife and older women who quietly care for a family member? Would the girl next door grow up perceiving herself as more heroic than she now does? Would her brother do the same? More importantly, once beyond the rigid gender-defined years of childhood, would men and women respect each other for the diverse forms of heroism of which both are capable—and as a result, would they act more heroically in all the public and private ways Eagley studied?

Until more research is done, one can only speculate. But this much at least seems reasonable: recognizing broader notions of heroism would likely attune us to our own personal power, a vital step toward facing up to and tackling our many collective challenges. At a time of super-sized and urgent issues—from global warming to the decline in America's reputation around the globe—that can't be a bad thing.

THE BANALITY OF HEROISM

Zeno Franco and Philip Zimbardo

THIRTY-FIVE YEARS AGO, one of us (Philip Zimbardo) launched what is known as the Stanford Prison Experiment.

Twenty-four young men, who had responded to a newspaper ad calling for participants in a study, were randomly assigned roles as "prisoners" or "guards" in a simulated jail in Stanford University's psychology department. The "prisoners" were arrested at their homes by real police officers, booked, and brought to the jail. Everything from the deliberately humiliating prison uniforms to the cell numbers on the laboratory doors to the mandatory strip searches and delousing were designed to replicate the depersonalizing experience of being in a real prison. The men who were assigned to be guards were given khaki uniforms, mirrored glasses, and billy clubs.

The idea was to study the psychology of imprisonment to see what happens when you put good people in a dehumanizing place. But within a matter of hours, what had been intended as a controlled experiment in human behavior took on a disturbing life of its own. After a prisoner rebellion on the second day of the experiment, the guards began using increasingly degrading forms of punishment, and the prisoners became more and more passive. Each group rapidly took on the behaviors associated with

their role, not because of any particular internal predisposition or instructions from the experimenters, but rather because the situation itself so powerfully called for the two groups to assume their new identities. Interestingly, even the experimenters were so caught up in the drama that they lost objectivity, only terminating the out-of-control study when an objective outsider stepped in, reminding them of their duty to treat the participants humanely and ethically. The experiment, scheduled to last two weeks, ended abruptly after six days.

As we have come to understand the psychology of evil, we have realized that such transformations of human character are not as rare as we would like to believe. Historical inquiry and behavioral science have demonstrated the "banality of evil"; that is, under certain conditions and social pressures, ordinary people can commit acts that would otherwise be unthinkable.

In addition to the Stanford Prison Experiment, studies conducted in the 1960s by Stanley Milgram at Yale University also revealed the banality of evil. The Milgram experiments asked participants to play the role of a "teacher" who was responsible for administering electric shocks to a "learner" when the learner failed to answer test questions correctly. The participants were not aware that the learner was working with the experimenters and did not actually receive any shocks. As the learners failed more and more, the teachers were instructed to increase the voltage intensity of the shocks—even when the learners started screaming, pleading to have the shocks stop, and eventually stopped responding altogether. Pressed by the experimenters—serious-looking men in lab coats who said they'd assume responsibility for the consequences—most participants did not stop administering shocks until they reached 300 volts or above—already in the lethal range. The majority of teachers delivered the maximum shock of 450 volts.

We all like to think that the line between good and evil is impermeable—that people who do terrible things, such as commit murder, treason, or kidnapping, are on the evil side of this line, and the rest of us could never cross it. But the Stanford Prison Experiment and the Milgram studies revealed the permeability of that line. Some people are on the good side only because situations have never coerced or seduced them to cross over.

This is true not only for perpetrators of torture and other horrible acts, but for people who commit a more common kind of wrong—the wrong of taking no action when action is called for. Whether we consider Nazi Germany or Abu Ghraib prison, there were many people who observed what was happening and said nothing. At Abu Ghraib, one photo shows two soldiers smiling before a pyramid of naked prisoners while a dozen other soldiers stand around watching passively. If you observe such abuses and don't say, "This is wrong! Stop it!" you give tacit approval to continue. You are part of the silent majority that makes evil deeds more acceptable.

In the Stanford Prison Experiment, for instance, there were the "good guards" who maintained the prison. Good guards, on the shifts when the worst abuses occurred, never did anything bad to the prisoners, but not once over the whole week did they confront the other guards and say, "What are you doing? We get paid the same money without knocking ourselves out." Or, "Hey, remember those are college students, not prisoners." No good guard ever intervened to stop the activities of the bad guards. No good guard ever arrived a minute late, left a minute early, or publicly complained. In a sense, then, it's the good guard who allowed such abuses to happen. The situation dictated their inaction, and their inaction facilitated evil.

But because evil is so fascinating, we have been obsessed with focusing on and analyzing evildoers. Perhaps because of the tragic experiences of the Second World War, we have neglected to consider the flip side of the banality of evil: Is it also possible that heroic acts are something that anyone can perform, given the right mind-set and conditions? Could there also be a "banality of heroism"?

The banality of heroism concept suggests that we are all potential heroes waiting for a moment in life to perform a heroic deed. The decision to act heroically is a choice that many of us will be called upon to make at some point in time. By conceiving of heroism as a universal attribute of human nature, not as a rare feature of the few "heroic elect," heroism becomes something that seems in the range of possibilities for every person, perhaps inspiring more of us to answer that call.

Even people who have led less than exemplary lives can be heroic in a particular moment. For example, during Hurricane Katrina, a young man named Jabar Gibson, who had a history of felony arrests, did something many people in Louisiana considered heroic: he commandeered a bus, loaded it with residents of his poor New Orleans neighborhood, and drove them to safety in Houston. Gibson's "renegade bus" arrived at a relief site in Houston before any government-sanctioned evacuation efforts.

The idea of the banality of heroism debunks the myth of the "heroic elect," a myth that reinforces two basic human tendencies. The first is to ascribe very rare personal characteristics to people who do something special—to see them as superhuman, practically beyond comparison to the rest of us. The second is the trap of inaction—sometimes known as the "bystander effect." Research has shown that the bystander effect is often motivated by diffusion of responsibility, when different people witnessing an emergency all assume someone else will help. Like the "good guards," we fall into the trap of inaction when we assume it's someone else's responsibility to act the hero.

In search of an alternative to this inaction and complicity with evil, we have been investigating the banality of heroism. Our initial research has allowed us to review example after example of people who have done something truly heroic, from individuals who enjoy international fame to those whose names have never even graced the headlines in a local newspaper. This has led us to think more critically about the definition of heroism and to consider the situational and personal characteristics that encourage or facilitate heroic behavior.

Heroism is an idea as old as humanity itself, and some of its subtleties are becoming lost or transmuted by popular culture. Being a hero is not simply being a good role model or a popular sports figure. We believe it has become necessary to revisit the historical meanings of the word and to make it come alive in modern terms. By concentrating more on this high watermark of human behavior, it is possible to foster what we term "heroic imagination," or the development of a personal heroic ideal. This heroic ideal can help guide a person's behavior in times of trouble or moral uncertainty.

WHAT IS HEROISM?

Frank De Martini was an architect who had restored his own Brooklyn brownstone. He enjoyed old cars, motorcycles, sailing, and spending time with his wife, Nicole, and their two children.

After the hijacked planes struck the World Trade Center on September 11, 2001, De Martini, a Port Authority construction manager at the center, painstakingly searched the upper floors of the North Tower to help victims trapped by the attack. De Martini was joined by three colleagues: Pablo Ortiz, Carlos DaCosta, and Pete Negron. Authors Jim Dwyer and Kevin Flynn piece together the movements of De Martini and his colleagues in their book *102 Minutes: The Untold Story of the Fight to Survive Inside the Twin Towers*. The evidence suggests that these four men were able to save 70 lives, moving from problem to problem, using just crowbars and flashlights—the only tools available. There are indications that De Martini was becoming increasingly concerned about the structural integrity of the building, yet he and his men continued to work to save others rather than evacuating when they had the chance. All four men died in the collapse of the tower.

These were not men who were known previously as larger-than-life heroes, but surely, most of us would call their actions on September 11 heroic. But just what is heroism?

Heroism is different from altruism. Where altruism emphasizes selfless acts that assist others, heroism entails the potential for deeper personal sacrifice. The core of heroism revolves around the individual's commitment to a noble purpose and the willingness to accept the consequences of fighting for that purpose.

Historically, heroism has been most closely associated with military service; however, social heroism also deserves close examination. While Achilles is held up as the archetypal war hero, Socrates' willingness to die for his values was also a heroic deed. Heroism in service to a noble idea is usually not as dramatic as heroism that involves immediate physical peril. Yet social heroism is costly in its own way, often involving loss of financial stability, lowered social status, loss of credibility, arrest, torture, risks to family members, and, in some cases, death.

These different ways of engaging with the heroic ideal suggest a deeper, more intricate definition of heroism. Based on our own analysis of many acts that we deem heroic, we believe that heroism is made up of at least four independent dimensions.

First, heroism involves some type of quest, which may range

from the preservation of life (Frank De Martini's efforts at the World Trade Center) to the preservation of an ideal (Martin Luther King Jr.'s pursuit of equal rights for African-Americans).

Second, heroism must have some form of actual or anticipated sacrifice or risk. This can be either some form of physical peril or a profound social sacrifice. The physical risks that firefighters take in the line of duty are clearly heroic in nature. Social sacrifices are more subtle. For example, in 2002, Tom Cahill, a researcher at the University of California, Davis, risked his credibility as a career scientist by calling a press conference to openly challenge the EPA's findings that the air near ground zero was safe to breathe in the aftermath of the September 11 attacks. His willingness to "go public" was challenged by the government and by some fellow scientists. Like Cahill, whistleblowers in government and business often face ostracism, physical threat, and the loss of their jobs.

Third, the heroic act can either be passive or active. We often think of heroics as a valiant activity, something that is clearly observable. But some forms of heroism involve passive resistance or an unwillingness to be moved. Consider Revolutionary War officer Nathan Hale's actions before his execution by the British army. There was nothing to be done in that moment except to decide how he submitted to death—with fortitude or with fear. The words he uttered in his final moments (borrowed from Joseph Addison's play *Cato*), "I regret that I have but one life to give for my country," are remembered more than two centuries later as a symbol of strength.

Finally, heroism can be a sudden, one-time act or something that persists over a longer period of time. This could mean that heroism may be an almost instantaneous reaction to a situation, such as when a self-described "average guy" named Dale Sayler pulled an unconscious driver from a vehicle about to be hit by an oncoming train. Alternatively, it may be a well-thought-out series of actions taking place over days, months, or a lifetime. For instance, in 1940, a Japanese consul official in Lithuania, Chiune Sugihara, signed more than 2,000 visas for Jews hoping to escape the Nazi invasion, despite his government's direct orders not to do so. Every morning when Sugihara got up and made the same decision to help, every time he signed a visa, he acted heroically and increased the likelihood of dire consequences for himself and his family. At the end of the war, he was unceremoniously fired from the Japanese civil service.

WHAT MAKES A HERO?

Our efforts to catalog and categorize heroic activity have led us to explore the factors that come together to create heroes. It must be emphasized that this is initial, exploratory work; at best, it allows us to propose a few speculations that warrant further investigation.

We have been able to learn from a body of prior research how certain situations can induce the bystander effect, which we mentioned earlier. But just as they can create bystanders, situations also have immense power to bring out heroic actions in people who never would have considered themselves heroes. In fact, the first response of many people who are called heroes is to deny their own uniqueness with statements such as, "I am not a hero; anyone in the same situation would have done what I did," or, "I just did what needed to be done." Immediate life-and-death situations, such as when people are stranded in a burning house or a car wreck, are clear examples of situations that galvanize people into heroic action. But other situations—such as being witness to discrimination, corporate corruption, government malfeasance, or military atrocities—not only bring out the worst in people; they sometimes bring out the best. We believe that these situations create a "bright-line" ethical test that pushes some individuals toward action in an attempt to stop the evil being perpetrated. But why are some people able to see this line while others are blind to it? Why do some people take responsibility for a situation when others succumb to the bystander effect?

Just as in the Stanford Prison Experiment and the Milgram

studies, the situation and the personal characteristics of each person caught up in the situation interact in unique ways. We remain unsure how these personal characteristics combine with the situation to generate heroic action, but we have some preliminary ideas. The case of Sugihara's intervention on behalf of the Jews is particularly instructive.

Accounts of Sugihara's life show us that his efforts to save Jewish refugees was a dramatic finale to a long list of smaller efforts, each of which demonstrated a willingness to occasionally defy the strict social constraints of Japanese society in the early twentieth century. For example, he did not follow his father's instructions to become a doctor, pursuing language study and civil service instead; his first wife was not Japanese; and in the 1930s, Sugihara resigned from a prestigious civil service position to protest the Japanese military's treatment of the Chinese during the occupation of Manchuria. These incidents suggest that Sugihara already possessed the internal strength and self-assurance necessary to be guided by his own moral compass in uncertain situations. We can speculate that Sugihara was more willing to assert his individual view than others around him who preferred to "go along to get along."

Also, Sugihara was bound to two different codes: he was a sworn representative of the Japanese government, but he was raised in a rural Samurai family. Should he obey his government's order to not help Jews (and, by extension, comply with his culture's age-old more not to bring shame on his family by disobeying authority)? Or should he follow the Samurai adage that haunted him, "Even a hunter cannot kill a bird which flies to him for refuge"? When the Japanese government denied repeated requests he made for permission to assist the refugees, Sugihara may have realized that these two codes of behavior were in conflict and that he faced a bright-line ethical test.

Interestingly, Sugihara did not act impulsively or spontaneously; instead, he carefully weighed the decision with his wife and family. In situations that auger for social heroism, the problem may create a "moral tickle" that the person cannot ignore—a sort of positive rumination, where we can't stop thinking about something because it does not sit right with us.

Yet this still leaves the question, What prompts people to take action? Many people in similar positions recognize the ethical problems associated with the situation and are deeply disturbed, but simply decide to ignore it. What characterizes the final step toward heroic action? Are those who do act more conscientious? Or are they simply less risk averse?

We don't know the answer to these vital questions—social science hasn't resolved them yet. However, we believe that an important factor that may encourage heroic action is the stimulation of heroic imagination—the capacity to imagine facing physically or socially risky situations, to struggle with the hypothetical problems these situations generate, and to consider one's actions and the consequences. By considering these issues in advance, the individual becomes more prepared to act when and if a moment that calls for heroism arises. Strengthening the heroic imagination may help to make people more aware of the ethical tests embedded in complex situations, while allowing the individual to have already considered, and to some degree transcended, the cost of his or her heroic action. Seeing oneself as capable of the resolve necessary for heroism may be the first step toward a heroic outcome.

HOW TO NURTURE THE HEROIC IMAGINATION

Over the last century, we have witnessed the subtle diminution of the word *hero*. This title was once reserved only for those who did great things at great personal risk. Gradually, as we have moved toward mechanized combat, especially during and after World War II, the original ideals of military heroism became more remote. At the same time, our view of social heroism has also been slowly watered down. We hold up inventors, athletes, actors, politicians, and scientists as examples of "heroes." These individuals are clearly role models, embodying important qualities we would all like to see in our children—curiosity, persistence, physical strength, being a Good Samaritan—but they do not demonstrate courage or fortitude. By diminishing the ideal of heroism, our society makes two mistakes. First, we dilute the important contribution of true heroes, whether they are luminary figures like Abraham Lincoln or the hero next door. Second, we keep ourselves from confronting the older, more demanding forms of this ideal. We do not have to challenge ourselves to see if, when faced with a situation that called for courage, we would meet that test. In prior generations, words like *bravery, fortitude, gallantry,* and *valor* stirred our souls. Children read of the exploits of great warriors and explorers and would set out to follow in those footsteps. But we spend little time thinking about the deep meanings these words once carried and focus less on trying to encourage ourselves to consider how we might engage in bravery in the social sphere, where most of us will have an opportunity to be heroic at one time or another. As our society dumbs down heroism, we fail to foster heroic imagination.

There are several concrete steps we can take to foster the heroic imagination. We can start by remaining mindful, carefully and critically evaluating each situation we encounter so that we don't gloss over an emergency requiring our action. We should try to develop our "discontinuity detector"—that is, an awareness of things that don't fit, are out of place, or don't make sense in a setting. This means asking questions to get the information we need to take responsible action.

Second, it is important not to fear interpersonal conflict and to develop the personal hardiness necessary to stand firm for principles we cherish. In fact, we shouldn't think of difficult interactions as conflicts but rather as attempts to challenge other people to support their own principles and ideology.

Third, we must remain aware of an extended time horizon, not just the present moment. We should be engaged in the current situation, yet also be able to detach part of our analytical focus to imagine alternative future scenarios that might play out, depending on different actions or failures to act that we take in the present. In addition, we should keep part of our mind on the past, as that may help us recall values and teachings instilled in us long ago, which may inform our actions in the current situation.

Fourth, we have to resist the urge to rationalize inaction or develop justifications that recast evil deeds as acceptable means to supposedly righteous ends.

Finally, we must try to transcend anticipating negative consequences associated with some forms of heroism, such as being socially ostracized. If our course is just, we must trust that others will eventually recognize the value of our heroic actions.

But beyond these basic steps, our society needs to consider ways of fostering heroic imagination in all of its citizens, most particularly in our young. The ancient Greeks and Anglo-Saxon tribes venerated their heroes in epic poems such as *The Iliad* and *Beowulf*. It is easy to see these stories as antiquated, but their instructions for the hero still hold up.

In these stories, the protagonist often encounters a mystical figure who attempts to seduce the hero away from his path. In our own lives, we must also avoid the seduction of evil, and we must recognize that the seduction will probably be quite ordinary—an unethical friend or coworker, for instance. By passing a series of smaller tests of our mettle, we can cultivate a personal habit of heroism.

Epic poems also often tell of the hero visiting the underworld. This metaphorical encounter with death represents an acceptance and transcendence of one's own mortality. To this day, some forms of heroism require paying the ultimate price. But we can also understand this as a hero's willingness to accept any of the consequences of heroic action—whether the sacrifices are physical or social.

Finally, from the primeval war stories of Achilles to Sugihara's compelling kindness toward the Jewish refugees in World War II, a code of conduct serves as the framework from which heroic action emerges. In this code, the hero follows a set of rules that serves as a reminder, sometimes even when he would prefer to forget, that something is wrong and that he must attempt to set it right. Today, it seems as if we are drifting further and further away from maintaining a set of teachings that serve as a litmus test for right and wrong.

But in a digital world, how do we connect ourselves and our children to what were once oral traditions? Hollywood has accomplished some of these tasks. The recent screen version of J. R. R. Tolkien's *The Lord of the Rings* brought us a classic story that is based on the epic tradition. Yet how many of us have stopped and talked with our children about the deeper meanings of this tale? As the sophistication of video gaming grows, can the power of this entertainment form be used to educate children about the pitfalls of following a herd mentality? Could these games help children develop their own internal compass in morally ambiguous situations? Or perhaps even help them think about their own ability to act heroically? And as we plow ahead in the digital era, how can the fundamental teachings of a code of honor remain relevant to human interactions?

If we lose the ability to imagine ourselves as heroes and to understand the meaning of true heroism, our society will be poorer for it. But if we can reconnect with these ancient ideals and make them fresh again, we can create a connection with the hero in ourselves. It is this vital, internal conduit between the modern work-a-day world and the mythical world that can prepare an ordinary person to be an everyday hero.

ILLUSTRATION CREDITS

INDEX

Page numbers in *italics* refer to illustrations.